Social Inequality
and Social Injustice

Also by Evelyn Kallen

The Anatomy of Racism: Canadian Dimensions (with D. R. Hughes)

Spanning the Generations: A Study in Jewish Identity

The Western Samoan Kinship Bridge: A Study in Migration, Social Change and the New Ethnicity

Ethnicity and Human Rights in Canada (3rd edn)

Label Me Human: Minority Rights of Stigmatized Canadians

Ethnicity, Opportunity and Successful Entrepreneurship in Canada (with M. J. Kelner)

Social Inequality and Social Injustice

A Human Rights Perspective

Evelyn Kallen

First published 2004 by
PALGRAVE MACMILLAN
Houndmills, Basingstoke, Hampshire RG21 6XS and
175 Fifth Avenue, New York, N.Y. 10010
Companies and representatives throughout the world

PALGRAVE MACMILLAN is the global academic imprint of the Palgrave Macmillan division of St. Martin's Press, LLC and of Palgrave Macmillan Ltd. Macmillan® is a registered trademark in the United States, United Kingdom and other countries. Palgrave is a registered trademark in the European Union and other countries.

ISBN 0–333–92426–6 hardback
ISBN 0–333–92428–2 paperback

This book is printed on paper suitable for recycling and made from fully managed and sustained forest sources.

A catalogue record for this book is available from the British Library.

Library of Congress Cataloging-in-Publication Data
Kallen, Evelyn.
   Social inequality and social injustice : a human rights perspective / Evelyn Kallen.
      p. cm.
   Includes bibliographical references and index.
   ISBN 0-333–92426–6 (hardback) — ISBN 0–333–92428–2 (pbk.)
      1. Equality. 2. Marginality, Social. 3. Social justice. 4. Human rights.
   I. Title.

HM821.K35 2003
305–dc22   2003058122

10 9 8 7 6 5 4 3 2
13 12 11 10 09 08 07 06 05 04

Printed in China

To my students, who challenged my ideas, offered new insights, and helped me formulate and refine my human rights approach to analysis of social issues

Contents

List of Tables and Figures

Tables

Figure

List of Key Human Rights Cases

List of Case Studies

Preface

For over three decades, I have attempted, in my university teaching and in my academic research and publications in the area of human relations, to provide an understanding of the ways in which human beings, intentionally or unintentionally, create barriers to loving relationships with other human beings. My concern stems from an abiding commitment to universal human rights principles, principles built on the cardinal premise that all human beings, as members of humankind, share the same fundamental human rights and freedoms. This being so, how then can we explain "man's inhumanity to man"? And, most importantly, what can we do about it? How can we ensure that the fundamental rights and freedoms of all human beings are equally recognized and protected?

Over the years, I have from time to time been asked by others who share my concern for human rights issues why I have focused my attention on infractions of human rights in democratic rather than in non-democratic societies, when human rights abuses allegedly are far more rampant in non-democratic contexts and are routinely carried out in such societies with relative impunity. Notwithstanding the legitimacy of this concern, which currently occupies the attention of increasing numbers of human rights activists and legal scholars, the problem this question raises for me is its implication that human rights violations in democratic societies pale by comparison with such violations elsewhere and that our time would better be spent in addressing the more urgent situations demanding international action. My own position, here, is that if all human rights scholars shifted their attention away from democratic societies, what could very well happen is that we neglect to "clean up our own back yards". It is relatively easy for people living in democratic contexts today to understand the occurrence of human rights abuses when they occur in politically repressive regimes where the right to dissent is virtually non-existent and glaring social inequalities are whitewashed. But how do we explain the continuing occurrence of violations of human rights in democratic societies whose laws and social policies are predicated upon human rights principles of justice and equity for all citizens?

In this book, my primary focus is on group-based inequalities within democratic societies. These human rights concerns are intra-national rather than international in substance. Notwithstanding, for comparative purposes, I outline parallel issues at the international level. Here, I introduce case studies to illustrate the similarities and differences in the nature of human rights violations in Western/democratic versus non-Western/non-democratic societies.

My use of the international framework of human rights throughout this book is designed to demonstrate how societies and governments can redress group-level inequalities and injustices amongst their own populations, rather than upon international action. My approach to the analysis of human rights issues presented in this book utilizes a broad, social scientific perspective rather than a narrower, legalistic one It thus differs from that of legal scholars who focus on international human rights issues and on international action. In short, in this book I use international human rights principles as a means of conceptualizing issues of group-level inequality and injustice within national contexts and, most importantly, as a means of redressing these human rights violations.

The significance and design of this book

The social issues addressed in this book – issues of prejudice, discrimination, and the promotion of hatred and harm against identified groups of citizens; issues of racism, sexism, heterosexism, ageism and the like – are of immediate and pressing concern to governments and concerned citizens in today's democratic societies. These issues are not only timely from a humanitarian viewpoint, but they are, currently, political "hot topics" in many democratic societies. The burning question addressed by this book is one which is constantly in the forefront of public consciousness: how do we explain the paradox of continuing human rights violations, continuing denial of equal justice for all, in democratic countries which openly espouse and endorse human rights principles? And, most importantly, what can we do about it?

In this book, I attempt to analyze and to document these issues in a clear and straightforward manner. The goals of the analysis presented in the book are threefold: first, to explain the ways in which members of more powerful human populations use unsubstantiated, negative prejudices against members of less powerful human populations to discredit them, to invalidate them, and to justify unequal, discriminatory treatment of them; second, to explain the ways in which long-term, categorical discrimination against particular human populations leads to the social construction of a hierarchy of group-level social inequality and to the subordinate group status of invalidated populations within it; third, and most critical, to explain the ways in which human rights protections, guaranteed through public policy, law and practice, can serve to provide just redress against past injustices and provide new hope for equitable treatment of members of subordinate groups.

Finally, and most importantly, the overarching purpose of this book, rooted in its human rights approach, is to make an innovative contribution to the social scientific understanding of dominant/subordinate relations which will further the process of societal change from a power-oriented model of social inequality and social injustice to a human rights-oriented model of social equality and social justice.

EVELYN KALLEN

The author and publishers wish to thank Oxford University Press Canada for permission to use adapted versions of two case studies from the author's *Ethnicity and Human Rights in Canada*, Third Edition, copyright Oxford University Press Canada 2003.

Introduction: A Human Rights Approach

Social equality and social justice

The primary contribution of a human rights approach to the social scientific analysis of issues of social inequality and social injustice confronting subordinate populations throughout the globe is that this approach is rooted in the internationally recognized and endorsed human rights principles of *social equality* and *social justice* endorsed in the provisions of the Charter of the United Nations (1945), the International Bill of Human Rights (United Nations, 1978, 1988) and related treaties and covenants. These international human rights principles are advocated by UN authoritative bodies as moral guidelines, the universal human rights standards to which all systems of justice should conform. As currently endorsed by the United Nations, fundamental human rights represent universally agreed upon ideals for systems of justice throughout the globe.

What this means with regard to furthering the social scientific understanding of social inequality and social injustice, is that issues of group-level inequality and injustice confronting virtually all subordinate populations throughout the globe can be conceptualized and studied within the same overarching interpretive framework. Whether the social construction of subordinate status derives from attributes of race, religion, language, gender, sexual orientation, age or any other unjustly invalidated human or cultural characteristic, the human rights violations experienced by members of these subordinate populations can be addressed, and hopefully redressed, under the rubric of social equality and social justice endorsed in international human rights principles.

The author's experience, over some twenty years of teaching social science courses on issues of social inequality and social injustice pertaining to a broad range of subordinate populations, revealed that there were two serious lacunae in the prevailing social scientific approaches which needed to be addressed. First, because social scientists traditionally focused their analytic attention upon social issues pertaining to *either* ethnic or non-ethnic populations, they had developed and applied quite different theoretical perspectives. In order to facilitate the analysis of issues of social inequality and social injustice pertaining to *both* ethnic and non-ethnic populations, there was a real need for a more comprehensive theoretical framework. Second, traditional approaches to the study of subordinate populations were decidedly negative in thrust: emphasis was placed on socially constructed invalidation and disadvantage. But no positive lever was offered which could enable members of subordinate human populations to take steps to gain equitable treatment as full and equal members of humankind. What appeared to be needed was a more positive approach, recognizing the inalienable human rights of all human beings, whether dominant or subordinate in status. Insofar as the issues of social inequality and social injustice are essentially human rights issues, I reasoned that a human rights-oriented approach could provide the missing lever by offering members of subordinate populations an internationally recognized basis for making human rights claims to equitable treatment. Moreover, what was becoming increasingly clear was that the social issues facing subordinate populations were and are increasingly perceived as human rights issues by members of these populations. It thus seemed to me to be both timely and appropriate to attempt to incorporate pivotal human rights concepts into my social scientific framework for analysis.

In order to clarify the nature of the contribution of the human rights approach to the social scientific framework for analysis applied in this book, I now present a critical overview of the theories drawn upon in the development of my conceptual framework.

Social scientific approaches to the study of dominant/subordinate relations

As indicated earlier, social scientists have traditionally focused their analytic attention upon relations of dominance and subordination, either between groups defined on the basis of race and ethnicity, or between groups defined on the basis of other, so-called "deviant" human attributes (sexual orientation, criminality, mental or physical abilities or disabilities and so forth). Accordingly, their analyses have been informed by somewhat different conceptual perspectives. Subordinate racial and ethnic groups have been analyzed from the approach of ethnic relations and social stratification: from this viewpoint, these populations have long been conceptualized as "minorities". Subordinate non-ethnic groups targeted for study have been analyzed from the approaches of medical pathology and social deviance: from this viewpoint, these populations have long been conceptualized as "deviants".

The race and ethnic relations approach to dominant/subordinate relations

Racial and ethnic stratification

Race and ethnic relations theorists have contributed significantly to our understanding of the social processes through which systems of social and ethnic stratification are developed and maintained. They have shown that systems of social stratification can be based on a wide variety of criteria: race, ethnicity, gender, sexual orientation, age, class and/or other factors. Whatever the criteria selected, a hierarchy of unequal group relations is *rooted in group-level power differentials*, giving rise to a system of social stratification in which the different population groups come to occupy unequal ranking based on their relative degree of political, economic and social power (Parsons, 1953; Porter, 1965; Lipset, 1968).

How do systems of *racial and ethnic stratification* emerge? Race and ethnic relations theorists have shown that despite racial/ethnic differences between coexisting populations in the same region, *majority/minority* relations – relations of dominance and subordination – do not develop until one population imposes its will on another (Noel, 1968). Once different racial/ethnic groups begin to compete against one another, the most important variable in determining which will emerge as dominant is differential power. Initially, power may derive from the superior size, weapons, property, economic resources, technology, educa- tion, skills, customary or scientific knowledge of a group; but whatever its basis or bases, superior power is crucial not only to the establishment of a system of ethnic stratification, but also to its maintenance and entrenchment (Lieberson, 1961; Noel, 1968; Barth and Noel, 1972).

Competition between distinct racial/ethnic groups for scarce, mutu- ally valued resources may take place in many contexts: for example, war, territorial expansion, or migration. Over time, competition leads to an unequal distribution and control of resources with the more powerful racial/ethnic groups emerging as dominant. Once established, these distributive patterns are maintained through continued control of society's major institutions. The dominant or "majority" racial/ethnic group confers the status of societal-wide norms upon its own culture, social institutions and laws, and requires conformity to these standards by all other groups in the society. Eventually, prestige becomes associated with control of the society's major resources and social institutions. Thus, the dominant group becomes vested with a relative monopoly of political, economic and social power. When this happens, the subordi- nate position of the various racial/ethnic minority groups becomes firmly entrenched (Wagley and Harris, 1958; Shibutani and Kwan, 1965; Lenski, 1966).

The social construction of minorities

Once the system of racial/ethnic stratification is established, dominant authorities are able to wield various techniques of domination to ensure that minorities "know their place and stay in their place" and that the existing structure of inequality is maintained (Shibutani and Kwan, 1965; Simpson and Yinger, 1972; Yetman and Steele, 1975). Historically, a number of insidious techniques of domination have provided domi- nant racial/ethnic groups with effective means of guaranteeing their ascendancy. These include: control of communications media, dissemi- nation of racist propaganda (invalidating and vilifying minorities), denial of franchise, denial of equal educational opportunities, denial of equal employment opportunities and wages, denial of adequate housing, control of immigration, persecution, extermination and expulsion. Racial/ethnic relations theorists have shown that these techniques of domination rely heavily on the use of prejudiced invalidation ideologies of racism to "justify" institutionalized forms of discrimination against racial and ethnic minorities. Racist ideologies fabricate a "natural" hier- archy of racial/ethnic groups based on erroneous assumptions of innate biological and cultural superiority and inferiority (Van den Berghe, 1967; Simpson and Yinger, 1972). This racial/ethnic ranking model is then used to justify the existing system of stratification and the unequal relations between dominant and subordinate populations within the system. Over time, institutionalized discrimination against racial and ethnic minorities through various techniques of domination results in the *self-fulfilling prophecy* of invalidation and unequal treatment. What Glaser and Possony (1979) refer to as the ethnic "minority syndrome" – invalidated , subordinated and collectively disadvantaged minority status – becomes full-blown.

Barriers to ethnic integration

An important contribution made by ethnic relations theorists focusing largely on immigrant ethnic minorities is to facilitate our understanding of the social processes through which ethnic diversity can be accommodated in society. Beginning with the seminal works of Park (1950) and Gordon (1961), many social scientists have, over the years, developed models of ethnic integration. Despite marked differences in the "schools" of theoretical approaches adopted, there is general agreement among social scientists that processes of ethnic integration within an ethnically stratified society are limited and controlled by various boundary maintaining mechanisms – barriers to integration posed by restrictive ideologies, policies and practices – imposed by both dominant and subordinate ethnic groups. In the case of subordinate groups, boundary maintaining mechanisms serve largely to protect the distinctive cultures of ethnic communities by keeping insiders in and outsiders out (Barth, 1969). However, it is the barriers of discrimination arbitrarily imposed by majority powers that restrict minority opportunities in public life. Accordingly, these are the barriers that violate the fundamental human right of all citizens to equality of opportunity for such participation. And it is these dominant-imposed barriers that present formidable obstacles to upward social mobility for ethnic minorities, thus impeding their attainment of the prestige and advantages associated with the top ranking social positions (Schermerhorn, 1961; Shibutani and Kwan, 1965; Rex, 1983). At the same time, dominant-imposed, racist roadblocks to integration and upward mobility serve to reinforce distinctive ethnic identities among subordinate groups by keeping their members "united in defense" against discrimination and exclusion by the dominant group (Barth, 1969; Fishman, 1979).

Until the 1960s, it was commonly assumed by ethnic relations theorists focusing on patterns of immigrant ethnic integration that, by and large, most members of ethnic minorities, given the opportunity, would willingly shed their distinctive ethnic identities and would assimilate to the dominant cultural blueprint for living. By the early 1970s, however, an apparent resurgence of ethnicity throughout the globe was marked by efforts of ethnic minorities to revitalize aspects of their traditional cultures and to strengthen group members' sense of pride in their collective ethnic identity (Glazer and Moynihan, 1970, 1975; Isaacs, 1975). This resurgence of ethnicity frequently led to the politicization of ethnicity, and the rise of ethnic nationalism began to create new tensions on a global scale (Bell, 1975; Isaacs, 1975; Connor, 1978, 1993). In this changing social context, many ethnic relations theorists began to shift their focus of analysis to the study of ethnicity and ethnic identity retention (Bennett, 1975; Glazer and Moynihan, 1975; Isajiw, 1977a, 1977b). Over the next two decades, a polarization emerged among social scientists between those focusing largely on ethnicity and ethnic identity retention (Breton *et al.*, 1990; Isajiw, 1999) and those focusing largely on race, racism and social inequalities (Bolaria and Li, 1985; Satzewich, 1998). While the line between the two camps is anything but absolute, this polarization among theorists of racial and ethnic relations continues today.

The deviance approach to dominant/ subordinate relations

Early deviance theory

As indicated earlier, the social scientific study of majority/minority relations has traditionally focused upon racial and ethnic minorities. Accordingly, early definitions and explanatory models of majority/ minority relations were not designed to include non-ethnic population categories within their purview. Sagarin (1971) was among the first social scientists to argue that the themes of negative, group-based judgments, collective discrimination, collective consciousness of oppression and subordinate social status – commonly found in prevailing definitions of racial and ethnic minorities – were equally applicable to similarly disadvantaged and stigmatized non-ethnic populations. Following from this assertion, Sagarin argued persuasively that women, children, the aged, homosexuals, alcoholics, the mentally and physically disabled and so forth could be conceptualized and analyzed as "minorities."

Traditionally, the non-ethnic minorities which have provided key target populations for social scientific research have been analyzed for the most part from the perspective of deviance theory. The traditional sociological approach to deviance originated in social pathology and was concerned primarily with an etiological explanation for deviant behaviour. Heavily influenced by the medical model, the focus of theory and research was on the individual "deviant" (rather than on the category of deviant persons), for it was in individual pathology that the source (cause) of the deviance was assumed to be located. The medical model of deviance – whether derived from psychological, psychiatric or psychoanalytical theories – assumes that some identifiable psychological abnormality or mental disorder in the individual is the determining cause of the deviant behaviour (Clinard and Meier, 1979).

The social construction of deviance

Over time, social scientists became increasingly critical of this approach for, they argued, it was based on tautological reasoning. The medical model, they pointed out, "diagnosed" deviant behaviour as evidence of psychological disturbance (its assumed cause) without being able to measure the cause independently of the behaviour itself (Conrad and Schneider, 1980). Further, the medical model fails to take serious account of the *social* nature of deviance. The critical role of the social audience, with its norms and sanctions against deviance, the political processes of defining and controlling deviant behaviour, and even the possibility of learning deviant lifestyles – all of these social factors are overlooked (or discounted) in the preoccupation with internal, medical causes (Conrad and Schneider, 1980).

Labeling and conflict theory

In reaction against, and in contradistinction to the medical model, social scientists, over the years, have developed a number of alternative models of social deviance based on labeling theory and on conflict theory. Labeling theorists, such as Becker (1963), are among the most vehement opponents of the medical model of deviance. They argue that the approach derived from social pathology obscures the value judgments which form a crucial part of the *social construction* of deviance. Becker (1963) (among others) contends that when social scientists fail to question the label "deviant", they are *ipso facto* uncritically accepting the values of the labelers – i.e. the majority authorities making the judgments.

Central to labeling theory is the concept of *stigma*, originally defined by Goffman (1963) as deep discreditation. Labeling theorists, following Goffman's seminal conceptualization, argue that stigma has its roots not in the particular characteristic singled out for deep discreditation, but in the discrediting label imposed upon assumed bearers of the attribute by dominant authorities – i.e. "deviant" minority status is socially constructed by societal authorities with the power to do so (discrediting sources). Dominant authorities are thus able to violate the human rights of members of deviant-labeled populations by defining them as somewhat less than human, hence unworthy of equal respect, equal treatment and equal life chance opportunities accorded members of "fully human" populations. Dominant authorities proceed to prescribe "appropriate" social placement and treatment (control) for deviant-labeled minorities. On the unsubstantiated assumptions that such populations were dangerous, unstable, threatening to themselves and or society and/or that they were inferior, incompetent, unable to care for themselves, social placement by majority authorities – for the "protection" of minorities and/or for the "protection" of society-at-large – traditionally took the form of incarceration of minority members in a socially and spatially isolated *total institution* (Goffman, 1961), such as a prison, mental hospital, nursing home, residential facility for the mentally and/or physically disabled persons and so forth. Within institutional confines, Goffman argues, the treatment of "deviant" minorities is characterized by the systemic denial of the fundamental human rights of freedom, equality and dignity.

Within or outside of the context of a total institution, labeling theorists argue that stigmatization leads to minority ostracization, discrimination and degradation. Thus, a *self-fulfilling prophecy* of stigmatization is set in motion, whereby the systemic denial of opportunities and of human dignity blunts capabilities, breeds apathy and eventually creates dependency. Minority members come to accept their stigmatized, dominant-imposed label (primary deviance) which becomes central to their stigmatized self-identity. They begin to "act out" their deviant roles (secondary deviance) and to develop deviant careers. The self-fulfilling prophecy of stigmatization reaches fruition when minority members come to embrace a deviant minority sub-culture as a personally appropriate, alternate lifestyle. At the group level, the long-term consequence of stigmatization and collective discrimination is the social creation of a subordinate population characterized by collective disadvantage, subordination and degradation.

In recent years, labeling theorists have been sharply criticized for their contention that the fulfillment of the self-fulfilling prophecy of stigmatization is almost inevitable. The assumption that deviant labeling sets up a process of deeper and deeper involvement in deviance has been called into critical question by increasing numbers of scholars. One of the most vehement of these critics is Prus (1983). Using Becker's (1963) organizing concept of "career contingencies" as a starting point, Prus identifies a number of personal and social factors which must be examined in order to account fully for the degree of a person's subsequent involvement in deviance and the particular pattern of his/her deviant career. Another criticism, again related to the position of labeling theorists on the virtual inevitability of the self-fulfilling prophecy of stigmatization, is that this static view of deviant minority status leaves no opening for theorists to address the social process of *destigmatization*, a crucial first step in the creation of positive minority identities, the precondition for the development of activist minority organizations (Trice and Roman, 1970).

While labeling theory has made a major contribution to our understanding of the social construction of deviant minority status at the micro-level of social psychological analysis, it has limited usefulness at the macro-level. For social scientific studies focusing on unequal relations of dominance and subordination at the *group-level*, conflict theory, as exemplified in Kinloch (1979), provides a constructive conceptual design applicable in the analysis of both ethnic and non-ethnic minorities.

Conflict models, such as that provided by Kinloch (1979), posit the social creation of deviance by dominant authorities with the power to define, treat, control and punish what they view as social deviancy. Dominant authorities create societal-wide policies and laws which reflect their own moral and ideological values and which serve their own instrumental interests. In their role as official gatekeepers for societal-wide norms, dominant authorities are able "officially" to label non-conformist behaviour as socially deviant. Once deviant labels are imposed, dominant authorities can discredit and control deviant-labeled (non-conformist) behaviour which is perceived to threaten their moral, ideological, political and economic hegemony.

In Kinloch's model, majority/minority group relations are seen to evolve out of macro-level demographic and economic developments in which assumed physical and/or psychological inferiority is used by the majority (authorities) to legitimize material inequality and thereby to maintain their own position of dominance in the institutionalized hierarchy of power, privilege and prestige. Kinloch's scheme affords a useful beginning for the integration of social deviance and ethnic relations perspectives, by explaining how majority authorities create, define and control minorities whose characteristics are assumed to deviate in unacceptable ways from majority norms.

Limitations of social scientific approaches to the analysis of dominant/subordinate relations

Boundaries of "otherness"

Examining, first, the minority concept as developed by race and ethnic relations and social stratification theorists (Shibutani and Kwan, 1965; Banton, 1967; Simpson and Yinger, 1972; Yetman and Steele, 1975), it has become apparent that the racial/ethnic conceptualization of minority status limits its applicability to other, non-racial/ethnic minorities.

Another lacuna evident in traditional social scientific designs for analysis of racial/ethnic minorities, and one which still persists to a large degree, is the omission of *aboriginal peoples* from among the ethnic populations studied. Initially, using what are now criticized as racist theories of social and cultural evolution, early anthropologists and other social theorists conceptualized aboriginal peoples as "primitives" – distinct from and somewhat less human than other "civilized" populations. In the post-colonial era, aboriginal peoples began to be, and to a large extent continue to be conceptualized as subordinated "colonized peoples", within a framework of paternalism/colonialism (Blauner, 1972; Patterson, 1972; Frideres, 1993). While some theorists focusing on ethnicity now tend to include aboriginal ethnic groups as targets for study (Elliott and Fleras, 1992; McLemore, Romo and Baker, 2000), all too frequently, aboriginal peoples are still considered to be somewhat marginal to the ethnic rubric and tend to be omitted from, or treated only nominally, in works focusing on their immigrant ethnic counterparts (Schaefer, 1995; Isajiw, 1999).

Turning our examination to the conceptualization of various non-ethnic populations as "deviant", traditionally these populations have been analyzed from the approaches of medical pathology and social deviance (Goffman, 1961, 1963; Becker, 1963; Lemert, 1967; Conrad and Schneider, 1980; Prus, 1983). I have long shared the view of those theorists as well as spokespersons for so-called "deviant populations" who argue that the term "deviance" can never be value free. Even in the seemingly innocuous concept of statistical deviation from a given societal norm, the deviant label connotes less value than the norm from which it differs, while the legitimacy and the arbitrary imposition of the norm itself remain critically unquestioned.

However, what has beleaguered me most about this division of subordinate human populations into different conceptual categories for analysis is that it arbitrarily creates boundaries of *otherness*, erroneously implying that there are *distinct genres of human beings*. By highlighting differences between the socially constructed categories of study, what is overlooked are their members' fundamental similarities as individual human beings – members of the family of humankind. Also glossed over are their evident affinities as members of invalidated and subordinate populations.

A human rights-oriented, social science approach

In the attempt to teach an undergraduate course which addressed human rights issues germane to both ethnic and non-ethnic populations, and which included aboriginal peoples among the ethnic populations studied, I deemed it essential to develop a comprehensive conceptual design which would integrate pertinent aspects of the different social scientific approaches to social inequality and social injustice and could also offer a positive approach to the understanding of subordinate populations as human beings. Towards this end, I undertook the seminal task of integrating pivotal international human rights concepts into my conceptual framework.

There were several considerations which led to my development of a unique human rights-oriented, social science approach. A primary consideration was the fact that international human rights principles are positive tenets built on the twin foundations of human unity and cultural diversity. What this means is that all human beings and all human populations can be conceptualized and studied as equals within the same comprehensive framework. This framework leaves no room for the treatment of any human being or population as the *other*. The principle of biological unity of humankind emphasizes the oneness of all human beings as members of the same human species and recognizes the close affinities between members of all human populations. The principle of cultural diversity respects the unique contributions to all of humankind made by each ethnocultural community throughout the globe.

As indicated earlier, another important consideration in developing a human rights-oriented framework was that it provides members of subordinate populations with an internationally recognized basis for making human rights claims to equitable treatment. For subordinate populations, by definition, lacking the power to make vast change to their disadvantaged status, the human rights approach provides a positive avenue through which to seek redress against past human rights violations and through which to seek new protections for their fundamental human rights in law and public policy.

This new, human rights-oriented framework was developed and

applied in previous publications in which I dealt separately with subordinate ethnic and non-ethnic populations (Kallen, 1989, 2003). In the present book, the conceptual design has been augmented so as to meet the challenge of applying a comprehensive, human rights-oriented, social scientific framework to the analysis of issues of social inequality and social injustice pertaining to the full gamut of subordinate populations throughout the globe.

In Chapter 1, I will provide an examination of the key provisions of international human rights instruments which have been drawn upon in developing my theoretical framework for analysis. I will show how these provisions have become incorporated into the laws of states ratifying them, and how, as *legal rights*, they can be used by members of subordinate populations within states to gain protection for their human rights and to gain redress against past violations of their rights.

CHAPTER 1

The Human Rights Perspective: International Human Rights

Universal human rights

International human rights are rights that belong to every human being solely by virtue of his or her membership in humankind. These universally endorsed human rights are expressed in the pivotal principles of social equality and social justice enshrined in the provisions of the Charter of the United Nations (1945), the International Bill of Human Rights (United Nations, 1978, 1988) and related treaties and covenants.

This conception of universal human rights is a twentieth-century phenomenon: it should not be equated with the historical concept of *natural rights* because to do so would be to overlook the crucial fact that so-called "natural rights" were not rights held solely by virtue of one's humanity. Indeed, race, gender and nationality were also relevant criteria. Natural rights, in reality, were the rights of dominant Westerners: white European men. Some 80 percent of all human beings were excluded.

International human rights principles set down in the provisions of the various international human rights treaties and covenants are *prior to law*: essentially, they serve to challenge states to revise laws in ways which offer guaranteed protections for the rights of citizens, especially members of subordinate groups, against abuses of state power. Principles are advocated by UN authoritative bodies as *moral guidelines*, the universal human rights standards, to which all systems of justice should conform. While UN international human rights principles are put forward as global moral standards, this is not to say that these principles are absolute or that they leave nothing further to be desired.

Indeed, these principles are continuously evolving as nations and concerned citizens within nations reconsider them and develop ever-newer covenants to protect more explicitly the human rights of persons and groups throughout the globe.

The human rights approach which I adopt in this book accepts the key human rights principles advanced in current UN international human rights instruments as universal moral guidelines for human relations. Taking these principles as the international standards for systems of law and justice, this book will examine how powerful authorities within states endorsing these international standards can continue to justify and thereby to perpetuate group-level inequality and injustice within their societies.

The development of international human rights covenants

The various human rights covenants in which international principles of human rights are put forward were developed soon after the Second World War, in response to the world's outrage when the full account of Nazi atrocities – enslavement, torture, genocide – became public knowledge. These resolutions represent the attempt by the world's nations to prevent such *crimes against humanity* from ever happening again.

On December 9, 1948, the UN General Assembly approved the Convention on the Prevention and Punishment of the Crime of Genocide. On the very next day, December 10, 1948, the UN General Assembly adopted and proclaimed the Universal Declaration of Human Rights (UDHR), a declaration which represents a statement of principles or moral guidelines for the recognition and protection of fundamental human rights throughout the globe.

Articles 1 and 2 of the UDHR (see Appendix A, p. 186) set out the three cardinal principles of human rights – freedom, equality and dignity – as rights and freedoms to which everyone is entitled without distinction of any kind. The 28 articles which follow identify particular rights and freedoms exemplifying the three central principles. Since its proclamation, the Universal Declaration has had an international impact, influencing national constitutions and laws – as well as, later, more specific international declarations which build upon its central principles.

The content of human rights provisions

The bulk of the declarations advanced in current international human rights instruments addresses a common, threefold theme: the right of every human being to participate in the shaping of decisions affecting their own life and that of their society (freedom to decide); reasonable access to the economic resources that make that participation possible (equality/equity of opportunity); and affirmation of the essential human worth and dignity of every person, regardless of individual qualities and/or group membership (dignity of person) (Kallen, 1989: 6–9).

Clearly, the single most basic human right is the *right to life*. The fundamental principle behind the human right to life requires that every human being should have access to the economic resources that maintain life. For without adequate economic maintenance – work, food, shelter, clothing – the other rights and freedoms are virtually meaningless.

Under current international human rights instruments, the human right to economic maintenance includes not only the right to the minimal, life maintaining essentials (which were provided even to "chattels", under slavery) but also, the right to an adequate standard of living, and to the kinds of public services, such as medical and health care, social services and, especially, education – which afford the basic supports for a decent living standard in modern society.

Freedom to decide and to determine one's own destiny is another fundamental human rights principle. Indeed, the right to *self-determination* of all individuals – regardless of their race or class – was one of the earliest of the fundamental human rights to gain universal recognition, for it provided the cornerstone of the early movement to abolish slavery. The exercise of this right requires access to political power; hence, within the context of the political process, it translates into the right to the franchise. But, beyond the political process, this right extends into decision-making in all life spheres: home and family, work, school, church, club and choice of lifestyle.

The right to *human dignity* is another fundamental human rights principle. It embodies the right of each individual to be held worthy, and to feel worthy; to be held in esteem and accorded respect by others, and to experience a personal sense of self-esteem and self-respect.

Many of the invalidating labels commonly used in identifying members of subordinate groups can be seen to violate the labeled population's fundamental right to human dignity. For example, the term "invalid" (literally: in-valid), used to describe very sick or severely disabled persons suggests worthlessness, uselessness and burdensomeness. This term, and others like it – cripple, crazy, idiot, faggot, dyke, nigger, kike – serve to discredit, to invalidate and to deny the very humanity of their bearers.

Freedom to decide is essential to the enhancement of dignity. While it is likely that slaves could receive adequate amounts of food, clothing and shelter, it is unlikely that they would ever acquire an adequate amount of respect for their own unique human personalities. One's sense of self-worth and dignity requires some control over one's own destiny. To be held worthy, and to feel worthy, each human being should be free to determine their own life in their own way. Each person should be free to decide whether and whom to marry, whether and how to worship, whether and what to read, write, watch, hear, see, or say.

Justifiable restrictions on human rights

Under current UN human rights covenants, the three pivotal human rights principles – freedom to decide, equality of opportunity and dignity of person – are held to be inalienable: these fundamental human rights are held to be rights which belong to every human being, solely by virtue of his or her *humanity*. This is the precise sense in which they are said to be "universal" (Murumba, 1998). What this means is that these fundamental human rights can be claimed equally by all human beings, regardless of demonstrated or assumed differences among individual persons in their talents, abilities, skills and resources and regardless of their membership in different human populations. As moral principles, fundamental rights can be said to be inalienable, individual rights, but they are not absolute: in the exercise of his or her fundamental rights, each human being must not violate – indeed, must respect – the funda-mental human rights of others. Human rights, then, are not uncondi-tional: they are conditional on the exercise of social responsibilities or duties to others.

Articles 29 and 30 of the UDHR emphasize that individual rights can be developed fully only in community with others. They emphasize the essential reciprocity of human rights and fundamental freedoms on the one hand, and of human duties and responsibilities to others in the community on the other. Just as each individual owes duties to the community, the community has an obligation to recognize its duty towards the individual and to ensure that the individual has the oppor-tunity to learn of his/her rights and duties.

These fundamental principles of the interdependence of the individual and community, and of the reciprocity of rights and duties, provide the underpinnings for moral justification of necessary *restrictions* on individual human rights. For, from a human rights view, any restriction or denial of the exercise of the fundamental human rights to freedom, equality and dignity of any human being can be justified only in instances where violations of the human rights of others can be fully substantiated. In such cases, restrictions may justifiably be imposed on the violator's exercise of human rights, but only to the extent necessary to prevent further violations of the rights of others.

Suppose, for example, that a student looks forward to the summer vacation as a time for partying with friends. He invites a group of friends to a late-night party where they can enjoy dancing to rock music. The party is in full swing at 2 a.m., with loud rock music blasting through the open windows. The loud music disturbs the elderly neighbours living next door and prevents them from sleeping. Should the student's individual freedom, then, include the right to play loud rock music, which can be heard by neighbors attempting to sleep at 2 a.m.? The student's freedom to do so immediately clashes with the freedoms of others – neighbours, trying to get to sleep in peace and quiet. Obviously, our freedoms cannot co-exist. One must give way to the other (Borovoy, 1978).

Everyday life provides us with endless examples of rights in conflict. For instance: does the freedom of the individual include the freedom to kill, maim, rape, and assault? The assailant and the victim cannot both have absolute freedom of choice. Thus, we must face the fundamental paradox. The existence of freedom demands the imposition of restrictions. In order to accomplish this task, democratic societies have developed *systems of justice* – laws, law enforcement agencies, courts and so forth. However, a critical question remains concerning the kind and the extent of restrictions or laws we should have. To put it even more specifically, what restrictions are appropriate in a democracy where the object is to promote the greatest possible freedom of the individual and, at the same time, to promote the greatest good of the society as a whole?

In some of the foregoing examples, the restrictions we enact enjoy a virtually universal consensus. In order to prevent physical harm to others, we prohibit the individual from engaging in physical attacks upon other people. In order to prevent economic harm to others, we outlaw theft, robbery, forgery, and so on. These kinds of examples form the basis of our criminal law.

During the twentieth century, however, we went much further. In order to prevent the harm caused to industrial workers by the conditions of modern industry, we imposed restrictions upon the conduct of individuals engaged in business activity. We required employers to install safety equipment, pay minimum wages, observe maximum hours and bargain collectively with unions. Employers lost the freedom to determine unilaterally the conditions of work for their employees. In order to prevent the harm caused by racial discrimination, we imposed restrictions upon the selection of employees by employers and tenants by landlords. Employers and landlords lost their freedom to base their selections on considerations of race, creed and color. Indeed, the entire apparatus of the modern democratic state represents a series of intrusions upon the freedoms of some sectors of society in order to promote the welfare of other sectors of society, and to promote the welfare of the society as a whole.

The crucial question at any given time is which freedoms to be exercised by which persons in which situations are to be given more weight. Is the harm inflicted in the absence of restrictions greater than the harm inflicted through the adoption of restrictions? Put another way, which decision would lead to the greater good ... which would more likely achieve the democratic aims of peace and order, security and safety and harmonious relations between all individuals and groups in the society?

This question brings us to the relationship between *freedom and equality*. The restrictions which a democracy imposes upon its citizens must reflect an equal concern for everyone affected. On the moral and social scales, we all weigh the same. Since one person's freedom may be another's restriction, administrators of justice cannot help assessing the relative importance of the interests in conflict. Thus, while it is impossible to avoid restrictions that may benefit some and burden others, democratic societies believe in the principle of equal consideration. Even if people are sometimes subject to differential treatment, they must receive equal consideration through equivalent treatment.

The right to equality principle is probably one of the most misunderstood (and variously interpreted) of all tenets of fundamental human rights. The right to equality essentially represents equality/equity of opportunity and results. Equality does not necessarily mean sameness. In some instances, equal (standard or same) treatment (e.g. equal access to jobs and promotions for equally qualified persons, without reference to race, gender or sexual orientation) is appropriate, but in other instances, equivalent (special) compensatory treatment may be required (e.g. architectural adaptation of public buildings; provision of ramps and handrails as well as stairs to enable access to the facility by wheelchair-bound and mobility-impaired persons, as well as by ambulatory persons). The latter is but one example of the multitude of documented instances where, in order to offset the handicapping effects of a disability, special, compensatory measures must be provided. In these cases, equivalent, rather than equal (standard) treatment is required to ensure real equality of opportunity and results.

Twin principles of human rights: human unity and cultural diversity

Fundamental *individual* human rights are rooted in the distinctive biological attributes shared by all members of humankind as a single species, *Homo sapiens* (Kallen 2003: Introduction). Recognition of the essential biological oneness of humankind provides the scientific basis for the universal principle of fundamental individual human rights. A primary assumption, then, behind international human rights covenants is that of the fundamental unity and kinship among all members of humankind.

Yet every human being is born not only into the human species, but also into a particular human population and ethnocultural community. *Collective, cultural* rights represent the principle of cultural diversity, the differentness of unique ethnocultures or blueprints for living developed by the various ethnic populations of humankind. Taken together, individual and collective human rights represent the twin global principles of human unity and cultural diversity.

While the key principles of the *universality* of individual and collective, cultural rights are central tenets of current international human rights instruments, they have long been the subject of both political and scholarly controversy, and, even today, the debate continues. Accordingly, before I proceed to elaborate on the internationally endorsed concepts of cultural diversity and collective cultural rights, I will digress briefly, in order to highlight the main arguments in this ongoing debate.

The debate over the universality of human rights

The international system of protection for the universality of human rights created by the United Nations has spawned a vigorous scholarly debate over the question of the normative and conceptual universality of human rights (Kallen, 2003: Ch. 1). This controversy has deep, historical roots in the age-old tension between "social cohesion and individual liberty" (in Bertrand Russell's words, 1972: xv). Today, in its contemporary version, it is expressed in the lively debate between libertarians and liberal individualists such as Rawls (1971), Nozick (1974) and Dworkin (1977), on the one hand, and communitarians such as Sandel (1992) and Taylor (1995) on the other (Murumba, 1998: 208).

Murumba's analysis

Murumba (1998) offers an incisive analysis and critique of both sides of this debate. He exposes the deficiencies in the thesis of incompatibility between individual rights and collective cultural and national rights posited by proponents of both positions. He proposes a new "symbiotic model" for the twenty-first century, in which culture and human rights are mutually reinforcing rather than mutually exclusive (Murumba 1998: 209).

Murumba begins by pointing out the problems in what he refers to as the "incompatibility thesis" – the professed "heterogeneity thesis". Of particular importance to this thesis is the alleged incompatibility of Western (presumably "individualistic") and non-Western (presumably "communitarian") societies and cultures. Murumba argues that its major defect lies in its premise of the Western singularity of human rights. While Western culture, he argues, must be credited with the conceptualization of a central component of rights, as claims upon society, the normative content of rights has older and more diverse roots. Human rights are claims against society, but claims against society are not human rights unless they are predicated upon one's *humanity*. Rights predicated on any other attribute, such as race, class, or gender, are not rights.

The second premise on which the incompatibility thesis rests is that of the conflict between the communitarian concept of culture and individual human rights. Murumba explains that the liberal vision of society is of a collectivity created by independent individuals who come together to form a society in order to gain benefits through common action which they could not secure individually. In direct contrast to this atomistic, liberal individualist vision, the distinctive feature of the communitarian vision is that it reverses the priority between individual and society. In the communitarian vision, the community or society comes first, the individual second. Its organizing principle is that of a "people" – not a loose coalition of independent individuals, but a closely known community of culturally connected persons who are born into and become an integral part of a complex web of social entanglements. The rights of individuals in the communitarian vision of society are derived from and contingent upon the nature of the society, but the society always comes before the individual.

Murumba suggests that both the liberal individualist and the communitarian versions of society are flawed, because they fail to acknowledge the inescapable fact that, just as the communitarian society can not mask the uniqueness of each individual member, so the individualistic society can not mask the shaping influence of the society and culture on each individual member.

Murumba concludes his analysis of the libertarian/communitarian debate by arguing that while their rival images of individuals and society compete with one another, they cannot live without each other. This, he contends, is because they both have roots deep in the human psyche, in the motivational duality of individualistic drives and communitarian drives. He then proceeds to defend a concept of human rights which reflects this fundamental duality.

To begin, Murumba emphasizes the primacy of human rights over particular cultural and social formations. Since human rights are rights which all human beings have solely by virtue of their *humanity*, they must *ipso facto* transcend cultural practices or forms which conflict with fundamental human rights. Human rights claims are claims of individuals against society, whether that society is organized along state, ethnic, or cultural lines. Indefensible cultural practices, allowed, or even prescribed by culture – such as female circumcision, racial discrimination or the execution of minors, constitute human rights violations and cannot be immune to censure from the international community. In such cases of *bona fide* conflict between individual and culture, the primacy of human rights must prevail.

But this possibility of conflict, Murumba contends, must not obscure the fact that the greater part of the relationship between culture and human rights is positive, even symbiotic. Murumba proposes that there is a human rights dimension of culture (human rights in the service of culture) and a corresponding cultural dimension of human rights (culture in the service of human rights). The human rights dimension of culture is demonstrated in the now widely acknowledged fact – at the heart of multiculturalism – that culture plays a crucial role in shaping personality and identity. Put another way, one's personhood is not developed in a cultural vacuum, each individual's personhood is shaped by the cultural particularities of his or her socialization. The cultural dimension of human rights emerges in the distinctive cultural conceptions of what it means to be human. Murumba points out that it was these competing visions of "true humanity" which haunted international human rights norms from their inception. The ensuing dispute between the "West and the rest" was responsible for the creation of two separate covenants – the International Covenant on Civil and Political Rights (ICCPR) and the International Covenant on Economic Social and Cultural Rights (ICESCR) – reflecting the Western and non-Western conceptions of human rights, respectively.

At the beginning of the twenty-first century, Murumba suggests that we should adopt a cross-cultural approach, incorporating both conceptions. This would reveal that they are indispensable components of the same notion – what it means to be human. This approach would thus provide a richer and more accurate conception of human rights.

In closing, Murumba draws attention to the fact that human rights themselves are, in the last analysis, a cross-cultural invention. Without cultures, which shape and define the very personhood for which human rights were invented, there would be no human rights. However, he contends, for cultures to operate effectively in the multi-cultural, global environment of the twenty-first century, they must become more flexible, for culturally shaped personality and identity will need to be open to the possibility of multiple allegiances. Put another way, he says, in the twenty-first century "we shall need to wear our cultures lightly" (Murumba, 1998: 240).

The United Nations: attempts to gain universal acceptance for the implementation of human rights in different socio-cultural contexts

The conception of the universality of humanity and of human rights currently built into virtually all international human rights documents had its core articulation in the Charter of the United Nations (Espiell, 1998). The UN Charter (1945), which serves as the written constitution of the international community, was drawn up for the purpose of promoting international cooperation in the realization of human rights and fundamental freedoms for all members of humankind, without distinction of any kind. The 1948 Universal Declaration of Human Rights (UDHR) followed and reinforced the universalist viewpoint of the Charter. This essential character of the Declaration was reaffirmed by the adoption of the term "universal", rather than "international" in its title (Espiell, 1998).

The universalistic objective of the Declaration is to unite all individuals, over and above their identity differences; to combine unity and diversity in the name of equal dignity, the crux of humanity (Espiell, 1998).

In the fifty-five years since its adoption, the Declaration has reached a general level of international acceptance, well beyond the expectations of its original adopters. It was thus thanks to the Declaration that the universality of human rights became a generally accepted axiom. In recent years, only a particular group of non-Western nations have questioned the universal character and international force of the Declaration (Espiell, 1998). This group sees the UDHR conception of universal human rights as part of the ideological patrimony of Western civilization. They argue that the principles enshrined in the UDHR reflect Western values, and not their own (Cerna, 1994). They claim that the West is interfering in their internal affairs by imposing their definition of human rights upon them, and they argue that because of their countries' social and cultural differences from the West, they should not be held to Western standards. This attempt to undermine the internationally enshrined notion of the universality of human rights is attributed to such countries as China, Columbia, Cuba, Indonesia, Iran, Iraq, Libya, Malaysia, Mexico, Myanmar, Pakistan, Singapore, Syria, Vietnam and Yemen. But the strongest advocates of this position are the Asian states experiencing the most dynamic economic growth (Cerna, 1994).

The challenge to the concept of universality of human rights, coming primarily from Asia, had to do with "private" rights. It is these provisions of the UDHR that have not become universally accepted. The private sphere deals with issues such as religion, culture, the status of women, marriage, divorce, and remarriage, the protection of children, family planning, and the like. These rights have traditionally been covered by religious law and, in some countries, they still are (Cerna, 1994). This tension between the universality of rights in the private sphere and the competing religious and/or traditional law means that some societies are unwilling to assume international human rights obligations in the private sphere.

Cerna (1994), in commenting on this seeming impasse, concludes that achieving universal acceptance of international human rights norms is a *process*, and that different norms occupy different places on the continuum. While the international community may censure countries for practices based on norms which violate human rights, they cannot impose international human rights norms to replace traditional ones. Acceptance of these norms must come from within the countries themselves. It seems clear, in the early twenty-first century, that international norms dealing with rights that affect the private sphere of life will take the longest time to achieve universal acceptance.

Later, in this chapter, we will offer a case study which should enable the reader to consider the issues in debate over the universality of human rights in the context of modern multicultural democracies. At this juncture, however, we will return to our earlier discussion of cultural diversity and elaborate on the meaning of the concepts of cultural diversity and collective, cultural rights, as currently articulated and endorsed under international human rights instruments.

Cultural diversity and collective rights

Culture as ethnoculture

Cultural diversity, as a human rights principle, and as the basis for collective human rights claims, rests on the anthropological conceptualization of culture as *ethnoculture*. The concept of ethnoculture refers to the distinctive culture developed and maintained by a particular people or ethnic group. Ethnoculture refers to the distinctive ways of viewing and doing things – eating, dressing, speaking, worshipping, loving – shared by members of a particular ethnic community and transmitted by them from one generation to the next; it is the unique design for living of a particular ethnic group. This concept of culture as ethnoculture underscores protections for collective cultural rights endorsed in the provisions of Article 27 of the International Covenant on Civil and Political Rights (United Nations, 1978, 1988) and reinforced in the provisions of the Declaration on the Rights of Persons Belonging to National, Ethnic, Religious and Linguistic Minorities (United Nations, 1992).

The reader should note that this conceptualization of culture as ethnoculture means that, under the provisions of current international human rights instruments, the various *sub-cultures* of the world's non-ethnic populations are not recognized or protected. Non-ethnic groups or communities therefore have no legitimate basis for making *collective rights* claims. (I will return to this point in Chapter 6 in order to offer a critique of this position in connection with my analysis of the gay and lesbian rights liberation movement).

The most important point about ethnoculture, from a human rights perspective, is that it is *learned*; it is acquired, for the most part, through the ordinary processes of growing up and participating in the daily life of a particular ethnic community (Kallen, 2003: 36–7). Insofar as culture is part of the condition of being human, then all individuals must learn to be human. But culture is not learned in the abstract, for no human being is born into a cultural vacuum. Every member of humankind learns to be human by learning the language, religion, values and customs of a particular culture.

Collective human rights

The principle of collective human rights recognizes the collective right of every human population, every ethnic community, to practice and to perpetuate the distinctive culture or way of life developed and shared by its members. From a human rights view, just as every individual human being is equally human, every human culture is equally human: no human being or human culture is superior or inferior to any other. Put another way, all human beings and all human cultures are equally valid. Just as all human beings, as members of humankind, must respect the fundamental individual rights of all other human beings, so, also, all human beings, as members of particular human cultures, must respect all of the different human cultures shared by other human beings.

Similar parallels can be drawn between individual and collective human rights with regard to the imposition of justifiable restrictions on their exercise in order to prevent human rights violations. In the increasingly multicultural context of modern democratic societies, just as we can justifiably impose restrictions on one human being's exercise of individual rights in order to prevent harm to others, so we can, justifiably, impose restrictions on one population's exercise of cultural rights in order to prevent harm to other human beings. So, for example, if the traditional cultural practices of a particular community include female infanticide, or the branding of slaves, or the burning at the stake of homosexuals, we can, justifiably, impose restrictions to prevent such human rights violations. Freedom of cultural expression, like freedom of speech, is not absolute. All human rights, both individual and collective, are *conditional on the cardinal principle of non-violation of the rights of others*.

Human rights as legal rights

At this point, it is important to distinguish clearly between international human rights principles and public policies or laws enacted by governments. For laws and government policies may violate human rights. Human rights principles are international, moral guidelines which are prior to law. They represent the global standards to which all laws of all countries should conform. However, as this book will amply demonstrate, laws do not always incorporate human rights principles: while some laws are modeled on human rights guidelines (e.g. anti-discriminatory laws prohibiting discrimination against particular categories of persons on specified grounds – race, sex, religion, nationality, sexual orientation, age, disability and so forth) others violate human rights principles (e.g. laws which discriminate against particular categories of persons on specified grounds). When human rights principles become incorporated into law, they become *legal rights* which can be invoked by persons or groups who perceive that their human rights have been violated in order to seek redress for the alleged violation.

Individual versus collective (cultural group) rights

A critical question surfaces at this point: given the increasingly multicultural nature of modern democracies, are there basic conflicts which arise between our commitment to the fundamental rights of freedom, equity and dignity of each individual citizen and our increasing desire to respect the distinctive customs and lifestyles of different ethnocultural communities? As suggested earlier, respect for culture can never be unconditional and condone acts of inhumanity and oppression. However, once we move beyond the incontrovertible cases of patent physical and psychological harm, inter-cultural moral judgments become problematic. We must be careful not to impose arbitrarily the values of democratic liberalism upon the immensely rich and varied moral universe introduced by multiculturalism.

To illustrate the kinds of conflicts which can develop from the tension between individual rights and collective cultural rights, we will now offer a case study (Case Study 2.1). This case study should enable the reader to consider the issues in the debate over the universality of human rights (addressed earlier) in the context of modern multicultural democracies.

Case Study 2.1   Human rights of women in a multicultural context

Okin (in Okin *et al.* 1999) argues that many practices and conditions which clearly violate international human rights principles – polygamy, forced marriage, female genital mutilation, punishing women for being raped, differential access for men and women to health care and education, unequal rights of ownership, assembly and political participation, unequal vulnerability to violence – are standard in some parts of the world. This observation, she submits, raises the following critical questions: Do demands for multiculturalism make these sexist customs more likely to continue and to spread to liberal democracies? Are there fundamental conflicts between our commitment to gender equity and our increasing desire to respect the customs of minority cultures or religions?

Okin asserts that some group [sic] rights can, in fact, endanger women. Okin argues that if we agree with a liberal, egalitarian and feminist approach which mandates that women should not be disadvantaged because of their sex, then we should not accept group rights that permit oppressive practices on the grounds that they are fundamental to minority cultures whose existence may otherwise be threatened.

By way of response to Okin's position, Parekh (in Okin *et al.* 1999) concedes that all "liberals" agree that minority communities should have a right to preserve their cultures, but disagree about the basis and limits of that right. Some suggest that cultures should enjoy the right to preservation so long as they meet the basic condition of civility and do not practice murder, incite hatred against outsiders, live as free-riders, and so on. Others require that cultures should also allow their dissenting members the right of exit. Yet others go further and ask minority communities to organize themselves internally along liberal lines. This involves respecting fundamental freedoms, encouraging personal autonomy, practising equality between the sexes and so on.

Although sympathetic to this last approach, Susan Okin thinks that it is not enough. Many cultures, she argues, are deeply sexist, and perpetuate women's subordination through a variety of practices too subtle for the law to catch, let alone disallow. They also condition their women into taking a low view of themselves and rationalizing and accepting their subordinate status, with the result that their well-being is damaged and they grow up without a strong sense of self-respect and self-esteem. In Okin's view, liberal democratic societies should ensure that respect for cultural diversity does not become a shield for sexism. She also implies that deeply sexist cultures should not qualify for cultural group rights.

In response, Parekh contends that Okin concentrates on extreme cases and, by doing so, ignores the problems involved in judging other cultures. Parekh agrees, for example, that clitorectomy on children is unacceptable, but points out that in some societies adult and sane women (including academics) freely undergo it after the birth of their last child as a way of regulating their sexuality and reminding themselves that from now onwards they are primarily mothers rather than wives. Should we deny them this right to choose? Again, he agrees with Okin that polygamy, meaning a man having multiple wives, is sexist and unacceptable but, he asks, what about polygamy which allows both sexes the same freedom? It violates no liberal equity principle, for it is based on uncoerced choices of adults, causes no apparent harm, encourages experiments in living and relates to the realm of privacy with which the liberal democratic state should not interfere. Should we also deny them this right to choose? In short, Parekh contends, once we move beyond the incontrovertible cases of patent physical and psychological harm, cross-cultural moral judgments become problematic.

There is also the further question, Parekh suggests, of how women themselves perceive their situation. If some of them do not share the liberal, feminist view, should we assume that they are brainwashed, victims of culturally generated false consciousness and in need of liberation? To do so uncritically, he argues, denies these women the very equality we espouse.

Parekh agrees with Okin that the way a culture treats women is of considerable importance. However, he insists, a culture comprises much more: it provides a blueprint for living and for finding meaning in one's life. As expressed in a living community, it also gives its members an ongoing opportunity to participate in the institutional life of the community, thus reinforcing a sense of collective identity, rootedness and he argues, therefore, that it is a serious mistake to judge any culture solely or even primarily in terms of, and to make its rights dependent on, its treatment of women.

Kymlicka (in Okin *et al.* 1999) agrees with the basic claim of Okin's paper – that a liberal egalitarian (and feminist) approach to multiculturalism must look carefully at intra-group inequalities, and specifically at gender inequalities. Justice *within* ethnocultural groups, he argues, is as important as justice *between* ethnocultural groups. Kymlicka emphasizes this point by distinguishing between two kinds of group-level rights.

The first kind of group rights, which Kymlicka (1999) calls "internal restrictions", consist of ethnocultural group rights against its own members – in particular, the right to restrict individual choice in the name of cultural "tradition" or cultural "integrity". Such collective rights restrict the ability of individuals within the group (particularly women) to question, revise or abandon traditional cultural roles and practices. Such internal restrictions, Kymlicka argues, are unacceptable in a liberal democracy since they violate the autonomy of individuals, and create injustice within the group.

A second kind of group rights, which Kymlicka calls "external protections", refers to rights which are claimed by a minority cultural group against the larger society in order to reduce its vulnerability to the economic or political power of the larger society. Such group rights can take the form of language rights, guaranteed political representation, funding of ethnic media, land claims, compensation for historical injustice, or the regional devolution of power. Kymlicka contends that all of these collective rights are acceptable in a liberal democracy because they can help to promote justice between ethnocultural groups, by ensuring that members of the minority have the same effective capacity to promote their interests as do members of the majority.

Kymlicka takes issue with Okin's inference that feminists should be deeply skeptical about the very category of cultural group rights. He argues instead that both feminism and multiculturalism are making the same point about the inadequacy of the traditional liberal conception of individual rights. In both cases, it is argued that the distinctive needs and interests of women and ethnocultural minorities are simply never addressed through standard, equal treatment, focussing on individual rights. The result is that liberalism has been blind to grave injustices which limit the freedom and harm the self-respect of women and ethnocultural minorities. Other minorities, Kymlicka points out, including persons with disabilities and gays and lesbians, have made similar arguments about the need for group-specific rights and benefits. All of these movements are challenging the traditional liberal assumption that equality requires identical treatment. They are arguing instead for *equity of treatment*.

Source: Okin *et al.* (1999) and adapted from Kallen (2003: ch. 1).

Group-level rights and claims: distinguishing between collective and categorical group rights

As far as it goes, Kymlicka's argument for equity of treatment of women and ethnocultural minorities (outlined in Case Study 2.1) is on firm ground. However, what he fails to address is the conceptual distinction between the nature of group-level rights raised by women and other non-ethnic minorities on the one hand, and by ethnocultural minorities on the other.

The basic principle behind *collective cultural rights* is the group-level right of ethnic communities as such to legitimate and free expression of their *ethnocultural* distinctiveness. As recognized in the provisions of Article 27 of the ICCPR, the distinctive elements of ethnocultures may be expressed in language, religion, politico-economic design, territorial links or any combination of these and/or other defining group attributes. Regardless of the specific cultural attributes emphasized at any given time, insofar as a people's ethnoculture is in itself consistent with human rights principles, every ethnic group has the collective right to develop, express and transmit through time its distinctive design for living.

The basic principle behind *categorical group rights* (Kallen, 2003: 17) is the group-level right of members of all distinctive social categories based on particular human attributes such as age, sex, sexual orientation, mental and physical abilities and so forth, to be treated equitably with their societal counterparts (for example, women and men, same-sex oriented and other-sex oriented, and so on). Unlike collective rights, categorical rights are not based on shared ethnocultural attributes; rather, they are based on shared physical, behavioural, and/or *subcultural* attributes.

This conceptual distinction between collective and categorical rights may become clearer when we look at the differential nature of the claims that can be raised in response to violations of rights.

Categorical rights claims, while put forward at the group level, essentially represent claims for redress against violations of fundamental individual human rights: the rights to freedom of choice, equity of opportunity or dignity of person. By way of contrast, *collective rights claims* seek redress against violations of a people's collective cultural rights – rights to language, religion, territory (including nationhood).

Concluding commentary

Our examination of internationally endorsed human rights principles advanced in the provisions of the UN Charter, the International Bill of Human Rights and related treaties and covenants, confirms that the international human rights system is rooted in the fundamental human rights precepts of *social equality* and *social justice*. These international human rights principles are advocated by UN authoritative bodies as moral guidelines, the universal human rights standards, to which all systems of law and justice should conform.

International human rights principles provide an overarching paradigm for social equality and social justice for all of humanity, rooted in the twin foundations of human unity and cultural diversity. The principle of biological unity of humankind emphasizes the oneness of all human beings as members of the same human species and recognizes the close affinities between members of all human populations. The principle of cultural diversity respects the unique contributions to all of humankind made by each ethnocultural community throughout the globe. Embraced together, these cardinal principles underscore the theme of *unity in diversity*, recognizing and embracing the essential oneness of all of humanity, while at the same time celebrating the uniqueness of each human being and of each human group.

What this means with regard to furthering the social scientific understanding of social inequality and social injustice is that issues of group-level inequality and injustice confronting virtually all subordinate populations throughout the globe can be conceptualized and studied within the same overarching interpretive framework. Whether the social construction of subordinate status derives from attributes of race, religion, language, gender, sexual orientation, age or any other unjustly invalidated human or cultural characteristic, the human rights violations experienced by members of these subordinate populations can be addressed, and hopefully redressed, under the rubric of social equality and social justice endorsed in international human rights principles.

In light of the current endorsement of these international human rights principles and their incorporation into human rights laws by the bulk of the world's democratic nations, how do we explain continuing violations of human rights in democracies throughout the globe? In order to answer this question, in Chapter 2, we will turn our attention to the ways in which the more powerful members of a society are able to *justify injustice and inequality* by invalidating others, defining them as somewhat less than human, thus rendering them undeserving of human rights.

CHAPTER 2

The Social Construction of Inequality

Introduction: the invalidation of difference

Group-level inequalities

Scientific evidence on the biological attributes of the world's various racial and ethnic population groups demonstrates beyond doubt that no human population is innately superior or inferior to any other human population (UNESCO, 1978). All human beings, despite differences in their ethnic, racial or other group membership, belong to the same biological species, *homo sapiens*. Accordingly, all humans share the same, fundamental biological traits which identify them as human beings. No human individual or human population group is any less human or any more human than any other. Within every human population, there is a range of variation for each human characteristic (e.g. intelligence, physical strength, emotional endurance): accordingly, every human population has some members who are very intelligent and others who are not as intelligent; some who are very strong and others who are not as strong, and so forth for every human trait. When discussing group differences among human beings, what is most important to understand is that the differences in characteristics *within* populations are far greater than the differences *between* populations. Put another way, the strong biological affinities between all human populations as members of the same human species are far greater than the differences between them.

This having been said, how, then, do we explain group-level inequalities between different populations in society? Social scientists, today, generally agree that group-level inequalities between populations are *socially constructed* (Kallen, 1995: 108–9): they are *not* a result of innate differences in the superiority/inferiority of group attributes of populations. They are arbitrarily created by human beings with the power to define and to invalidate others on the basis of *assumed or perceived group differences*, in order to protect their own vested interests. When powerful decision-makers in a society *invalidate* a particular population by defining its members as innately *inferior* with regard to their (perceived or assumed) shared human attributes, they are then able to rationalize acts of categorical discrimination against the population by denying its members their fundamental human rights – that is, by denying members of invalidated populations the same opportunities, rewards and esteem accorded others. As a result of these human rights violations, over time, the invalidated population comes to occupy a subordinate and collectively disadvantaged position in the society. The more powerful population, on the other hand, comes to occupy a dominant status in the society. Over time, these group-level inequalities become institutionalized in a hierarchy of unequal *social relations* between dominant and subordinate populations in which the dominant populations are able to wield their greater power and higher status position to control the life destinies of subordinate populations and to protect their own vested interests.

Dominant/subordinate relations: the structure of social inequality

The majority/minority relations paradigm

In my discussion of the development of my theoretical framework for analysis, presented in the Introduction, I noted that, traditionally, ethnic stratification theorists tended to conceptualize dominant/subordinate relations as *majority/minority relations* (Simpson and Yinger, 1972; Yetman and Steele, 1975). In my previous works (Kallen, 1989, 2003), I followed in the footsteps of theorists like Sagarin (1971) and Winslow (1972), who were among the first social scientists to extend the application of the "minority" concept beyond the racial/ethnic realm. Like these theorists, I applied the majority/minority paradigm in the study of both ethnic and non-ethnic populations, and included for study many populations previously categorized and studied as "deviant".

Over the years, in teaching courses on majority/minority relations, I found that the widespread lay use as well as the political use of the terms "majority" and "minority" to refer to inequalities in *population numbers* tended to confuse the issues when these concepts were applied to unequal *power relations*. In the present work, in order to make absolutely clear to the reader that my analysis of unequal relations between groups focuses on unequal power relations and not on inequalities in numbers (population size), I have chosen to conceptualize my analysis in terms of dominant/subordinate relations.

The relativity of the concepts of dominance and subordination

Dominant/subordinate relations are unequal relations between population groups in the society, based on group-level inequalities in political (decision-making) power, economic power (resources) and social power (prestige or esteem). Domination and subordination are *relative notions*: each has meaning only in relation to the other. With regard to any human attribute (such as, for example, skin color, religion, national origin, age, sex, sexual orientation), the dominant population is the more powerful population whose members' human rights are recognized and protected in the society; and whose members' physical, cultural and behavioral attributes provide the recognized cultural standards for all individuals and populations in the society. Because it is the dominant population who defines the rules governing life in the society, for any socially significant human characteristic it is the dominant attribute which provides the positive value standard against which subordinate differences are judged as inferior (Kallen, 1989: 49–51).

It is important to point out, at this juncture, that it is the dominant population's *perceptions* or *assumptions* about subordinate group attributes, and not the attributes themselves, which lead to the imposition, by dominant authorities, of inferiorizing/invalidating labels on these subordinate attributes and on the members of the population assumed to share them.

To understand the evaluative process underscoring dominant/subordinate relations, let us consider the six human attributes mentioned earlier. Viewed in the social context of Euro-Western societies, the reader should be able to identify, for each attribute, the dominant population and the corresponding subordinate population (Table 2.1).

In Table 2.1, the dominant attributes are found in the first column, and the subordinate attributes in the second column. This table illustrates well the very important observation that domination and

Table 2.1 Human attributes (as perceived and defined by dominant powers)

Skin color:	White	Non-white
Religion:	Christian	Islam
National origin:	British	Asian
Age:	Adult (18–65)	Children and elderly (under 18/over 65)
Sex:	Male	Female
Sexual orientation:	Heterosexual	Homosexual

subordination are *relative* conditions: the subordinate label has meaning only in relation to a corresponding dominant label, and vice versa. Accordingly, we may define a dominant population, in relation to a corresponding, subordinate population as follows (Kallen, 1989: 49–51):

The concept *dominant* refers to any population within a society:

(1) whose members have the power to *define their population as innately superior* and to define all other populations whose members' perceived or assumed attributes deviate from dominant physical, cultural and behavioral norms as inferior (and/or dangerous);

(2) whose members have the power to *invalidate* populations defined as inferior and, by so doing, to justify categorical discrimination against them;

(3) whose members have the power to impose their will, their cultural standards and their laws on society-at-large and to *deny the expression of alternative cultural values and lifestyles*;

(4) whose members are able to exercise the greatest degree of political, economic and social power in the society and thus are able to *control the life destinies* of invalidated subordinate populations.

In relation to a corresponding dominant population, we may define a subordinate population as follows:

The concept *subordinate* refers to any population within a society:

(1) whose members are set apart and defined by the dominant population as inferior (and/or dangerous) on the basis of perceived or assumed physical, cultural and/or behavioral *differences from dominant norms*;

(2) whose members are invalidated and categorically discriminated against by dominant authorities and are thereby subject to *violations of their fundamental human rights* to freedom, equality, dignity and cultural expression;

(3) whose members, as a result, become *collectively disadvantaged* and come to occupy a subordinate and marginalized social status in the society.

Invalidation: the key to unequal relations

History has demonstrated, time and again, that one of the most powerful tools of decision-makers in a society is the *power to define*. Those with the most power are able to wield that power by imposing inferiorizing and *invalidating* labels on those with less power, and to do so arbitrarily, on the basis of their own unsubstantiated and often highly prejudiced assumptions about the shared attributes of members of invalidated populations.

Once invalidating labels are imposed, dominant authorities can *justify injustice*: they can rationalize human rights violations – denial of the freedom to decide, equality of opportunity and the right to human dignity – to populations arbitrarily defined as in-valid, less-than-human beings.

A classic example is provided by the former apartheid regime in South Africa, which began with the artificial (and scientifically erroneous) classification of populations into socially constructed and legally defined "races": white, colored and black. These so-called "races" were then ranked, on the basis of colour, on a socially constructed scale of racial superiority and inferiority, with "whites" (those with the authority to define the "races" and to construct the racial hierarchy) at the top and "blacks" (those presumed to be most inferior to "whites") at the bottom. Under apartheid in South Africa, human rights violations took the form of legal discrimination, justifying separate and unequal treatment of those classified as colored (and, even more so, those classified as black), in the form of forced segregation, denial of franchise, unequal economic opportunity and continual affronts to human dignity.

Over time, continuing human rights violations, which deny members of invalidated populations the opportunities, rewards and esteem accorded others, act collectively to disadvantage them. The long-term consequence is that invalidated, disadvantaged populations come to occupy a subordinate and marginal status in the society. All too commonly, subordinate status becomes a trap, from which it is very difficult to escape. What happens is that a *self-fulfilling prophecy* is set in motion, which serves to keep members of subordinate groups "in their place", at the bottom of the heap (Kallen, 1989: 29–30). How does this occur?

When members of subordinate groups are continually denied their fundamental human right to make decisions affecting their own life destinies; when they are continually denied adequate educational and job opportunities for meaningful participation in the society; when they are continually ridiculed, shunned, harassed or physically abused; when their culture has been forcibly mutilated or destroyed, what eventually happens is that they become the victims of a self-fulfilling prophecy whereby denial of opportunity and of human dignity begin to blunt their untapped capabilities and unused skills, and lead to a loss of motivation to get ahead. When this happens, members can, and too frequently do, lose all hope of status improvement. They simply give up trying. This results in a condition of *socially constructed dependency* whereby members of subordinate groups, no longer willing or able to make it on their own, become dependent on welfare handouts from governments, charitable organizations and the benevolence of others in order to survive. Not surprisingly, they often become depressed, withdrawn and alienated from society. They experience the pains of social and cultural *marginality*: a frustrating and humiliating experience of not belonging, not fitting in, being unable to find a meaningful niche in life, either within their own communities or within society-at-large. They may turn to alcohol, drugs or even suicide in order to seek solace from their chronic state of despair. The long-term outcome of the self-fulfilling prophecy is that members of subordinate groups all too frequently become entrapped in the predicament of collective disadvantage, socially constructed dependency and social marginality which characterizes their subordinate status.

Characteristics of subordinate status
Collective disadvantage, created dependency and marginality

In the course of this discussion, I have noted the factors leading to the conditions of created dependency and collective disadvantage which characterize the subordinate status of invalidated populations. I will now focus attention on another major outcome of the self-fulfilling prophecy of invalidation, the experience of *marginality*.

Social and cultural marginality is a notion which refers to the highly stressful and psychologically devastating situation of those members of subordinate groups who find themselves in a *status dilemma*, caught between two different communities, cultures, and lifestyles but unable to identify fully with, to gain acceptance in, or to find a comfortable niche for themselves within, either (Stonequist, 1937; Kallen, 1972).

This situation typically arises among children of immigrant parents, who are socialized at home and within their own ethnic community into one set of cultural values, but who are exposed to another, conflicting set of norms and values at school and in the dominant society-at-large. In this kind of case, marginality is usually only a temporary thing. Over time, some kind of cultural compromise is usually worked out, and the problem of marginality is resolved.

However, there are other cases in which the problem of marginality is much more difficult to resolve – and, indeed, may never be resolved. A special case of marginality may arise with regard to persons of mixed ancestry, the children of inter-racial and/or inter-ethnic unions. In some of these cases, children may be forced to renounce one side of their family/one ethnic community/one language/ one religion ... in favor of the other, or they may be rejected by both communities. Not able to fit in or gain acceptance by either community can be psychologically devastating.

The double life syndrome

Another example of social and cultural marginality is provided in the case of those subordinate groups whose invalidated attributes are invisible or can be hidden from public view, and who can, if they so choose, hide their subordinate identities. In many such cases – for example, gay and lesbian persons, recovering alcoholics, ex-prisoners, epileptics and others – this can lead to the *double life syndrome* (Kallen, 1989: 108–11). This term refers to the dual lifestyle of secretive (*closeted*) members of invalidated populations who participate in the alternate sub-culture of their subordinate community in their private lives, but who attempt to mask their subordinate status and identities and to pass for members of the dominant population in their public lives.

Closeted gay and lesbian youth, unable to identify fully with, or to feel a sense of belonging to either the adult gay (homosexual) or straight (heterosexual) communities, and fearing rejection by their families and straight peers should their sexual orientation be disclosed, too frequently exist in a condition of marginality. They feel all alone in the world and unable to disclose their invalidated identities to others. They feel alienated from society, a condition which results in low self-esteem, inadequate coping mechanisms, substance abuse and even suicide (Schneider, 1988). Research studies about the incidence of suicide by gay/lesbian/bisexual/transgendered teens in the USA reveal that 30 percent of teen suicides are by such youth, when even conservative estimates place such teens at 5 percent of the total population (Remafedi, 1994).

The anatomy of invalidation

My examination of the practices leading to the social construction of unequal, dominant/subordinate relations, indicates that there are three major steps in this process: first, the official labeling of particular populations as invalid; second, categorical discrimination against the invalidated population, involving long-term denial of members' fundamental human rights and leading to socially constructed, collective disadvantage; third, the process of the self-fulfilling prophecy of invalidation, ensuring that members of invalidated and disadvantaged populations

"know their place, and stay in their place", i.e. that they remain within
the socially constructed trap of collective disadvantage, dependency and
marginality which defines their subordinate status.

In order to demonstrate how this process works in everyday life, I
will examine the case of the black population in North America. One of
North America's most persistent *invalidation myth*s holds that "As a group,
whites are smarter than blacks." The underlying assumption behind this
statement is that whites are innately superior to blacks in intelligence.
Can we provide scientific evidence for this? We cannot. There has been
no instrument developed, as yet, that can accurately measure intellectual
capacity. What one may be able to find are data on *comparative performance*
of white and black students on intelligence tests. Suppose, then, that
these data consistently reveal superior performance by white students?
Does this prove that whites are smarter? It does not. What is revealed by
so-called "intelligence test scores" is relative performance on a culturally
biased test, favoring the dominant "white", middle-class populations in
the society, in a culturally biased, test situation, probably under the
supervision of a white middle-class test administrator. The crucial factor
which is not revealed by test scores is the highly negative influence of
unequal educational opportunities on the test scores of disadvantaged
black students (Elliot and Fleras, 1992: 41–2). Most significantly, a
compendium of articles, entitled *Race and IQ* (1999) edited by the
renowned anthropologist, Ashley Montagu, debunks the mythology
attributing differences in IQ scores to racial differences. What emerges
in chapter after chapter is a deep skepticism about the scientific validity
of intelligence tests, especially as applied to evaluating innate intelligence, if only because scientists still cannot distinguish between genetic
and environmental contributions to the development of the human
mind.

What this example is meant to illustrate is that invalidating assumptions about the innate intellectual inferiority of members of the black
population are not supported by scientific evidence. So-called "intelligence tests" are invariably prejudiced in favor of the dominant white
population because evaluations are made in terms of the dominant
population's social and cultural values and expectations. As a result,
these culturally biased tests serve to "blame the victim" (Bolaria and Li,
1985: 9), by failing to take into account the disadvantaging consequences
for the subordinate black population of long-term denial of the human
right to equality of opportunity.

The myth of racial inferiority and superiority

I pointed out earlier that scientific evidence on the biological attributes of the world's various racial and ethnic population groups demonstrates beyond doubt that no human population is innately superior or inferior to any other human population (UNESCO, 1978). In order to invalidate any particular human population, therefore, one must rely on erroneous and negatively prejudiced invalidation myths about the inferiority of that population's human attributes. Myths of racial superiority and inferiority have long been used by those in power to justify unjust and often cruel acts of discrimination against particular racial and ethnic groups. In order to demonstrate the scientifically erroneous *premises* behind racist myths and ideologies, it is important to clarify the social scientific meaning of the key concepts of *race* and *ethnicity* which are distorted and manipulated in these invalidation myths and ideologies. While there has long been and continues to be considerable variation among theorists on social scientific definitions of these concepts, there is general agreement today that the concepts must be distinguished from one another and that the concept of race, if it is to be employed at all, should refer only to biological human attributes and not to cultural attributes (Wilson, 1973; Biddiss, 1979; Miles, 1989; Satzewich, 1998).

What is "race"?

The scientific term *race* refers to any arbitrary classification of human populations using biological measures such as observable physical traits and/or genetic indicators (gene frequencies for particular traits). It is very important to point out that this scientific definition of race is based solely on biological differences between human populations , and not on cultural differences (Kallen, 2003: 35).

The three most commonly used racial categories today are Caucasoid ("white"), Mongoloid ("yellow") and Negroid ("black"). Clearly, these categories are not based on cultural criteria. There is no white culture or black culture or yellow culture, based solely on race. However, each of these broad racial categories can be sub-divided along lines of ethnic origin, national origin, religion and many other variables. Once we begin to differentiate among various populations within the broad racial categories, we introduce the component of *culture*. For example, within the "white" category, we find Italians, Irish, Jews, English, Spanish and many other national, ethnic and religious groups. Within the "yellow" category, we find such diverse populations as Chinese, Inuit, Japanese and Vietnamese. Within the "black" racial category we find a similar range of variation: Jamaican, Nigerian, Afro-American, Trinidadian and so forth. All of these diverse populations within each of the three broad racial categories can be distinguished, at least in part, by cultural differences. Some of these differences pertain to ethnicity.

What is ethnicity?

The social scientific term *ethnicity* refers to any arbitrary classification of human populations based on the biological factor of common ancestry in conjunction with cultural factors such as language or religion. Ethnicity, then, has both biological and cultural dimensions. It refers to one's biological ancestors, their ancestral territory or homeland, and their ancestral culture or ethnoculture (Kallen, 2003: 36).

The root of this notion of ethnicity is the term *ethnic*, which simply refers to a people. Probably the easiest way to grasp this rather complex idea is to think of your own family and your family background. Can you name the particular people (*ethnic group*) with which your parents identified themselves? What about your grandparents and great-grandparents, and your ancestors before them? What part of the world would they have identified as their *homeland*? Where did they come from? What language did they speak amongst themselves? What religion did they practice? How did they dress and what kinds of foods did they eat?

Common ancestry links members of a given ethnic group, through time, to their biological ancestors, to their ancestral cultural heritage and to their ancestral territory or homeland. But, at any given time, ethnicity is expressed in the form of living ethnic communities whose members maintain distinctive, but ever-changing, ever-adapting ethnocultures. With changing circumstances – modernization, immigration and so forth – ethnic communities and their distinctive cultures become transformed, even transported, so as to adapt to changes around them. However, as long as enough members of a given ethnic group continue to identify with and to maintain even selected aspects of their distinctive culture, their common ethnicity is maintained through bonds of kinship and culture.

Race, ethnicity and human rights

Exposing the myths of racial superiority and inferiority

I emphasized earlier that fundamental human rights are rooted in the indisputable biological fact of the unity of humankind. All humans share the same, fundamental *biological traits* which identify them as human beings. No human individual or human population group is any less human or any more human than any other; no human individual or population group is innately superior or inferior to any other.

Invalidating labels which define some human populations as superior and others as inferior are erroneous and misleading because they ignore not only the natural range of individual differences *within* all populations, but, even more importantly, the strong human family ties and likenesses *between* all populations as members of the same human species. Because these scientific facts are overlooked, invalidating labels unjustly taint the labeled population as a whole. This leads, almost invariably, to *categorical discrimination.*

Categorical discrimination

Let me digress, for a moment, to explain the concept of categorical discrimination, a concept crucial for the comprehension of the social construction of subordinate status. "Categorical discrimination" refers to differential and unequal treatment which serves to advantage or to disadvantage persons because of their assumed membership in a particular human population. Such discriminatory treatment, whether positive or negative in thrust, is "categorical" because it ignores the natural range of variation within any human population and thus treats all assumed members of the population as alike. Categorical discrimination, then, is not based on the unique, individual traits of the person or persons who are the victim/s of the discriminatory act, for these are beside the point. The real target of discrimination is the invalidated population group to which the victim is assumed to belong. Categorical discrimination totally ignores the range of differences in individual personalities, interests or skills among members of the invalidated population, because the negatively prejudiced assumptions upon which the act of discrimination is based are assumptions made about the invalidated population *as a whole.*

Thus, for example, when an aboriginal or black candidate, with equal or better qualifications than a white candidate for the same job, is refused the job given to the white applicant, on the *arbitrary basis of skin color*, this is a clear example of categorical discrimination. The prejudiced assumption is that "whites are smarter than blacks." Similarly, when a female student with higher grades than a male student in the same class, applies to engineering school or medical school or law school, and is rejected, in favor of the male student on the *arbitrary basis of gender*, this is a clear case of categorical discrimination. The prejudiced assumption here is that "women are the weaker sex" and/or "men are the natural thinkers and decision-makers."

Turning back to our discussion of the myth of racial inferiority and superiority: if this *racist* myth is truly unfounded, and contrary to the scientific evidence about the biological unity of humankind and the strong ties and similarities between human populations, how can we explain its dogged persistence? The explanation may seem obvious. We all know that people often react with fear and mistrust to things that seem strange or foreign to them, things they do not understand and that they do not like. When people see other human beings who look very different from themselves and/or who act very differently from themselves, in ways that they do not understand and that they do not like, they tend to fear and mistrust these differences and to judge them as signs of human inferiority.

Comparative evaluation

As far as it goes, this explanation is on the right track. What it fails to take into account, however, is the very important role played by the process of *comparative evaluation* through which members of one population judge members of another population in terms of their own, culturally biased, group values and standards. The more another population is seen to deviate, in unacceptable ways, from one's own cultural standards, the more likely it will be that the "deviant" population will be labeled as inferior. When those doing the labeling have the greater power, they can exercise that power to invalidate members of the less powerful population by officially defining and invalidating them as innately inferior.

The dogged persistence of unfounded beliefs in human inferiority and superiority can be explained in large part by two facts: first, they are sanctioned and supported by dominant authorities in the society as a means of protecting their own vested interests and their superior status; and second, over time, they become entrenched in invalidation myths, deeply-rooted in the public mind. Invalidation myths are unscientific and erroneous statements which authoritatively assert that some human populations are *inherently inferior to others* with regards to particular human attributes.

Thus far, I have focused my argument on the myth of racial superiority and inferiority. By and large, however, the same kind of argument can be made with reference to myths of human superiority and inferiority based on a host of other human attributes: sex/gender, sexual orientation, age, mental and physical abilities and disabilities, ethnocultural group status and so forth.

Invalidation myths

To illustrate this point, let us examine a number of invalidation myths which have historically been used to justify the erroneous and invalidating belief that men are superior to women: women are the weaker sex; women are by nature emotional and submissive, and are innately predisposed to adopt "mothering" roles (child-rearing, nursing and the like). Men, by contrast, are the stronger and more aggressive sex; the natural protectors of women and children; and are innately predisposed to be the thinkers and decision-makers in public life (Swann, Langlois and Gilbert, 1999).

What these myths imply is that the subordinate status of women in society is "justifiable": it is a direct result of their innate inferiority based on their sex. In reality, however, the subordinate status of women is a social construct: it based upon gender ... a culturally defined sex role difference. Historically, invalidating assumptions about innate, sex-based female inferiority have been used by dominant male authorities to deny women the same opportunities, rewards and esteem accorded men. Unequal treatment, which has violated women's fundamental rights to freedom, equality and human dignity, has led to the socially constructed gender role subordination of women. Based on dominant males' culturally biased assumptions about the "proper role" for females, their "natural place" in society, women became confined to subordinate, gender roles (unpaid child-rearer and home-maker for the head of the household, secretary for the boss, nurse for the doctor). Thus, it is not sex differences *per se*, but negatively prejudiced, male assumptions about sex-based female inferiority, which have been responsible for the social construction of subordinate gender roles for women. And it is gender role subordination which has led to the subordinate status of women, and the socially constructed dependency, disadvantage and marginality historically associated with that status. That this tendency persists, despite the remarkable advances made by women today, will be elaborated in later chapters of this book.

Invalidation ideologies

Weapons of discrimination, subordination and extermination

In my earlier discussion of invalidation myths, I alluded to the terms "racism" and "sexism". I will now attempt to demonstrate how dominant authorities can build upon invalidation myths to create invalidation ideologies such as racism, sexism, heterosexism, ageism, handicappism and so forth (Kallen, 2003: 40). Such invalidation ideologies are misleading theories which falsely claim to "prove" invalidation myths by fabricating pseudo-scientific and pseudo-religious "evidence" for them. Invalidation ideologies are designed to give teeth to invalidation myths in order to sharpen their effectiveness as weapons of categorical discrimination and human rights violation.

Invalidation ideologies are based on the erroneous and scientifically untenable assumption that some human populations are innately inferior to others with regard to particular human attributes (for example, race, sex, sexual orientation, disability, or age). A second presumption behind these theories is that human populations can be ranked in terms of their members' innate ("natural") superiority and inferiority. Based on these false premises, an invalidation ideology is socially constructed which affords allegedly superior populations a legitimizing rationale, a platform for discriminatory action against allegedly inferior populations. Accordingly, discriminatory laws, public policies and practices are developed which legitimize *unequal relations* between allegedly superior/dominant and allegedly inferior/subordinate populations.

In order to illustrate these arguments, I will provide examples of invalidation ideologies of sexism, racism, anti-Semitism and heterosexism which have been used by dominant authorities to legitimize laws and public policies which categorically discriminate against, and thereby violate, the human rights of women, non-whites, Jews and gay populations.

One flesh ... one person: the pseudo-religious ideology of sexism

In Christian countries, the law has institutionalized the dependent status of women since Biblical times. In the Biblical account of the creation myth, Eve is created from the rib of Adam, and thus represents a part of Adam as a whole person. The biblical concept of marriage as a sacrament uniting husband and wife as one flesh, one person, symbolizes the reuniting of Adam and Eve as one person; namely, Adam. This "one flesh, one person" concept was institutionalized in the common law of England, the civil law and Napoleonic Code of France and (later) in North American laws. Legally, then, when a woman married she was absorbed into her husband's legal identity and they became, in law, one person. This one person was the husband. The woman/wife was a nonperson (Eberts, 1979).

Legitimized by pseudo-religious invalidation ideology and institutionalized through legal tradition, the inferiorized patriarchal conception of women has led to their confinement to the private sphere of life. They have been (until very recently) virtually excluded from public life. For example, under Canadian law, only "persons" could participate in public life; women were thus excluded from public life because the unwritten law defined "persons" as men. Well into the 20th century, women, whether married or single, could not vote, could not hold an elected or appointed political or judiciary office, practice law, serve as a police constable, or sit on a jury (Eberts, 1979). In North America, as in other democratic countries with a Christian tradition, a woman's employment opportunities outside the home were very limited, concentrated in areas resembling her domestic functions: housework, light manufacture, child care, nursing and teaching. Until the 1950s, women suffered economic discrimination in the form of job segregation and lower pay, largely through their relegation to the low-paid "pink ghettoes" of "woman's work". Moreover, the husband traditionally had the right to the wife's wages from her work outside the home, even if the wife and husband were separated.

Even within the private sphere of family life, the assumed "woman's place", legal precedent dictated that women assume a subordinate and dependent role. At marriage, a woman customarily lost her own nationality, surname and domicile and took those of her husband. She became unable, during marriage, to leave property by will or to make binding contracts, because, at marriage, a husband assumed virtually total control over his wife's real and personal property. In return, the wife was legally entitled to a level of financial support appropriate to her husband's income, on condition that she remained absolutely chaste and faithful. (This "moral" condition, of course, did not apply to her husband, the patriarch, who could pursue extra-marital encounters with impunity). Until 1891, the husband had the legal right to administer "moderate physical correction" (read: wife-battering) to a disobedient wife (Eberts, 1979).

In North America, as in other democratic societies, there have been significant changes in law and social policy, affording women the status of persons, and hence the franchise; affording women greater opportunities for participation in the workforce and greater equality within marriage. Yet, as will be elaborated later in this book, status disparities between men and women remain, even today.

White racism

A Euro-Western instrument of subjugation and control of non-whites

Both pseudo-religious and pseudo-scientific racist ideologies of white supremacy have long been employed by white Euro-Christian authorities to invalidate non-white populations and to justify and legitimize highly discriminatory acts and policies against them. Social Darwinism was a particularly popular brand of pseudo-scientific racism in the late nineteenth and early twentieth centuries. Social Darwinist theories were based on erroneous interpretation and misapplication of Charles Darwin's notion of "survival of the fittest", which Darwin used to explain the survival of some species over others in the process of evolution of species of animals and plants. Social Darwinists attempted to apply Darwin's model, based on *species*, to human societies and cultures *within* the human species. This led to the idea that some sub-species of humankind (the so-called "white races") and some human cultures (the so-called "civilized" cultures) were more "evolved" and more "human" than others (non-white races/cultures). Non-white races were held to be innately inferior to white races because of a presumed "evolutionary lag" which predestined them (as less-than-human beings) to be subservient to whites (assumed to be full human beings). This kind of theorizing, however erroneously founded, has been employed to justify racist colonial and post-colonial government policies throughout the world, policies which violate the human rights of subordinated non-white populations through such cruel discriminatory measures as forced relocation and segregation of populations, enslavement, cultural genocide and even genocide (Kallen, 2003: 43).

The "new racism"

In contrast to traditional, pseudo-scientific racism which proposes a hierarchy of human superiority and inferiority based on immutable racial differences, the "new racism" (Baker, 1981; Gilroy, 1991; Thompson, 2001) proposes the existence of "natural" boundaries between human populations (nations), rooted in immutable cultural differences. This scheme proposes that human beings have a natural "instinct" to form a bonded community, a nation, aware of its differences from other nations. Each national community, it is argued, has a natural home and its members share a natural instinct to preserve their common, national identity and to defend their territory (homeland). The language of this theory is race-free; but its covert agenda links together race/

ethnicity/culture and nation, based on "legitimate", "natural" human instincts.

Baker (1981) and Gilroy (1991), two British scholars, represent an increasing number of social scientists who suggest that the "new racism" is used by dominant authorities in a democratic society to maintain the "status quo" of racial and ethnic inequality in the face of espoused democratic ideals of anti-racism and egalitarianism. As Baker so astutely observes, the language of innocence in which the new racism is couched leaves racists free of any imputation of racial superiority/inferiority, or even of dislike or blame against those who pose the threat of "cultural alienness". The argument suggests that our biological instincts predispose us to defend our national way of life, traditions and institutions against outsiders, not because they are inferior but because they are naturally different.

Gilroy uses the example of "black criminality" to illustrate this point. Gilroy argues that the new racism endorses the view that law represents the cultural ideals of national unity and equality of citizens in a democratic nation. The identification of racially distinct crimes and criminals ("black criminality") is attributed not to "race", but to the economically disadvantaged and politically marginalized status of blacks which, in turn, is attributed to their distinctive inner-city culture ("deviant", single-parent, female-headed families; lack of work ethic, street gangs bent on revenge against the white oppressor, drug sub-culture and so forth). Deviant black culture, it is argued, is expressed in particular forms of crime – drugs, street violence and robbery ("mugging"), which have resulted in national chaos, a crisis in law and order and a real threat to the distinctive, national way of life cherished by loyal and law-abiding citizens.

Gilroy's position is illuminated by some very astute observations put forward by Thompson (2001: 63–4), who emphasizes the importance of seeing race and ethnicity in conjunction because, he argues, the cultural differences of ethnicity are manipulated as political weapons (techniques of domination) by majority authorities to reinforce their power and control over minorities, insofar as these ethnocultural differences are seen as deviations from the ethnocentric majority norm. Failure to recognize this covert shift from ethnicity to race, Thompson argues, serves to mask racism and its subtle influences.

Racism and social reality

Today, in Britain, North America and elsewhere throughout the globe, the old and the new racism flourish side by side. Dyed-in-the-wool bigots (Aryan Nations, Ku Klux Klan, Heritage Front and other organized racist groups) continue to promote the pseudo-religious and pseudo-scientific theories behind the established models of racism, while polite racists, as well as many self-professed anti-racists, cloak their parallel views in the discourse of culture promoted by exponents of the new racism. Yet, the source of both forms of racist discourse is the same: *xenophobia*.

From a human rights perspective, what appears to distinguish the two forms of xenophobia is this: the established models of racism "racialize" culture (e.g. Jews as a vile and depraved "race"); the new models of racism "culturalize" race (e.g. blacks as a dangerous and deviant "sub-culture"). But the end result is the same: blaming the victim for the disadvantaging consequences of institutionalized and systemic racism.

Anti-Semitism

Nazi instrument of Jewish genocide

The term "anti-Semitism" originated with an anti-Jewish political movement that surfaced in Germany in 1873. The pseudo-scientific invalidation ideology of anti-Semitism used by the Nazi regime in Germany to justify their covert policy of Jewish genocide, posited a racist ranking order in which Germans, classified as the élite of the supreme Aryan or Nordic "race", were ranked at the very top; all other "races" were subordinated, accordingly (Kallen, 2003: 43). Jews, singled out as an evil, dangerous and demonic race, were ranked at the bottom of the scale. Their very presence in Germany was considered to present a threat of contamination and degeneration of the "superior" German civilization. They were, accordingly, defined and treated as social outcasts.

The ideology of anti-Semitism

The pseudo-scientific foundation for this ideology was provided in the writings of Houston Stewart Chamberlain (1899), who argued that the Jews were waging a permanent war for the destruction of Aryan civilization, and advocated "expelling this alien and noxious element from the body of European society". The ideology of anti-Semitism was used to justify repeated acts of hostility toward and persecution of Jews in the nineteenth century, and in the twentieth century by Adolph Hitler, to justify the racist policy of genocide that culminated in the death of millions of Jews during the Second World War. Like the thinking that underscored colonial suppression of the world's aboriginal peoples, the

Nazi theory of Aryan glorification was an extreme variation of the common invalidation ideology of white supremacy.

Heterosexism

A Euro-Christian instrument of homosexual genocide

The pseudo-religious invalidation ideology most commonly used to condemn homosexuals as sinners and to justify violations of their fundamental human rights is largely based on heterosexist and highly homophobic interpretations of eight quotations from the Judaic–Christian Bible (Toothman, see website references; see also Daniel, Helminiac and Spong (2000). The passages in the St James version of the Bible referred to as the "Big Eight" are listed in Table 2.2.

Legitimizing discrimination

The passages referred to in these quotations have been variously interpreted by biblical scholars, some of whom support heterosexist interpretations, but many of whom support alternative interpretations. In general, the passages condemn, as sinful, a number of acts and practices which, in the particular cultural context of the time, contradicted accepted religious teachings. Such practices generally involved the use or abuse of one person by another as objects or property, without love, and included such acts as male and female temple prostitution associated with pagan fertility cults, as well as all sexual acts, both heterosexual and homosexual, which violated the sanctity of marriage (sexual acts outside of marriage by unmarried or married persons).

The narrow and misleading, heterosexist interpretation of these passages clearly reflects the biased influence of deeply-rooted anti-homosexual prejudice. Nevertheless, it has been the heterosexist interpretation of these biblical messages which has served, since biblical

Table 2.2   The "Big Eight" passages in the St James Bible

Deuteronomy 23: 17–18
Genesis 19: 4–11
Judges 19: 22
(related passages are Jude 6–7 and II Peter 2: 4, 6–8)
Leviticus 18: 22, 20: 13
I Corinthians 6: 9
I Timothy 1: 10
Romans 1: 26–7

---

times, as a powerful weapon used to justify and to legitimize inhumane acts of discrimination against homosexuals, including genocide (Kallen, 1989, 59, n. 4)

Hate propaganda

Invalidation ideologies and the promotion of hate and harm

Hate propaganda represents probably the most malignant expression of invalidation ideology, for it not only brands invalidated populations as inferior, but it also singles them out as *dangerous and threatening* to society. Not surprisingly, it follows from this premise that hate propaganda urges its audience to take steps to eliminate the alleged threat. What begins as negative prejudice is thereby translated into categorical discrimination through the promotion of hate propaganda which incites harmful, violent and even genocidal acts of discrimination against the invalidated target population. The invalidation theories currently promoted in hate propaganda, and widely distributed by organized hate groups through-out the globe, tend be put forward in a sequence of three main stages (Kallen, 1997):

(1) *Invalidation myth* (negative prejudice): definition of the invalidated target population as inferior and dangerous;
(2) *Invalidation ideology* (fabricated theory): development of a theory of invalidation and concoction of supporting "evidence" to "justify" denial of fundamental human rights to members of the target population;
(3) *Incitement to hate and platform for action* (strategy for discrimination): incitement to hatred and harm, and outline of proposed plan for discriminatory action against the invalidated target population.

Hate messages: 1

To illustrate the way in which hate is manipulated in order to provoke discriminatory action against target groups, I will offer, by way of example, an adapted passage from a heterosexist hate message recently promoted over the internet by an organized, homophobic hate group. (Westboro Baptist Church website: July 9, 2002): The passage declares that the Westboro Baptist Church of Topeka, Kansas engages in daily, peaceful sidewalk demonstrations opposing the homosexual lifestyle of "soul-damning, nation-destroying filth". The demonstrators display large colourful signs containing "Bible words and sentiments" such as God hates fags … AIDS cures fags … Fag=AIDS=Death … Fags are nature freaks and so on.

This hate message provides a clear example of a homophobic, religious invalidation ideology, an ideology of heterosexism. Pseudo-religious "evidence" is presented to demonstrate the palpable threat to society posed by homosexuals, and to justify acts of genocide designed to exterminate this "dangerous" population.

The message well illustrates the sequence of arguments typically found in hate propaganda:

(1) *Invalidation myth*: homosexuals are abnormal ("nature freaks"). The homosexual lifestyle is sinful, shameful, rooted in "soul-damning, nation-destroying filth";
(2) *Invalidation ideology*: heterosexism;
(3) *Incitement to hate and platform for action*: God has sent AIDS (=death) as a "cure" for homosexuality. Death to homosexuals.

A few words about homophobia

Despite variations in the invalidation myths promoted, the common denominator in the views proclaimed by heterosexist authorities has been homophobia – irrational fear and hatred of persons labeled as homosexuals. I would argue that the most damaging myths behind homophobic invalidation ideologies are based on the unsubstantiated assumption that "homosexuality is unnatural". While pseudo-religious "evidence" for this assumption abounds, scientific evidence is lacking. Whatever is found in nature is natural. It is natural for a heterosexual person, one whose sexual and affectional preference is for persons of the opposite sex, to relate intimately to a heterosexual person of the oppo-site sex. In exactly the same way, it is natural for a homosexual person, one whose sexual and affectional preference is for persons of the same sex, to relate intimately to a homosexual person of the same sex. There is simply no scientific evidence whatever to support the presumption that homosexuality is unnatural.

The nature/nurture question

As soon as the subject of homosexuality is raised, the almost inevitable question asked is: What makes people gay or lesbian? Are they born that way or do they choose their same-sex orientation?

Today, the virtually unanimous view of gays and lesbians themselves is that their same-sex orientation is neither a choice nor a disease but an identity, deeply held for as far back as they can remember. It is not just behavior, nor merely what they do in their love-making, but who they are as human beings, pervading every aspect of their human nature.

The origins of homosexuality may never be fully understood, and its forms of expression are so complex and varied that no single neat explanation is ever likely to suffice. But the search for understanding advanced considerably with the recent release of new genetic studies that make the most compelling case yet that same-sex orientation is at least partly genetic (*Time Magazine*, June 12, 1995). These new studies are said to provide the strongest evidence to date that there is a genetic determinant which is at least partly responsible for sexual orientation among gay men. The preliminary results from a similar study of lesbians still in progress suggest that female same-sex orientation also is genetically influenced. These studies lend new, scientific support to the prevailing view among gays and lesbians that their same-sex orientation is "natural"; it is part of their inherent human nature. Research findings such as those noted above are ignored/discounted by hate propagandists who cling to their own homophobic views about gays and lesbians with dogged tenacity.

Hate messages: 2

To return to my analysis of hate propaganda, my next (second) example is based on anti-Semitic hate messages currently widely distributed, especially over the internet, by an organized hate group called the Church of Jesus Christ Christian–Aryan Nations. (ADL website, Poisoning the Web/aryan nations: July 7, 2002). In 1985, this hate group was the subject of considerable media attention in North America, because twenty-three of its members were on trial, charged with crimes that included machine-gunning to death a Jewish radio talk host, bombing a synagogue (the Jewish House of Worship), robbing banks, killing a state trooper and a variety of other crimes.

The pseudo-religious, racist ideology of anti-Semitism advanced by the Aryan Nations church preaches that the white race is God's chosen people, the good "seed" of Adam and Eve, while the Jewish race is Satan's people, the evil "seed" of Eve and the serpent or Satan. Jews are the source of all evil. The Aryan Nations church preaches further, that Jews have enslaved the world and that the US government has fallen under Jewish power. This evil Jewish takeover of America is bringing about decadence, and blinding "white people" to their fallen state. It is the religious duty of the "Aryans" (the superior white race) to join in a race war to overthrow the Jewish-controlled government of the USA, referred to by the Aryan church as the "Zionist Occupation Government" or "ZOG".

This hate message represents a prime example of a pseudo-religious, racist invalidation ideology of anti-Semitism. The arguments manipulate and distort biblical creation myths in order to justify discriminatory, anti-Semitic actions: they incite hatred and harm against the "evil" Jewish target population. The audience is urged to take immediate, collective action: to engage in a "race war" against the alleged evil Jewish takeover of America by overthrowing the "Jewish-controlled" government of the USA.

The message well illustrates the sequence of arguments typically found in hate propaganda:

(1) *Invalidation myth*: Jews (Satan's people/the bad seed of Eve and Satan) are the source of all evil;
(2) *Invalidation ideology*: racism in the form of anti-Semitism;
(3) *Incitement to hate and platform for action*: the Jewish race, the source of all evil, has usurped control of the US government and is bringing about decadence in America and the fall of the superior white race. Immediate action must be taken to eradicate the immediate danger and threat to the superior white race and to American society posed by evil Jewish control. It is the religious duty of the "Aryans" (the superior white race) to join in a race war to overthrow the Jewish-controlled government of the USA.

Hate messages: 3

My third and final hate message is currently promoted over the internet by a white racist hate group, the Knights of the Ku Klux Klan. (Ku Klux Klan website: July 7, 2002). The body of the message is preceded by a few words about the selection of members of the KKK. It declares that only pure White Christian people of non-Jewish, non-negro, non-Asian descent who are at least eighteen years old and who pledge to dedicate their lives to this cause can enter the Knights of the Ku Klux Klan.

The message suggests that "niggers", equated with savage jungle beasts, and "kikes", our number one enemies, the powerful pigs who promote the defiling activities of "niggers" and faggots", should be destroyed. These sub-human creatures, the message suggests, have taken over and corrupted our nation. They must not be allowed to teach and corrupt our children. Destruction of these allegedly polluting and menacing races will bring purity to "white people".

This hate message clearly demonstrates how unsubstantiated white racist, anti-Semitic and heterosexist invalidation myths are ideologically manipulated, in a typical 3-stage sequence of arguments, to justify injustice, to incite the audience to take immediate, collective action to exterminate non-whites, Jews and homosexuals in order to eradicate the alleged threat to white, Christian, heterosexual society posed by these "dangerous" populations:

(1) *Invalidation myth*: blacks (niggers), Jews (kikes) and gay men (faggots) are sub-human savages and pigs – polluting and defiling races;
(2) *Invalidation ideology*: racism, anti-Semitism and heterosexism;
(3) *Incitement to hate and platform for action*: the message suggests that these sub-human creatures have taken over the nation built by the pure white Christian race. These sub-human pigs are corrupting our children with their impure teachings. They threaten our future and our children's future. We must take back our nation and save our children. We must take action to destroy these enemies and to purify our white Christian nation and race.

The argumentation of hate messages

The examples which I have cited reveal the insidious and manipulative nature of the argumentation typically employed in messages of hate. They demonstrate my proposition that hate messages follow a sequence of three stages, beginning with an *invalidating definition and depiction* of the target population as dangerous and threatening to society. They then build upon this invalidation myth to develop an *invalidation ideology* by providing pseudo-scientific and pseudo-religious "evidence" for their arguments. In this process, they manipulate their "evidence" so as to depict the target population as truly dangerous and to incite hatred for the target group in their audience. Finally, they outline a *platform for discriminatory and harmful action* against the target population proposed as necessary in order to eliminate the "threat" to society posed by them.

Concluding commentary

In this chapter, I have attempted to demonstrate how social inequalities are created and maintained, even in contemporary democratic societies that endorse international human rights principles. My arguments have demonstrated that there are a number of basic steps in the process of social construction of group-level inequalities. First, the arbitrary imposition, by dominant authorities, of invalidating labels on particular populations. Second, the use of invalidation ideologies to justify injustice, to discriminate against invalidated populations and to deny their members fundamental human rights. Third, the self-fulfilling prophecy of invalidation which leads to the creation and maintenance of subordinate group status, a status marked by collective disadvantage, created dependency and marginality. Fourth, and finally, the social construction of a hierarchy of dominance and subordination characterized by unequal relations between dominant and subordinate groups and maintained and enforced by the discriminatory laws, policies and acts of the dominant powers.

In Chapter 3, I will attempt to demonstrate how prejudice and discrimination form the building blocks for the process of *invalidation of difference*, eventuating in the social construction of group-level inequalities between different human populations.

Prejudice and Discrimination: Building Blocks of Social Inequality

Introduction

In previous chapters, I have tried to demonstrate the way in which dominant authorities are able to justify human rights violations through *categorical discrimination* against subordinate populations, by employing *invalidation ideologies* to "prove" that members of these invalidated populations are unworthy of treatment as full and equal human beings.

In this chapter, I want to elaborate on some of the key concepts behind invalidation ideologies, the concepts of prejudice, stereotype and discrimination (Kallen, 1995: Ch. 2). These same concepts provide the building blocks for the social construction of subordinate status. Before I begin, I want to emphasize the *categorical nature* of prejudice, stereotype and discrimination which leads to the social construction of subordinate status.

Prejudice and discrimination

Categorical and personal prejudice

Prejudice and discrimination are most ordinarily thought of as biased beliefs, feelings and actions of one individual for or against another individual. This common form of prejudice and discrimination refers to *personal* prejudice and discrimination. But the *categorical* form of prejudice and discrimination can be far more harmful. This form refers to biased beliefs, feelings and actions of members of one population group for or against members of another population group. In this, second form, the real target of prejudice and discrimination is not the individual victim, but the particular *population group* with which the victim is identified.

To illustrate the difference between personal and categorical forms of prejudice and discrimination, let us consider the following example. Suppose that a student has been warned by gossiping friends that a new student at their school is "dangerous", he is a drug user and dealer, and that it is wise to stay away from him. If the student in question simply accepts this gossip, without questioning it, and then acts upon it by avoiding the newcomer, he has carried out an act of *personal* discrimination based on *personal* prejudice.

Suppose, however, that the student in question had never heard gossip about the newcomer, but that he has seen him and identified him as black. His preconceived notions about blacks suggest that "they" are involved in acts of violence and in the illegal drug trade. He then acts upon these notions by avoiding the new, black student, and having nothing at all to do with him. In this case, the student in question has carried out an act of *categorical* discrimination based on *categorical* prejudice. His actions against his fellow student are not motivated by any feelings or ideas which he has about him as a an unique person but, rather, they are motivated by his negative *prejudgments* about the particular population (blacks) with which he identifies the newcomer.

I thus caution the reader to remember that my focus of discussion throughout this book will be on *categorical* prejudice, stereotype and discrimination which are the concepts that provide the building blocks for the social construction and maintenance of subordinate group status.

The concepts of prejudice and discrimination

While prejudice and discrimination are related concepts, it is important to recognize that, in practice, they are not invariably found together. That is to say, a prejudiced person may not discriminate, and an unprejudiced person may discriminate.

Prejudice

The concept of *prejudice* refers to biased attitudes, feelings and/or beliefs towards particular human populations on the basis of unsubstantiated assumptions and prejudgments concerning the nature of members' collective, physical, cultural and/or behavioral characteristics. Prejudice can be positive or negative in thrust: that is to say, the bias can be in favor of or against particular human groups. Probably the most insidious feature of prejudice is the fact that it is based on unsubstantiated opinion. Because prejudice, for the most part, is learned through the normal process of socialization – that is, by the examples, advice, and actions of persons whom the growing child trusts and respects – the prejudiced beliefs remain unquestioned and untested. Thus, for example, when children hear racist or heterosexist comments or jokes as part of the family conversation or when they are taught racist or heterosexist ideas at school, it is not surprising to find that they become prejudiced against non-white and gay and lesbian persons.

Another aspect of prejudice that reinforces the unsubstantiated prejudgment, often even in the face of scientific facts to the contrary, is its emotional underpinnings. When the emotional component of prejudice is strong, unsubstantiated ideas increase in strength and resistance to change. Because of the strength of the emotional component in prejudice in general, confronting the prejudiced person or group with facts that invalidate their untested prejudgments is a tactic which is likely to prove ineffective in reducing or eliminating the prejudice.

We all live in human societies in which prejudiced beliefs and myths flourish, and are passed on by word of mouth and by public media from one generation to the next. Children do not tend to question the statements of adult authorities, and adults tend to just take prejudiced beliefs for granted . . . assuming that they are "common knowledge," part of the "conventional wisdom". We do not have to feel guilty about holding prejudiced ideas: after all, we didn't invent them. But when we become aware of them, we can begin to question them critically and to ask ourselves whether we are able to provide concrete evidence to substantiate these ideas. And, most importantly, we can refuse to act on unsubstantiated prejudgments in ways that would discriminate against others.

It is important to emphasize, here, that every human being, regardless of differential group membership and regardless of dominant or subordinate status in society, can be categorically prejudiced for or against members of other populations and can act to discriminate for or against them. Because this book focuses on the disadvantaging collective impact on members of subordinate groups of unequal social relations, the tendency is to highlight forms of categorical prejudice and discrimination employed by dominant authorities in the society against members of subordinate populations in order to maintain the existing hierarchy of group inequality and their dominant position at the top of it. However, members of subordinate groups may also be prejudiced and may also discriminate against members of other groups, including subordinate sub-populations *within* their own communities. For example, blacks may discriminate against gay and lesbian members of the black community, and gay men and lesbians may discriminate against black members of gay and lesbian communities. However, at the level of society as a whole, members of dominant groups are far more likely than members of subordinate groups to be represented among the dominant authorities wielding decision-making power behind the laws and public policies which affect the life destinies of all citizens. And it is these powerful authorities who are able to justify injustice and thereby to enact the discriminatory laws and public policies against members of subordinate populations which create and maintain their disadvantaged status. Having clarified this important point, let us now return to the discussion in progress.

Stereotypes

In relation to the concept of prejudice, the concept of stereotype can be said to represent the pictorial content of the prejudiced attitude or belief, the mental image of the population which is the target of prejudice. While stereotypes generally contain a "kernel of truth", they invariably represent distorted images or caricatures which exaggerate some group attributes and disregard others. For example, until quite recently, traditional images of aboriginal peoples depicted them as hatchet-wielding, head-feathered, savages, complete with painted faces and wearing only the barest of loincloths. While this historical stereotype has become replaced by the modern image of indigenous peoples as "a bunch of drunken bums, living on welfare handouts", the current stereotype is equally distorted and equally damaging: it masks wide variations in the life conditions and lifestyles of aboriginal peoples and it violates their fundamental right to dignity.

Some traditional stereotypes seem to be more resistant to change than others. Even today, stereotyped images of women in "mothering" roles; elderly persons as forgetful, incompetent and in need of care; and physically disabled persons as mentally incompetent continue to be promoted, especially in the mass media. Insofar as these, and other group stereotypes of subordinate populations focus on *invalidated* attributes, they serve to underscore negatively prejudiced feelings and attitudes towards target populations. It does not necessarily follow, however, that the bearer of prejudice will act upon his or her biased feelings and stereotyped images of particular populations.

Prejudice does not necessarily lead to discrimination. Put simply, the distinction between prejudice and discrimination lies in the difference between what one thinks, feels and believes and what one does.

Discrimination

The concept of *discrimination* refers to biased acts or practices towards particular human populations which afford categorical advantage or disadvantage on the basis of unsubstantiated assumptions about members' collective physical, cultural and/or behavioral characteristics.

From a human rights view, a critical distinction between prejudice and discrimination is that prejudice, in and of itself, does not violate human rights; discrimination (whether positive or negative) invariably violates human rights principles. Let me explain. A person may be highly prejudiced against any number of categories of people but, unless that person acts upon one of these prejudiced beliefs or feelings by carrying out an act of discrimination against a member of one of these populations, the prejudice, in itself, violates no other person's human rights. On the other hand, if a person performs acts or carries out practices which categorically disadvantage particular categories of people – politically, economically, socially, or culturally, then the discriminatory acts themselves violate the human rights of members of the target population.

If an aboriginal student for example, wants to become a nuclear physicist, he might apply to an elite university where the Department of Physics is staffed by highly racist, and decidedly anti-aboriginal professors. However, unless one of these professors discriminates against him because he is an aboriginal person, whatever racist notions exist in the professors' heads do not affect the aboriginal student and do not violate his human rights. However, if one of the professors tries to exclude the aboriginal student from enrolling in the Department on the basis of his race/aboriginality, or if he succeeds in becoming a graduate student majoring in physics, and one of the professors gives him low grades or refuses to give him job references because of his race/aboriginality, then his human rights are unquestionably violated. The student is denied the fundamental human right to equality (equality of educational and employment opportunity).

Forms and levels of discrimination

Individual, institutional and systemic (structural) discrimination

Discrimination can be manifested in a wide variety of forms. At the level of the individual, an act of discrimination may stem from conscious, personal prejudice. This form of discrimination may be termed *individ-*

ual discrimination. For example, an employer who is prejudiced in favor of males and against females acts upon this personal prejudice to exclude equally-qualified or more highly-qualified female applicants for positions with the firm. This case provides an example of individual discrimination based on sexist prejudice. Another example of individual discrimination is that of a hospital nurse who is prejudiced against the fragile elderly (elderly persons in need of total care) and who acts upon this prejudice to ignore the persistent ringing of the nurse's bell from the room of an elderly patient confined to bed. Younger patients, on the other hand, need press their bell only once or twice before the nurse appears to respond to their needs. This case provides an example of individual discrimination based on ageist prejudice.

Often, however, an act of discrimination does not derive from the personal prejudice of the actor, but from the carrying out by the actor of the dictates of others who are prejudiced or of a prejudiced social institution (business, educational institution, government agency and so on). This form of discrimination may be termed *institutional discrimination*. Suppose an openly lesbian high school teacher applies for a position at a private girls' school. The headmistress is not prejudiced against lesbians (indeed, she happens to be lesbian herself, but she has never openly declared her lesbian identity). The headmistress refuses to hire the lesbian teacher, despite her excellent credentials, because of a covert agreement between the school board and the students' parents excluding lesbians from staff positions. This case provides an example of institutional discrimination based on heterosexist prejudice. In this case, the person who performed the discriminatory act was not prejudiced against lesbians, however the discriminator acted in accordance with the prejudiced (heterosexist) policy of the (educational) institution.

To illustrate a different point, I will change this scenario by just one variable. Let us suppose that the closeted lesbian headmistress in the case is herself prejudiced against lesbians. She has come to internalize and to accept the invalidation myth which holds that same-sex oriented persons – lesbians and gay men – are sick, perverted sinners, but she regards herself as a clear "exception". Moreover, she fears that if an openly lesbian applicant should be hired, her own lesbian identity may be discovered. The headmistress, then, is predisposed to discriminate against lesbians and her own prejudice is supported by the heterosexist policy of the institution (private girls' school) she represents. This case constitutes an example of both individual and institutional discrimination.

Individual and institutional forms of discrimination can ultimately be attributed to prejudiced attitudes: either the actor is prejudiced, or he/she conforms to the sanctions of other prejudiced persons or institutions. Yet, discrimination can occur even in the absence of conscious prejudice. Over time, a prejudiced society can become permeated with structural or systemic forms of discrimination. The concept of *structural or systemic discrimination* refers to group inequalities which have become rooted in the system-wide operation of society as a long-term consequence of institutional discrimination against particular human populations.

When members of invalidated populations have been categorically denied opportunities to acquire or to use political, economic, educational and/or social skills and qualifications, the subordinate group, as a long-term result, as a whole becomes collectively disadvantaged. The collective, adverse impact of group disadvantage frequently becomes compounded through the self-fulfilling prophecy of invalidation through which members come to lose confidence in themselves, to lose the motivation to better their life conditions and to give up hope of status improvement. When this happens, members become locked into their increasingly disadvantaged subordinate status and excluded from large areas of significant political, economic and social participation.

In the area of equality rights (e.g. equality/equivalence of educational and employment opportunities), one way of looking at the difference between institutional and systemic forms of discrimination is this: institutional discrimination denies equal opportunities for dominant and subordinate group members with equal qualifications; systemic discrimination prevents subordinate group members from acquiring or utilizing qualifications which are equal/equivalent to those held by dominant members.

To illustrate, we will refer back to an earlier example. An aboriginal student succeeds in obtaining a PhD in nuclear physics and then applies for a position with a prestigious research institute. His credentials are superior to those of a Euro/white applicant for the same position, but the Euro/white applicant is hired because the covert policy of the Euro/white research institute is "Euro/whites only". This is an example of institutional discrimination. Suppose, however, that the aboriginal applicant had never succeeded in acquiring a university degree in nuclear physics because, as a rule, university Departments of Physics did not admit aboriginal students. The aboriginal applicant clearly would not have the qualifications for the position in the research institute, not because of his aboriginality, but because of the adverse impact of past discrimination upon aboriginal people as a whole, i.e. denial of the human right to equality of educational opportunity. In this case, even if the research institute in question removed its racist/anti-aboriginal hiring policy, the aboriginal applicant could not compete for the position as he would still lack the necessary qualifications.

In such cases, it has been argued that some form of positive intervention such as an *affirmative action* program (Kallen, 1995: 235–250). is necessary in order to ensure that aboriginal (and other subordinate group) students with the essential capabilities are represented as students in all university departments and are represented in occupations appropriate to their academic and professional qualifications in numbers equivalent to Euro/whites (i.e. proportionate to their numbers in the population). It is important to note, here, that such "equal opportunity" programs essentially represent "catching-up" measures: they are temporary programs which are put in place only until the goal of equality/equivalence in proportional representation of subordinate and dominant group members in any particular educational or occupational environment is reached.

Systemic or structural discrimination is not necessarily linked to prevailing prejudice (although it almost certainly can be traced to prejudice which existed in the past). The important point here is this: should all prevailing prejudice against a particular subordinate group suddenly be removed, the collectively disadvantaged position of the group as a whole would in no way be improved. For the adverse impact of systemic discrimination on the group – lack of skills, jobs and resources – would not be addressed. In order for the *collective disadvantage* of the subordinate group to be remedied, the provision of temporary, special opportunity programs for members of the subordinate group in the areas of education, job training, job recruitment and employment equity would have to be initiated.

Thus far, my coverage of forms of discrimination has focused on violations of fundamental, individual rights (e.g. equality rights). A parallel analysis can be made with regard to violations of collective, cultural rights.

Cultural discrimination

Cultural discrimination refers to the denial or restriction of the free expression of the distinctive cultural values and lifestyles of subordinate groups. When the moral and cultural values of dominant group(s) become sanctioned in law and incorporated into public institutions, they come to provide the normative guidelines for the whole society. Cultural discrimination occurs when legitimate alternatives – subordinate values and lifestyles which are consistent with human rights principles – are suppressed. Cultural discrimination, then, refers to the denial or restriction of the free expression by subordinate groups of their legitimate, alternate cultures or lifestyles. It constitutes a violation of collective cultural rights. Cultural discrimination, like discrimination representing violations of individual human rights, can also occur at the individual, institutional and systemic, or structural levels. Here is an example of individual discrimination. A group of students at London University in England go out to dinner to celebrate the end of term. The head waiter in the restaurant refuses to admit them because one of the female students is wearing an Indian sari and one of the male students has his hair styled in dreadlocks. The waiter is prejudiced against non-European cultural minorities. He believes that all "proper" British citizens should conform to currently acceptable, European hairstyles and dress codes. If we alter this scenario by just one variable, we can provide an example of institutional discrimination based on cultural prejudice. In this case, the policy of the restaurant in question is to strictly enforce Euro/Western dress codes. The waiter therefore acted not only on his own cultural prejudices, but also carried out the prejudiced policy of the institution (restaurant) he represented. This second example, then, illustrates both individual and institutional discrimination based upon cultural prejudice. In a third scenario, where the waiter was *not* prejudiced against non-European cultural minorities, but had simply carried out the prejudiced policy of the restaurant in which he was employed, we would have an example of institutional discrimination, without individual discrimination.

We can use this same example to illustrate systemic or structural discrimination. What would happen, over the long-term, if the discriminatory policy of the restaurant was enforced in all public institutions throughout Great Britain? What if all public institutions – schools, workplaces, government offices and so forth enforced strict conformity to prevailing Euro/Western dress codes, hairstyles, and so on? Members of subordinate cultural communities would be forced to conform to dominant British/Euro/Western cultural norms of attire and, over time, their distinctive ways of dressing and hairstyling would likely be lost. The same kinds of examples of violations of collective rights, leading to loss of the distinctive cultural practices of subordinate groups, could be provided with regard to language, religion and many other aspects of distinctive cultures. These violations of collective, cultural rights can lead, over time, to the destruction of a particular culture or way of life, i.e. *ethnocide* (cultural genocide) (United Nations San Jose Declaration, 1981).

Cultural genocide

Probably the most blatant historical example of cultural genocide on a global scale is that provided by the treatment of aboriginal peoples by colonial authorities in the era of the global expansion of European colonial powers into new territories occupied by aboriginal peoples (Glaser and Possony, 1979: 510–23). Primary among the colonial agents responsible for the cultural genocide of aboriginal peoples were Christian missionaries. European colonizers encouraged Christian missionaries from the colonizing country (the homeland) to undertake the task of civilizing (Christianizing and Westernizing) the aboriginal "savages". The civilizing goal of Christian missionaries extended far beyond their efforts at religious conversion. Bringing the "savages" into submission entailed a high degree of institutional control over the relocated aboriginal peoples and a concerted effort to eradicate aboriginal customs and to instil Euro/Western practices in their place. Aboriginal religious customs, sexual practices, ways of dressing, eating, speaking and virtually all other distinctive aspects of aboriginal ways of life were strictly forbidden by missionaries under the threat of penalties to be imposed by "divine sanction". Children enroled as students in mission schools were forbidden, under threat of harsh punishment by mission teachers, to speak their native languages and to engage in other customary behaviours. They were made to feel ashamed of their traditions, and often came to be ashamed of their own parents, many of whom continued (if only covertly) to carry out traditional ways of doing things. The end result of all of these concerted efforts of missionaries and of other colonial agents to destroy aboriginal ways of life was cultural genocide ... a crime against humanity, under current international human rights instruments (United Nations San Jose Declaration, 1981).

Discrimination of silence

Human rights violations by acts of omission

An important, *covert* form of discrimination which has only recently begun to receive the attention of scholars and human rights activists is the discrimination of silence whereby dominant authorities – those with the legitimate power to do something – choose to say nothing and do nothing about discrimination against members of subordinate populations. By such discriminatory acts of *omission*, the human rights of members of subordinate groups continue to be violated. How can we explain this silence, this resistance to speaking out on behalf of invalidated and subordinated groups? In part, this may be explained by the general resistance of many human beings to becoming "involved" in other people's issues. Additionally, uncertainty about the consequences of speaking out, and the fear of doing so inhibits many, even well-informed professionals who are sympathetic with the human rights concerns of subordinate groups.

Invalidation-by-association

Discrimination by omission may also be deeply rooted in the fear of *invalidation-by-association* – the fear that you will be invalidated simply by your association with invalidated persons and subordinate group issues. As a result of all of these fears and uncertainties, the discrimination of silence continues and nothing is done by those who could do so much to curb harmful violations of the human rights of subordinate populations.

In a 1982 report of the American Sociological Association's Task Group on Homosexuality (American Sociological Association, 1982), substantial evidence was provided to support the task group's research finding that invalidation of the same-sex-oriented population had led to widespread discrimination against gay and lesbian professors. The report also revealed that the fear of invalidation-by-association presented a formidable barrier to the undertaking by sociologists of academic research on homosexuality. Findings, based primarily on three surveys conducted by the Task Group of sociologists, revealed that the vast majority of Sociology Department heads in American universities perceived real barriers to the hiring and promotion of known gays and lesbians. That this situation compelled same-sex-oriented sociologists to remain "closeted" is beyond doubt. Survey findings further revealed that the frequently expressed academic disapproval of homosexuality as a legitimate research topic appeared to divert sociologists (heterosexuals as well as homosexuals) from pursuing research in this area. In this connection, a number of heterosexual sociologists reported that they, personally, and their academic reputations, had been discredited (invalidated) as a result of their association with such research. Fear of invalidation, then, was probably responsible, at least in part, for the reportedly small number of university courses dealing with homosexuality. This discrimination of silence on the part of the very scholars whose potential researches and teachings in the area of homosexuality could contribute the most to the public understanding of gay and lesbian issues seriously hinders the prospects for reducing overt and covert discrimination against same-sex-oriented persons.

While social scientists and other educators, through their research, teaching and public-speaking activities, could come to constitute a strong force in dispelling negative prejudices and stereotypes by providing responsible, factual information about subordinate groups, and about the nature of dominant/subordinate relationships, this responsibility is not theirs alone. Besides these and other powerful dominant authorities – policy-makers, judges, law enforcers, professional care givers and the like – there are also those among the families and close friends of invalidated persons who participate, often unintentionally, in the discrimination of silence. Well-meaning parents, relatives and even partners of gay and lesbian persons, for example, can contribute to the discriminatory conspiracy of silence by engaging in the deceptive mechanisms designed to keep the invalidated friend or relative in the closet. By so doing, "the secret" remains highly suspect to outsiders, and negative prejudices and stereotypes persist.

The relationship between prejudice and discrimination

In my earlier discussion of forms or levels of discrimination, I drew attention to the relevance of these distinctions with regard to their relationship to prejudice. I will now attempt to demonstrate the importance of the relationship between prejudice and discrimination with regard to the development of law, social policy and practice. In order to help in this task, I will use Figure 3.1, a chart originally developed by the sociologist Robert Merton, to demonstrate various pertinent relationships between prejudice and discrimination (Merton, 1949).

Discussion of Figure 3.1

The situations represented by the (++) and (--) boxes are virtually self-explanatory: (++) a person acts upon a particular prejudice he/she holds to discriminate against the members of the population which is the target of the prejudice; (--) a person holding no prejudice against a particular population does not discriminate against members of that population. The more relevant situations, as regards the development of law, public policy and practice, are the situations represented in boxes (-+) and (+-). Under what social conditions would an unprejudiced person be likely to discriminate? Under what social conditions would a prejudiced person be unlikely to discriminate? To answer these questions, think about the way prevailing public

Figure 3.1   The relationship between prejudice and discrimination

		Prejudice	
		+ high	– low
Discrimination	+ high	+ +	– +
	– low	+ –	– –

Code: + +   prejudiced discriminator
  – +   unprejudiced discriminator
  + –   prejudiced non-discriminator
  – –   unprejudiced non-discriminator

(Kallen, 2003: 210–11)

policies and laws in a society can influence the relationship between prejudice and discrimination.

Law, public policy and practice

What Figure 3.1 can illustrate, in relation to law, public policy and practice, is that a prejudiced person can be *prevented* from discriminating by human rights legislation which imposes moral pressure and legal penalties against acts of discrimination. In contrast, an unprejudiced person can be *forced into* discriminating by discriminatory legislation which legitimizes acts of discrimination and imposes legal penalties for not discriminating. Finally, a prejudiced person can be *allowed* to discriminate by the *absence* of anti-discriminatory laws (institutional discrimination by omission).

To illustrate these points, let us consider the hypothetical impact of changes in laws and social policies towards same-sex-oriented persons (gay men and lesbians) in a given social context. Historically, in Western, Euro/Christian countries, criminal legislation prohibiting "unnatural sexual acts" between persons of the same sex not only imposed severe penalties (e.g. incarceration) on offenders but stigmatized them as "perverted" social outcasts. In this homophobic environment, any law enforcement officer who knowingly failed to arrest offenders was likely to be severely sanctioned as well as to risk becoming stigmatized-by-association. This social context virtually ensured that even an officer who was *not prejudiced* against gays/lesbians would discriminate against them by enforcing the law. The decriminalization of so-called "homosexual acts", in a given social context, did not, however, "magically" remove all discriminatory barriers against gay men and lesbians. Same-sex-oriented persons remained highly stigmatized and were frequently denied employment opportunities, housing and access to public venues (bars, restaurants, hotels, and so on). Insofar as no anti-discriminatory legislation existed to protect the rights of gays and lesbians, employers, landlords and others who were prejudiced against same-sex-oriented persons were allowed to discriminate against them. It was not until anti-discriminatory, human rights legislation was introduced, prohibiting discrimination on the ground of sexual orientation, in a given social context, that a prejudiced person was likely to be prevented from discriminating against gays and lesbians by the moral pressure and legal penalties imposed by the law against heterosexist discrimination.

What also should be emphasized, with specific regard to our discussion of *legal* protections for human rights, is that human rights legislation is designed to *prevent discrimination*, not to eradicate prejudice (Hill and Schiff, 1988: 28–9). It goes without saying, that you can't legislate what is in people's minds and hearts. Human rights laws can not force you to love your neighbor, but they can prevent you from violating your neighbor's human rights. And that is precisely what they are intended to do. Over the long term, human rights legislation may indirectly serve to reduce prevailing prejudices by helping to create a social environment which strongly disapproves of and discourages the invalidation of persons and groups in society. However, the primary purpose of human rights laws is to protect individuals and groups against harmful acts of discrimination; ideally, to prevent violations of the fundamental human rights of all persons and groups in the society.

However, laws are created by governments, and governments can change laws – not only from discriminatory to anti-discriminatory, but also vice versa. Case Study 3.1 provides a shameful example of the latter point.

Case Study 3.1   UK new anti-terror law rolls back rights

According to a Human Rights Watch press release, new anti-terrorism legislation adopted on December 13, 2001 in the UK marks another step in the UK's retreat from human rights and refugee protection obligations. Human Rights Watch expressed concern that, while the September 11 attacks in the US evoked grave security issues, the new legislation was not an appropriate response as it constituted a frontal assault on fundamental rights.

In a critique issued on November 16, in advance of the bill's parliamentary readings, Human Rights Watch urged parliamentarians to reject provisions that would define terrorism so broadly that individuals could be found "guilty by association". Human Rights Watch was also critical of provisions that would permit prolonged indefinite detention of terrorist suspects without charge. This, Human Rights Watch alleged, would allow the UK to derogate from certain obligations under the European Convention on Human Rights, and would severely undermine the right to seek asylum in the UK.

Human Rights Watch also expressed a broader concern that the UK's derogation from certain provisions of the European Convention sends a signal to other Council of Europe member states that obligations under the convention can be disregarded with ease. Human Rights Watch hailed the passage of the Human Rights Act in 2000 as a milestone, but expressed dismay that with the new legislation, the UK is departing from the European Convention and adopting a law that permits indefinite detention without trial and a denial in some cases of the right to seek asylum.

Human Rights Watch criticized Home Secretary David Blunkett for equating critics of the bill with supporters of terrorism. Among those critics was a number of members of the House of Lords who complained in debate that certain provisions could lead to human rights abuses, without significantly improving UK security. Many human rights and civil liberties organizations with large UK-based memberships also opposed the bill.

Human Rights Watch expressed concern for the law's impact on the right to seek asylum in the UK and the obligation not to return a refugee to a country where his or her life or freedom could be threatened. The new law, Human Rights Watch alleged, clearly undermines the Refugee Convention at the expense of those the convention was designed to help. The new law, Human Rights Watch alleged, also offends the long human rights tradition in Britain.

Source: Human Rights Watch press release, New York, December 14, 2001.

Prejudice or discrimination?

The promotion of hate against subordinate target groups

The fact that human rights-oriented laws are designed to prevent discrimination, and not to eradicate prejudice, has important bearing on the considerations to be taken into account when such laws are being formulated and enacted. An important case in point concerns anti-hate promotion legislation. If we consider the incitement to hatred and harm of identified target groups to be an expression of prejudice, then the argument follows that anti-hate promotion laws are both inappropriate and ineffective means for the eradication of such prejudice. If, however, we consider the promotion of hatred and harm to identified target groups to be acts of discrimination, then it can be argued that anti-promotion laws are both necessary and effective means for the prevention of discrimination. Continuing controversy over this question of definition has given rise to a heated debate concerning the appropriateness of anti-hate promotion legislation.

The hate propaganda debate

The question of whether or not to prohibit hate promotion activities legally is a currently pressing human rights issue which has sparked vehement debate among concerned citizens and legal scholars in democratic countries. The debate on this issue highlights the underlying theoretical question as to whether the promotion of hatred and harm against identified target groups constitutes prejudice or discrimination (Kallen, 1992; Kallen and Lam, 1993).

The hate propaganda debate centers on *rights in conflict*; namely, the right of members of identifiable target groups to freedom from the demonstrable harm caused by incitement to hatred, harassment and violence, as opposed to the right of hate promoters to freedom of expression. There are two contrasting positions among both legal scholars and concerned citizens on this question: (1) the "libertarian" view holds that freedom of speech takes precedence over all other rights and freedoms because all rights and freedoms depend on the existence of an effective right of dissent. From this view, the harmful effects of hate promotion are not deemed to be sufficiently grave to justify the imposition of legal (especially, criminal) restrictions on freedom of speech; (2) the opposing "egalitarian" view holds that the state has a valid interest in suppressing activities which incite hatred and harm against identified subordinate groups in order to protect target populations from demonstrable psychological damage, pain and suffering and in order to promote inter-group harmony in the society.

Another question underlying this debate is whether or not affronts to group dignity (*group defamation*) constitute violations of the individual human right to dignity of members of subordinate target groups. The egalitarian position is consistent with the view that an affront to group dignity is experienced by target group members as an affront to their individual dignity. The libertarian position is inconsistent with this view.

Incitement to hatred and harm: prejudice or discrimination?

When hate propaganda and its promotion are considered to be expressions of prejudice against identified target groups, it can be argued that it does not violate human rights. This, we suggest, is what the libertarians are saying. However, when hate promotion activities which incite hatred and harm are considered to be acts of discrimination against identified target groups, the promotion of hatred indisputably violates human rights. This, we suggest, is the line of argument put forward by proponents of the egalitarian view.

The harmful impact of hate propagandizing

The central question raised by the conflict of rights in the hate propaganda debate is whether or not the demonstrable harm to subordinate target groups and to inter-group harmony in society caused by hate promotion activities is sufficiently grave to justify the imposition of legal restrictions on the freedom of expression of the promoters of hatred and harm.

What evidence do we have that incitement to hatred and harm has harmful effects on members of target populations? Our evidence comes largely from research studies carried out by social psychologists (Kaufmann, 1966; Rosenthal, 1990). A great many psychologists embrace a theory of *general persuadability* as a personal characteristic. They argue that, in assessing the impact of hate promotion activities, account must be taken of the fact that human beings are emotional as well as rational in their predispositions, and that, particularly in times of stress and strain, they can be swept away by the emotional appeals of false, defamatory propaganda against identifiable target groups. Hitler's Germany, they suggest, provides a stark case in point. It is further argued that the uncontrolled harassment of subordinate target groups and the uncontrolled repetition of falsehoods and pseudo-facts can leave behind a residue of actual or potential prejudice among (non-target) recipients – a seed bed from which more widespread hatred and harm can flourish.

With regard to the psychological impact of hate messages on members of target groups, psychologists have argued that the promotion of hate and harm, and the exposure of target members to words, events and materials which incite hatred and harm against the target population as a whole, can inflict profound psychological and spiritual damage on individual members. Defamatory messages which violate the right to dignity of the target population as a whole, it is argued, are experienced by individual members as violations of their individual right to human dignity. These contentions are strongly borne out by the findings of research studies which examine the impact of hate on target subjects (Cotler, 1985; Kallen, 1992; Kallen and Lam, 1993).

The critical question which remains is: Just how great is this harm? Is the demonstrable psychological damage to target group members caused by incitement to hatred and harm grave enough to warrant the imposition of reasonable limits on the fundamental right of freedom of speech of the hate promoters? This question is not easy to answer, as "psychological harm" is an intensely personal experience, and one which is very difficult to measure. Nevertheless, in Chapter 4, I will attempt to draw upon the reports of the personal experiences of victims of incitement to hatred and harm in order to document the nature and extent of their experienced psychological damage.

Concluding commentary

In this chapter, I have focused my discussion on some of the key concepts behind invalidation ideologies, the concepts of prejudice, stereotype and discrimination. I have distinguished between three forms or levels of discrimination – individual, institutional and systemic or structural. I also have illustrated the various relationships between prejudice and discrimination, and the implications of these distinctions for the development of law, public policy and practice.

With specific reference to the ongoing hate propaganda debate, I have considered the policy implications of the question whether the promotion of hatred and harm against identified target groups constitutes prejudice or discrimination. In closing, I raised the burning question as to whether the demonstrable psychological damage to target group members caused by incitement to hatred and harm is sufficiently grave to warrant the imposition of reasonable limits on the fundamental right of freedom of speech of the hate promoters.

In Chapter 4, my focus of analysis will be on the personal *experience* of invalidation and human rights violation. I will use the reports of victims of hateful discrimination, degradation and abuse to document the damaging impact upon members of subordinate populations of these dehumanizing experiences of invalidation and human rights violation.

The Experience of Degradation, Abuse and the Harmful Impact of Hate

In previous chapters, I have focused on the ways in which dominant authorities have been able to use invalidation ideologies – such as racism, sexism, ageism, heterosexism and handicappism – in order to justify insidious and harmful forms of discrimination which violate the fundamental human rights of members of subordinate populations. In this chapter, my focus will be on the damaging impact upon target subjects of their experiences of human rights violations through degradation, abuse and the promotion of hatred and harm.

Violations of the rights of children

Among the key provisions of the UN Declaration of the Rights of the Child (UN, 1959) are the following:

Principle 2
The child shall enjoy special protection, and shall be given opportunities and facilities, by law and by other means, to enable him to develop physically, mentally, morally, spiritually and socially in a healthy and normal manner and in conditions of freedom and dignity. In the enactment of laws for this purpose the best interests of the child shall be the paramount consideration.

Principle 6
The child, for the full and harmonious development of his personality, needs love and understanding. He shall, wherever possible, grow up in the care and under the responsibility of his parents, and in any case in an atmosphere of affection and of moral and material security.

Principle 9
The child shall be protected against all forms of neglect, cruelty and exploitation. He shall not be the subject of traffic, in any form. The child shall not be
admitted to employment before an appropriate minimum age; he shall in no
case be caused or permitted to engage in any occupation or employment
which would prejudice his health or education, or interfere with his physical,
mental or moral development.

Despite the endorsement by democratic countries across the globe of
the UN Declaration of the Rights of the Child (1959) and of the later,
further elaborated UN Convention on the Rights of the Child (1989),
reported violations of children's rights continue, unabated.

Children, like adults, are fully entitled to the fundamental human
rights of freedom, equality and dignity. At the same time, however, in
order to grow up to be loving and caring adults, children must learn to
respect the human rights of others. Positive role models of loving and
caring adults are crucial to this learning process. Until they have reached
adulthood, children need, and have a right to, the protection, care and
guidance of parents and elders. In order to learn respect for others and
in order to prevent harm to themselves and harm to others, children
may have reasonable limits imposed on their fundamental human rights.
They should, however, not be arbitrarily denied their fundamental right
to make reasonable choices, according to their stage of development and
to their individual capacity to do so; nor should they be denied their
fundamental right to be treated as worthy beings, to be held in esteem
and to have their ideas listened to and considered seriously . . . not arbitrarily rejected or ignored.

Violations of the human rights of members of vulnerable subordinate groups

Paternalism

In the context of an earlier analysis of invalidation ideologies, in
Chapter 2, I drew attention to an important distinction between the
ways in which dominant authorities tend to treat those subordinate
populations labeled as "dangerous and threatening", as opposed to those
labeled as "inferior and incompetent, but relatively harmless". The
former, I argued, tend to be singled out as targets for particularly cruel
and damaging forms of discrimination, including hate crimes and even
genocide. Vulnerable human groups, those whose members have the

least power to defend themselves against harm, and who have the least power to strike out against dominant oppressors, tend to be labeled and treated as inferior/incompetent, but relatively harmless. The latter invalidating label tends to be followed up, in terms of public policy and practice, by paternalistic treatment. Let me elaborate briefly on the concept of *paternalism*.

The model for paternalistic treatment is found in the traditional, paternalistic, Roman family, commonly referred to in feminist literature as the "patriarchal family" (Saller, 1995). In this context, the father (*pater*) had absolute authority over his dependents, his wife, his children and any other members of his household, and he expected absolute, unquestioning obedience to his decisions by them. In return for their obedience, the father assumed full responsibility for the care and protection of his charges. Should his dependents disobey his orders, however, the father could use his absolute power and authority to violate their human rights with impunity. He could beat them, torture them, degrade them and neglect them. With specific regard to children, blatant violations of their fundamental human rights which, in democratic societies today, are considered to be forms of child abuse, were "justified" by the use of religious invalidation myths which held that children are, by nature, not only immature and incompetent, but also wild and bad, and that the most effective way to humanize these little "savages" and to teach them obedience to authority is to beat them into submissiveness. Until quite recently, such traditional mottos as "spare the rod and spoil the child" were commonly used to discipline children through the use of corporal punishment. In democratic societies today, corporal punishment as a legitimate and effective means of child discipline is under serious question, and child abuse, in the various forms to be described in the following section of this chapter, is legally prohibited. While child abuse continues to be widespread, it is not publically accepted today, and child abusers generally perform their violent acts "in the closet".

Paternalistic treatment of adult members of vulnerable populations rests on invalidation myths which depict these populations as "childlike", not "wild and bad" but inferior in competence, unable to make rational decisions on their own behalf, and in constant need of the care and protection of their (dominant) "superiors". As in the case of children, members of other vulnerable populations are expected, by their dominant care givers, to "know their place, and stay in their place": they are not expected to make independent decisions or to disobey the rules imposed by their dominant care givers. Should members of vulnerable populations begin to voice their protest against their discriminatory,

paternalistic treatment, they then may come to be perceived by dominant care givers as "threatening" to their own vested interests and dominant status. When this happens, vulnerable persons are likely to become
subject to various forms of abuse at the hands of their dominant care
givers. Like child abuse, abuse of adult members of vulnerable populations is not publically accepted, and abusers perform their violent acts
"in the closet".

Until quite recently, the shocking statistics on widespread child abuse
were a well-kept secret. Once the facts about child abuse were exposed,
however, other well-kept secrets about the abuse of women, abuse of the
elderly and abuse of persons with disabilities began to be revealed,
sometimes in graphic detail.

It goes without saying that of all vulnerable populations, children are
the most vulnerable. Accordingly, it has been the paradigm of child
abuse which has been extended and applied to members of other
vulnerable subordinate groups (Case Study 4.1).

**Case Study 4.1   Child abuse: physical, sexual, emotional
and neglect**

Physical abuse refers to non-accidental physical injury which may include
severe beatings, burns, biting, strangulation and scalding with resulting
bruises, welts, broken bones, scars or serious internal injuries. Under various
state and provincial laws in the USA and Canada, an "abused child" means a
child less than 18 years of age whose parent or other person legally responsible for the child's care inflicts or allows to be inflicted upon the child non-
accidental physical injury which causes or creates substantial risk of death,
serious disfigurement, impairment of physical health, or loss or impairment of
the function of any bodily organ. It is also considered "abuse" if such a care-
taker creates or allows to be created situations whereby a child is likely to be
in risk of the dangers mentioned above.

Sexual abuse is any sexual contact with a child or the use of a child for the
sexual pleasure of someone else. This may include exposing private parts to
the child or asking the child to expose him or herself, fondling of the genitals
or requests for the child to do so, oral sex or attempts to enter the vagina or
anus with fingers, objects or penis.

Neglect refers to the failure of a child's legal guardian to exercise a
minimum degree of care in supplying the child with adequate food, clothing,
shelter, or education or medical care. Neglect also occurs when the legal
guardian fails to provide the child with proper supervision or guardianship by
allowing the child to be harmed, or to be at risk of harm. "Neglected child"
means a child less than 18 years of age whose physical, mental or emotional
condition has been impaired or is in danger of becoming impaired as a result
of the above-mentioned forms of neglect.

Emotional abuse refers to acts which constitute attacks on a child's emotional development and sense of self-worth. Emotional abuse includes excessive, aggressive or unreasonable demands that place expectations on a child beyond his or her capacity. Constant criticizing, belittling, insulting, rejecting and teasing are some of the forms these verbal attacks can take. Emotional abuse also includes failure to provide the psychological nurturing necessary for a child's psychological growth and development – providing no love, support or guidance.

Source: Child Abuse & Mental Health website, 3 June, 2001.

Child abuse on an international scale

November 1999 marked the fortieth anniversary of the Declaration of Children's Rights and the tenth anniversary of the UN Convention on the Rights of the Child. Yet, throughout the globe, violations of children's rights remain a chronic, and in all too many cases an escalating, problem. In Western democratic societies, as suggested earlier, child abuse is not publically accepted, and abusers perform their violent acts "in the closet". Abuse of children by family members and family friends and abuse of children in institutional settings is most common.

The continuing, shocking revelations about sexual abuse of children, in the USA and elsewhere, by members of the Catholic clergy provides a telling case in point. Internationally, and especially in non-Western/non-democratic countries, child abuse is frequently represented in abusive forms of child labour including slavery or practices similar to slavery, such as the sale and trafficking of children, debt bondage, serfdom and forced or compulsory labour, and forced or compulsory recruitment of children for use in armed conflicts. Also high on the list are the use of a child for prostitution, production of pornography or pornographic performances; the use, procuring or offering of a child for illicit activities, in particular for the production and trafficking of drugs; and work which is likely to harm the health, safety or morals of children (Case Study 4.2).

Case Study 4.2   Sexual abuse and exploitation of children

Children around the world are sexually abused and exploited in ways that can cause permanent physical and psychological harm. In some cases, police demand sexual services from street children, threatening them with arrest if they do not comply. In detention and correctional facilities, children may be sexually abused by staff or are not protected from sexual abuse by other inmates. In refugee camps, many children are exploited by adults or sometimes forced to sell their bodies for food. Children in orphanages may be abused by staff members or other children. In conflict areas, children are kidnapped to serve as child soldiers and also as sexual servants for adult soldiers. Children working as domestics may be assaulted or raped by employers.

This grim picture is compounded by the use of children as prostitutes in countries throughout the world. An unknown but very large number of children are used for commercial sexual purposes every year, often ending up with their health destroyed, victims of HIV/AIDS and other sexually transmitted diseases. Younger and younger children are sought with the expectation that clients will not be exposed to HIV. Prostituted children can be raped, beaten, sodomized, emotionally abused, tortured and even killed by pimps, brothel owners and customers. Some have been trafficked from one country to another; both boys and girls are trafficked. Moreover, child prostitutes are frequently treated as criminals by law enforcement and judicial authorities, rather than as children who are victims of sexual exploitation.

Articles 34 and 35 of the UN Convention on the Rights of the Child forbid sexual exploitation or trafficking of children, and the Committee on the Rights of the Child has devoted time and effort to the issue, urging governments to crack down on the practice. But vast numbers of children are still trapped in this life-threatening sex trade.

Human Rights Watch has investigated the trafficking of women and girls from Burma to Thailand and from Nepal to India. In 1993, it found that thousands of Burmese women and young girls were trafficked into Thai brothels every year. They worked in conditions tantamount to slavery. Subject to debt bondage, illegal confinement, various forms of sexual and physical abuse and exposure to HIV in brothels, they then faced arrest as illegal immigrants if they tried to escape or if the brothels were raided by Thai police. Once arrested, the girls were sometimes subjected to further sexual abuse in Thai detention centers. They were then taken to the Thai–Burmese border where they were often lured back into prostitution by brothel agents who played on their fear of arrest on return to Burma. Thai police and border patrol officials were involved in both the trafficking and the brothel operations, but they routinely escaped punishment as do, for the most part, brothel agents, pimps and clients.

In 1995, Human Rights Watch looked into the trafficking of Nepali women and girls to brothels in India. The victims of this international trafficking network routinely suffered serious physical abuse, including rape, beatings, arbitrary imprisonment and exposure to HIV/AIDS. Held in debt bondage for years at a time, girls worked under constant surveillance: escape was virtually impossible. Both the Indian and Nepali governments were complicit in the abuses. Police and officials in India protected brothel owners and traffickers in return for bribes; Nepali border police accepted bribes to allow trafficking. Even when traffickers were identified, few arrests and even fewer prosecutions resulted.

Source: Human Rights Watch (HRW), August 20, 2002; See website references.

The experience of abuse by adult members of vulnerable populations

Elder abuse, often referred to as "gram-slamming" or "granny-bashing", goes beyond actual acts of physical assault to include financial and psychological or emotional forms of abuse (Elder Abuse, website, November 7, 2002; Elder and Vulnerable Adult Abuse, website, June 3, 2001). Physical abuse refers to the infliction of bodily pain upon an elderly person through any means, including neglect. Psychological or emotional abuse refers to actions that cause the elderly person mental anguish such as threats of placement in a nursing home or isolation from the family. Financial abuse refers to any form of exploitation of an elderly person's money or property, such as coercing elderly persons into signing over pension checks.

The first-ever National Elder Abuse Incidence Study (1996, see website references) propelled a severely under-reported problem out of the shadows. This study estimates that in the USA at least half a million older persons in domestic settings were abused and/or neglected, or experienced self-neglect during 1996, and that for every reported incident of elder abuse, neglect or self-neglect, approximately five went unreported. Research on elder abuse in both Canada and the USA has revealed that those who abuse the elderly are often their care givers: employees of homes for the aged and the adult children of the abused. Until very recently, abuse of the elderly by family members was a closely hidden secret. The shocking facts are now beginning to emerge but the biggest stumbling block is that elderly people are afraid to report abuse by family members because they fear that their families will eject them from their homes. Many elderly persons would rather stay with their families and be abused than go to a nursing home. Others are too ashamed to report abuses. They tend to blame themselves: they wonder what they could have done to bring up a child that would inflict such pain and suffering on them. Research carried out both in Canada and in the USA indicates that neglect is the most widespread form of elder abuse, with financial abuse second, and physical abuse third.

Recent Australian studies support the extensive North American work on the issues of elder abuse (Preventing Elder Abuse – Statistics; see website references). These studies have found that:

- 4.6 percent of people aged over 65 years, presenting to the Hornsby Ku-ring-gai Geriatric and Rehabilitation Service, over a one-year period, had experienced abuse
- 5.4 percent of people referred to the Central Coast Aged Care

Assessment Teams (ACAT) indicated they had experienced abuse. Differences were found between the care giver and the client who had experienced abuse as well as differences in abuser characteristics when comparing financial and non-financial abuse cases

- 2.5 percent of older people (n = 579) living in the general community in South Australia tested in a random sample stated they had experienced spousal abuse since turning 65 years

- Of 55 cases of abuse reported in a survey in Victoria, 30 older people were living with dementia – elder abuse was recorded in 1.2 percent of all referrals to four ACATs (n = 5,246). The ACATs came from three states, and covered both urban and rural areas. Risk factors contributing to the abuse were: mental health/alcohol abuse issues of the abuser (30 percent), dependency of the person experiencing abuse (25 percent), domestic violence (19 percent), care giver abuse (18 percent) and financial dependence (8 percent).

In another study, 100 case records were retrospectively analyzed. This represented approximately 20 percent of total clients over an 18-month period (since the inception of the (ARAS) Aged Rights Advocacy Service Abuse Prevention Program); 100 older people experienced 267 situations of abuse. (This means that when older people reported to ARAS that they were experiencing abuse, more than one type of abuse was noted.)

During 1998–9, 354 people sought assistance from ARAS about abuse of older people by family and friends. Of these 69 percent were female, 10 percent were from a non-English speaking background, 21 percent had a diagnosis of dementia, 53 percent experienced abuse from their son or daughter, 21 percent by other family members, 8 percent from their spouse, 6 percent friends and 11 percent from multiple family members. 354 people who sought assistance from ARAS during 1998–9 reported 658 different types of abuse. Older people reported they often experienced more than one form of abuse at a time from someone close to them, 35 percent were experiencing psychological abuse, 34 percent were experiencing financial abuse.

Woman abuse

Woman abuse, commonly referred to as wife abuse or wife battering, is a term which refers to the loss of dignity, control and safety, as well as the feeling of powerlessness and entrapment experienced by women who are the direct victims of ongoing or repeated physical, psychological, economic, sexual and/or verbal abuse (Fact Sheets: Wife Abuse/

Violence Against Women, Health Canada website, November 7, 2002). Woman abuse also includes being subjected to persistent threats of abuse, or the witnessing of acts of abuse against their children, relatives, friends, pets or cherished possessions by their boyfriends, husbands, live-in lovers, ex-husbands or ex-lovers. As in the cases of child abuse and elder abuse, woman abuse may be physical, psychological, economic, sexual and/or verbal, or may take the form of threats of abuse. It is currently estimated that one in every ten members of the female population in North America is a victim of woman abuse. As in the case of abused elders and their abusing children, abused wives usually stay with or return to their abusing husbands (see Case Study 4.3).

Case Study 4.3   Sexual abuse of women in US state prisons

This Human Rights Watch Report examined sexual abuse of female prisoners, largely at the hands of male correctional employees at eleven state prisons located in the north, south, east and west of the USA. It reflects research conducted over a two-and-a-half-year period from March 1994 to November 1996 and is based on interviews conducted by the Human Rights Watch Women's Rights Project and other Human Rights Watch staff with the US federal government, state departments of corrections and district attorneys, correctional officers, civil and women's rights lawyers, prisoner aid organizations and over sixty prisoners formerly or currently incarcerated in women's prisons in California, Georgia, Illinois, Michigan, New York and the District of Columbia, which is the nation's capital.

The report findings indicate that being a woman prisoner in US state prisons can be a terrifying experience. If you are sexually abused, you cannot escape from your abuser. Grievance or investigatory procedures, where they exist, are often ineffectual, and correctional employees continue to engage in abuse because they believe they will rarely be held accountable, administratively or criminally. Few people outside the prison walls know what is going on or care if they do know. Fewer still do anything to address the problem.

The USA has the dubious distinction of incarcerating the largest known number of prisoners in the world, of which an increasing number are women. Since 1980, the number of women entering US prisons has risen by almost 400 percent, roughly double the incarceration rate increase of males; 52 percent of these prisoners are African-American women, who constitute 14 percent of the total US population.

The custodial sexual misconduct documented in the report takes many forms. Human Rights Watch found that male correctional employees have vaginally, anally, and orally raped female prisoners and sexually assaulted and abused them. In the course of committing such gross misconduct, male officers have not only used actual or threatened physical force, but have also used their near total authority to provide or deny goods and privileges to female prisoners to compel them to have sex. In addition to engaging in sexual relations with prisoners, male officers have used mandatory pat-frisks or room searches to grope women's breasts, buttocks and vaginal areas and to view them inappropriately while in a state of undress in the housing or bathroom areas. Male correctional officers and staff have also engaged in regular verbal degradation and harassment of female prisoners, thus contributing to an aggressively hostile and humiliating custodial environment.

No one group of prisoners appears to suffer sexual misconduct more than any other, although those in prison for the first time and young or mentally ill prisoners are particularly vulnerable to abuse. Lesbian and transgendered prisoners have also been singled out for sexual misconduct by officers, as have prisoners who have in some way challenged an officer, either by informing on him for inappropriate conduct or for refusing to submit to demands for sexual relations. In some instances, women have been impregnated as a result of sexual misconduct, and some of these prisoners have faced additional abuse in the form of inappropriate segregation, denial of adequate health care and/or pressure to seek an abortion.

Human Rights Watch states that the organization has no objection *per se* to male officers guarding female prisoners, which is in accord with US anti-discrimination laws prohibiting employment discrimination on the basis of gender. Nor does Human Rights Watch believe that all male officers abuse female prisoners. However, it has expressed concern that the state's adherence to US anti-discrimination laws, in the absence of strong safeguards against custodial sexual misconduct, has often come at the expense of the fundamental rights of prisoners. The investigation revealed that where state departments of correction have employed male staff or officers to guard female prisoners, they have often done so without clear prohibitions on all forms of custodial sexual misconduct and without either training officers or educating prisoners about such prohibitions. Moreover, Human Rights Watch reports, few prisons have express policies protecting the privacy rights of prisoners, and fewer still deal expressly with the impropriety of verbal harassment and degradation.

The District of Columbia and all of the states investigated in the report, with the exception of Illinois, expressly criminalize sexual misconduct between officers and prisoners. However, state laws are rarely enforced, and when they are, they often carry very light penalties. States' failure to uphold their own laws regarding custodial sexual misconduct, Human Rights Watch contends, reflects their sexist view that, except in the most egregious cases, the prisoner was complicit in the sexual abuse committed against her. In this sense, state officials still widely view criminal sexual misconduct as a victimless crime. Thus, the sexual and verbal abuse and harassment of female prisoners by male custodians continues, unabated.

Source: Human Rights Watch, December 1996; see website references.

Violence against women on an international scale

Human Rights Watch contends that unremedied domestic violence essentially denies women equality before the law and reinforces their subordinate social status (Women's Human Rights: Domestic Violence; available at the Human Rights Watch website). Men use domestic violence to diminish women's autonomy and sense of self-worth. States that fail to prevent and prosecute domestic violence treat women as second-class citizens and send a clear message that the violence against them is of no concern to the broader society. Countries as diverse as Pakistan, South Africa, Jordan, Russia, Uzbekistan and Peru have one thing in common: a horrendous record on addressing domestic violence. In Pakistan, officials at all levels of the criminal justice system believe domestic violence is not a matter for criminal courts. In South Africa, the police and courts treat complaints by battered women as less serious than other assault complaints, and there are persistent problems with the provision of medical expertise to courts when women have been abused. In Jordan, "honor killings" occur when families deem women's behavior improper and, despite some legislative reforms, the perpetrators receive lenient sentencing before the courts. In Russia and Uzbekistan, police scoff at reports of domestic violence, and harass women who report such violence to stop them from filing complaints. In Peru, despite improvements in its domestic violence legislation, the law still does not protect women from marital rape and stalking. Discriminatory attitudes of law enforcement officials, prosecutors and judges, who often consider domestic violence a private matter beyond the reach of the law, reinforce the batterer's attempts to demean and control his victim.

Abuse of the disabled

Abuse of the disabled refers to the physical abuse, sexual abuse, emotional abuse or neglect of persons with disabilities (Abuse of the Disabled, Disability Resources website, November 12, 2002). Abuse of persons with disabilities is a global problem. Disabled women are particularly vulnerable to abuse. Studies have found that the most dangerous place for a disabled girl or woman is in her own home. The most likely abusers are her own mother and/or father. Female care givers are the next most likely assailants. Many disabled women experience assault at the hands of teachers, attendants, older brothers and others. It might be speculated that disabled women and girls are perceived as ideal targets because their disabilities may mean they are unable to flee or communicate easily. The very fact that they are female, smaller and socialized to be passive may, again, increase the risk of abuse. A study by the Seattle Rape Relief Development Disabilities Project in 1984 found that 90 percent of the girls and women referred to them had been exploited by relatives or individuals they knew (see Case Study 4.4).

Case Study 4.4 Abuse of persons with disabilities is a world wide problem

Physical and emotional abuse of persons with disabilities is a global problem. To mark European Day of Disabled People on December 3, 2000, the campaigning group Disability Awareness in Action (DAA) condensed the stories of discrimination into a powerful dossier of human misery. The DAA prepared for United Nations officials a report containing information about some of the worst human rights abuses suffered by people with disabilities around the world. The report was produced in response to the UN Human Rights Commission's Resolution on the Human Rights of Persons with Disabilities, which called for campaigners to keep commissioners informed about discrimination.

The following examples allegedly represent only the "tip of the iceberg" in relation to this massive human tragedy.

In Thailand, a disabled boy lives in an institution and is tied up every day to prevent him wandering out of the gates into the road outside. He gets no exercise and cannot go to visit friends, or help himself to visit the toilet or get water. Another boy is bound by his left arm and right leg to a metal bedstead and is forced to lie in a pool of his own urine on a hard tile floor. He reports that sometimes the staff tie the cloth too tight and his hands become blue and swollen. He says that it is unsafe and uncomfortable. A female resident has been trained by staff to remain in the same place, where she also sits soaked in her own urine.

Human rights abuses are by no means confined to the developing economies. In the Netherlands, a 34-year-old woman tells how she had to go to court to fight for an interpreter to help her study at the University of Utrecht. Initially, the government refused to pay. Allegedly, the woman was told that she could work in a factory.

In Australia, a 53-year-old woman with multiple sclerosis, who cannot write or use her hands, was denied the opportunity of a postal vote in a local council election. She asked if her husband, who has power of attorney, could sign and date the voting form on her behalf. The request was denied. The officials suggested that her husband place the pen in her mouth, so that she could make a mark on the ballot paper and he could then attest to the fact that this was her mark. The woman allegedly took exception to being asked to make her 'mark' like an illiterate person. She said that she was an educated person and felt that this treatment was very degrading.

A 60-year-old woman in hospital in the UK was denied the use of a text-phone to call her family after she developed a potentially fatal condition. She asked a nurse to phone on her behalf and request an urgent visit, but the family was not contacted.

The DAA has been putting together an international database of human rights abuses. The organization has used the Universal Declaration on Human Rights (1948) and the Standard Rules on the Equalization of Opportunities for Persons with Disabilities (1993) as yardsticks for measuring the treatment of people with disabilities. The database currently contains more than 1,200 reports concerning 2 million disabled people. According to Richard Light, DAA's Research Director, one of the most depressing findings to emerge from the project is the fact that human rights abuses are 1.5 times more likely to stop because of the death of the victim than as a result of a legal intervention.

DAA Project Director Rachel Hurst says full implementation of the Disability Rights Task Force's recommendations in the UK would make a huge difference. The Disability Rights Commission, has asked the government to extend its remit to allow it to use human rights legislation to benefit people with disabilities.

Source: Inman, K., December 1, 2000, SocietyGuardian.co.uk website.

How do we explain the abuse of the vulnerable?

From the perspective of dominant/subordinate relations, abuse of children, women, the elderly and the disabled is a function of the created dependency of these members of vulnerable subordinate populations in a paternalistic society, ruled by the dominant populations of adults, men and the able-bodied. In this societal context, members of the dominant populations of the able-bodied, adults and men have the power to use ageist, sexist and handicappist invalidation myths to rationalize flagrant violations of the human rights of members of these vulnerable populations. At the hands of dominant authorities, child abuse, women abuse, elder abuse and disabled abuse are easily wielded as instruments of social control, ensuring that members of vulnerable minorities "know their place, and stay in their place".

Abuse of members of vulnerable subordinate populations highlights two glaring facts: their *vulnerability* and their *socially constructed dependency*. In a paternalistic home, and elsewhere in a paternalistic society, these two characteristics enable dominant authorities to violate the human rights of members of vulnerable subordinate populations by committing abusive acts against them as means of social control and as a means of reinforcing their own dominant status and authority.

The experience of racial degradation and discrimination by members of aboriginal subordinate groups

Like the reports of members of vulnerable populations – children, women and the elderly and disabled – about their experiences as targets of ageist, sexist and handicappist degradation and discrimination, the reports of aboriginal peoples as targets of racial degradation and discrimination reveal that these experiences are both stressful and harmful: they cause pain and suffering, fear, shame and anger. And the psychological damage they cause is very long-lasting. The examples, in Case Study 4.5, drawn from the experiences of aboriginal men and women, should serve to illustrate this important point.

Case Study 4.5   Aboriginal subordinate groups: experiences of racial degradation and discrimination

Chief Dan George
"Do you know what it is like to have your race belittled and to come to learn that you are only a burden to the [white man's] country? . . . We were shoved aside because they thought we were dumb and could never learn . . . What is it like to be without pride in your race, pride in your family, pride and confidence in yourself? . . . I shall tell you what it is like. It is like not caring about tomorrow for what does tomorrow matter . . . It is like having a reserve that looks like a junk yard . . . It is like getting drunk . . . an escape from ugly reality . . . It is most of all like awaking next morning to the guilt of betrayal. For the alcohol did not fill the emptiness but only dug it deeper."

Source: Waubageshig (1970: 86). (Cited in Kallen, 2003: 78)

Shirley Bear
"The thing I remember the most [was] . . . being called dirty Indian kids, and not understanding. They would say 'dirty brown' or 'dirty black' – 'there go the dirty Indian kids' . . . I remember feeling really embarrassed . . . I think it is easy for a person of color to be embarrassed about themselves, to wish they were any color but I also remember going home and trying to wash it off . . . "

Source: Silman (1987: 55). (Cited in Kallen, 2003: 78)

Maria Campbell
Maria Campbell is best known for her autobiography *Halfbreed*, which relates her struggles as a Metis woman, a woman of mixed European and aboriginal ancestry, in Canadian society. The book provides a poignant case study of social and cultural marginality. Of Scottish, Indian and French descent and the eldest daughter in a family of seven children, Maria was born in Northern Saskatchewan. After her mother's death, she was forced to quit school at age

twelve to take care of her younger siblings. At age fifteen she married an alco-
holic, abusive "white man" in order to prevent her brothers and sisters from
being placed in an orphanage. Her attempt to keep her family united,
however, was unsuccessful; her husband reported her to the welfare authorities and her siblings were placed in foster care. After moving to Vancouver,
where her husband deserted her, Maria became a prostitute and drug addict.
After two suicide attempts and a nervous breakdown, she was hospitalized
and entered Alcoholics Anonymous. She began writing *Halfbreed* in an
attempt to deal with her anger, frustration, loneliness, and the pressure to
return to a life of drugs and prostitution. Maria says that she started writing a
letter to herself, because she had to have somebody to talk to, and there was
nobody to talk to. And that was how she wrote her now classic autobiography.

Relating the first thirty-three years of her life, *Halfbreed* recounts on a
personal level the racial discrimination to which the Metis have historically
been subjected. Infused with a strong undercurrent of anger and bitterness,
the book documents Maria's search for self-identity, her attempts to overcome
the poverty and harshness of Metis life and finally, albeit briefly, her work as a
political activist. Until she wrote the book, she points out proudly, "halfbreed"
was nothing but a common derogatory term; now it means a person "living
between two cultures."

Source: Maria Campbell (Metis), website, November 2, 2002.

The experience of anti-Semitic degradation and discrimination by members of the Jewish subordinate population

Invalidating labels

Before I begin this discussion, let me backtrack for a moment to re-
emphasize the distinction, made earlier, between the ways in which
dominant authorities tend to treat those subordinate populations labeled
as "dangerous and threatening", as opposed to those labeled as "inferior
and incompetent, but relatively harmless". I pointed out that vulnerable
human groups, those whose members have the least power to defend
themselves against harm, and who have the least power to strike out
against dominant oppressors, tend to be labeled and treated as inferior/
incompetent, but relatively harmless. This invalidating label tends to be
followed up, in terms of public policy and practice, by paternalistic treatment. By way of contrast, those subordinate populations perceived by
dominant authorities as posing some kind of danger or threat to the
established racial, cultural, or moral order of the society, and thereby
posing a threat to the dominant status and vested interests of established

authorities, tend to be viewed and treated more inhumanely. It is these "dangerous" populations, in contrast to vulnerable populations, which tend to be singled out as the target groups for incitement to hatred and harm. In an earlier chapter, I described some of the invalidation ideologies about blacks, Jews and gays and lesbians which are currently used to justify cruel acts of discrimination against members of these subordinate target groups. In the following section of this chapter, I will attempt to show how these same invalidation ideologies are manipulated through hate propaganda to promote hate and harm against members of these "dangerous", subordinate populations.

Anti-Semitic incitement to hate

As my first example, I will focus my discussion on anti-Semitic incitement to hate, and on the reported experiences of members of the Jewish target group subject to the promotion of hatred and harm against Jews. A major, current form of incitement to hate and harm against Jews is *Holocaust denial* (Lipstadt, 1994; Shermer, Grobman and Hertzberg, 2000). A great many anti-Semitic hate groups specialize in this form of hate promotion and the internet is replete with their ever-expanding websites through which they disseminate insidious anti-Semitic hate propaganda to readers across the globe (Nizkor website, May 31, 2001; NSWPP website, May 31, 2001; Zundel website, May 31, 2001). Holocaust denial is rooted in the false premise the "Holocaust never happened". Its main claim is that the Holocaust is a hoax created by the "Jewish lobby" to get the world's sympathy and to justify the existence of Israel. Followers of this movement deny that millions of Jews were killed by the Nazis, and claim that the ones who died in the concentration camps during the Second World War died because of typhus and other fatal diseases (Lipstadt, 1994; Shermer, Grobman and Hertzberg, 2000).

There is no issue or controversy among *bona fide* Holocaust scholars about the reality that the holocaust occurred (Laqueur and Baumel, 2001; McCarthy *et al.*, Nizkor website, May 31, 2001). Between 1941 and 1945, the German Nazis murdered about 5–6 million Jews and Gypsies, plus another million others. The largest number of murders took place by means of poison gases in six extermination concentration camps (KZs), of which Auschwitz is the best known, in present-day Poland. This genocide is among the best documented events in human history. Documents are stored in various archives of the victors and the vanquished of the Second World War. Eyewitness survivors of Auschwitz and other KZs have written memoirs as first-hand evidence of this atrocity. Films made of the camps show a ravaged, starving humanity which no fake or fiction film could re-enact (Nizkor website, May 31, 2001).

Pseudo-scholars who deny the Holocaust follow a sometimes undeclared agenda. If the Holocaust events can be minimized or denied, then the Nazi and other racist, anti-Semitic, invalidation ideologies may regain respectability. At the same time, it is hoped, the Jewish people, the perpetrators of the "holocaust hoax", will lose credibility and will be vilified and discriminated against by an ever larger audience (National Socialist White People's Party, NSWPP website, May 31, 2001). For members of the Jewish target group, Holocaust denial is experienced as a violation of their collective rights; a blatant denial of their group history and a violation of their group dignity. And for the vast majority of Jews, this flagrant affront to their group dignity is experienced as a denial of their individual right to human dignity.

To back up this observation, I will briefly refer to the findings of two Israeli studies (Herman, Yockaman and Yuchtman, 1965 and Deutsch, 1974), both designed to assess the social psychological impact of the trial of Adolph Eichmann – a Nazi war criminal – on Jews in Israel. The two studies, one conducted shortly after the Eichmann trial, and the other carried out two years later, produced analogous findings. With regard to the psychic impact of the trial on Israeli Jews, the findings revealed that the greater the "involvement" of the respondent in the events of the Holocaust – i.e. the more central the Holocaust was to their Jewish identity – the deeper the psychological wounds reopened by the trial, and the more emotional and intense their reaction.

While conducting preliminary research for my own research study, "Target For Hate", (Kallen and Lam, 1993) designed to assess the impact on Jews in Canada of the public trials of anti-Semitic hate propagandists, I hypothesized that the variable of Holocaust "involvement" would also prove to be significant in assessing the impact of these trials, which recall vividly the events of the Holocaust.

The "Target For Hate" study was based on the findings of a five-year research project which I carried out among Jewish respondents following the 1985 criminal trials of Ernst Zundel and James Keegstra in Canada (Kallen, 1992; Kallen and Lam, 1993). Zundel and Keegstra were charged and tried, under Canada's criminal code, for the promotion of hatred and harm against Jews. My research study was designed to assess the nature and extent of the impact upon a Jewish audience of the anti-Semitic hate promotion activities, including Holocaust denial, graphically depicted in these trials (Case Study 4.6).

Case Study 4.6   Research findings: impact of Holocaust denial

Although a majority of the Jewish respondents were born in Canada, the formidable psychological impact of the Holocaust upon their sense of Jewish identity is revealed in the finding that close to 50 percent of them agreed with the view that every Jew should regard himself or herself as a survivor of the Holocaust. Responses to questions about Holocaust documentation revealed that over 95 percent of respondents held the view that the events of the Holocaust were incontrovertible, 98.2 percent believed that the atrocities documented by Holocaust survivors were true and over 86 percent reported that they had lost kin or family members in the Holocaust. Accordingly, to question the established fact of the Holocaust was viewed by respondents as a contemptuous negation of their ethnic group history, an insult to their collective ethnic identity, and a violation of their right to group dignity.

Overall psycho-social impact of the trials showed that almost 80 percent of respondents reported that they experienced suffering /psychological harm as a result of following the trials. Qualitative responses to these questions revealed that Jewish respondents felt . . . silenced . . . targeted and exposed . . . insecure and fearful . . . angry and frustrated . . . deep, gut-wrenching agony and . . . too painful to say. Further, 89 percent of respondents expressed the belief that hate propagandizing activities have caused harm and suffering . . . "psychic harm and trauma" . . . "mental anguish" . . . to Jews as a people.

Source: Kallen and Lam, 1993.

The experience of heterosexist degradation and discrimination by members of the gay and lesbian subordinate population

The reports of gay men and lesbians about their harmful experiences as targets of heterosexist and homophobic degradation and discrimination reveal a somewhat different dimension of pain and suffering from the experiences reported earlier; they reveal the experienced agony of the "double life syndrome", alluded to briefly in my discussion of marginality in Chapter 2.

The double life syndrome
In the closet and "passing"
The double life syndrome involves the maintenance of a closeted (secret) same-sex-oriented identity and lifestyle in private life and the simultaneous maintenance of a pseudo-heterosexual identity and lifestyle in public

life (Kallen, 1989: Ch. 4). However, maintaining the double life syndrome can lead to a situation of agony and desperation, for attempting to maintain two conflicting lifestyles and identities means spinning endless webs of deception, while living in constant fear of the harmful and hurtful, discriminatory consequences of disclosure. To illustrate, I will present excerpts from the reported experiences of two members of the gay and lesbian population (Case Study 4.7).

Case Study 4.7   The double life syndrome

Jerry (a leading gay activist)
Basically, I lived in anguish, and lived a dual role. I would occasionally have these [homosexual] experiences. I felt extremely guilty about it. I still continued to date women and to lead a very heterosexual social life. . . I spent several years in psychoanalysis, trying [unsuccessfully] to become heterosexual . . . then I moved to New York City and [here] it was easy to develop a gay niche of social activity. I continued a heterosexual facade when it came to my business life . . . however, there was great ambivalence in having this heterosexual identity at business and having gay identity elsewhere . . . [At work] I was always cryptic over the phone to gay friends and generally would discourage calls at work from gay friends . . . I had to pretend I had a girlfriend. . . . I would always play the role with clients. . . . I would have a girl on my arm for these social occasions . . . I was even engaged to be married, three times.

Source: Kallen (1989: 110).

Jeri (a lesbian sociologist)
Some of us have spent time attempting to protect ourselves by keeping separate our private lives and our public academic lives, in order to keep our lesbian identities secret. We are all aware of the immense personal toll taken by the secretiveness and deception involved in leading a closeted existence. [One lesbian professor] described her precarious existence as "one foot in the closet, the other on a banana peel". [Besides torturous] anxiety and fracturing of one's sense of self, leading [a closeted] existence grants tremendous power to anyone who might discover the truth. I feel that the more people are secretive, the more you seal your own self into those box cars for them to take you away.

Source: Kallen (1989: 111).

Homophobic hate crimes

The damaging psychological impact of hate-motivated acts on target populations is nowhere more dramatically illustrated than in the case of victims of homophobic hate crimes. The findings of a four-year psychological study funded by the National Institute of Mental Health in the United States indicate that hate crimes based on sexual orientation have more negative impact on lesbians and gay men than other crimes (Herek *et al.*, 1997). Study findings showed more signs of psychological distress – including depression, stress and anger – among lesbian and gay survivors of hate crimes than among lesbian and gay survivors of comparable non-bias-motivated crimes in the same time period. Study findings also revealed that hate crimes have long-lasting effects. While all victims of serious crime are at risk for such distress, the problems associated with hate crimes appear to last longer than for random crimes. Research results also found that crime-related psychological problems dropped substantially among survivors of non-hate crimes within approximately two years after the crime. Hate crime victims, however, continued to have higher levels of depression, stress and anger for as long as five years after their victimization occurred.

Researchers have suggested that many of the problems observed by the research team may result from hate crimes victims' feelings of personal danger and vulnerability associated with their identity as a gay man or lesbian. All crime victims are likely to feel more vulnerable after their experience and to perceive the world as more dangerous, unpredictable and hostile, but hate crime victims, in addition, often link this sense of vulnerability and powerlessness to their gay or lesbian identity. This association can be psychologically harmful because sexual orientation is such an important part of their self-concept.

The experience of abuse, degradation and hateful discrimination by members of subordinate populations

Psychological damage

The reported experiences of members of invalidated, subordinate populations who have been subject to degradation, defamation and, in some instances, to abusive acts of neglect and violence, demonstrate unequivocally that these blatant violations of their fundamental human rights are personally experienced as painful, harmful and deeply damaging. In comparing the reported experiences of members of various subordinate groups, both vulnerable and alleged "dangerous" populations, a common denominator emerges: the virtually unanimous observation that an affront to group dignity (group defamation – whether through direct verbal abuse, the promotion of hatred and harm or other means) is experienced as a violation of the individual's fundamental right to human dignity. And, in cases where both physical and emotional abuse are reported, the abused person frequently points out that the harm, the pain and suffering of emotional abuse is experienced as far greater than that of physical abuse or neglect. Physical damage heals, sometimes completely, they say, but psychological damage strikes at the root of one's very being, and does not go away. The evidence from the victims of homophobic hate crimes strongly supports this position.

Are legal prohibitions against the promotion of hate "justifiable"?

In my closing comments in Chapter 3, I posed the crucial question raised by the hate propaganda debate as to whether the demonstrable psychological damage to target group members caused by incitement to hatrede and harm is sufficiently grave to warrant the imposition of reasonable limits on the fundamental right of freedom of speech of the hate promoters. I would suggest that the comparative evidence presented in this chapter, based on reported experiences of defamation and hate-inspired discrimination, offers strong support for the egalitarian position in the debate which argues that freedom of speech does not include the right to vilify. The evidence presented here suggests strongly that vilification (defamation) which denies a people's group right to human dignity is experienced by members of the target group as a violation of their personal right to human dignity. It causes demonstrable pain, anguish and suffering to the victims, as well as long-lasting psychological damage. These observations lend strong support for the egalitarian view which holds that justifiable restrictions must be imposed on freedom of speech in order to protect members of subordinate target populations from demonstrable harm and suffering, and also in order to safeguard harmonious relations between members of all of the different populations groups in the society.

Concluding commentary

Up until this point, my discussion in this book has centered on the ways in which invalidation and human rights violations lead to the social construction and the long-term maintenance of a hierarchy of unequal (dominant/subordinate) relations between various population groups in a society. In this chapter, my focus has been on the experience of invalidation and human rights violation. I have graphically documented the damaging impact upon members of subordinate populations of their personal experiences of degradation, abuse and hate-inspired discrimination.

The compelling question which remains is: What can we do about it? How can members of society – members of both dominant and subordinate groups – assist in the promotion of changes aimed at providing equal protections for the fundamental rights and freedoms of all individuals and groups in the society? In the following chapters of this book I will attempt to respond to this pressing question.

CHAPTER 5

Equality/Equity-Seeking Protest Movements 1: Women's Rights

Introduction

In previous chapters of this book, I have shown how dominant authorities, on a long-term basis, are able to wield their superior status and power in order to invalidate subordinate populations and to justify injustice against them. Through the enactment and enforcement of discriminatory laws, policies and practices, dominant authorities are able to maintain the established hierarchy of unequal (dominant/subordinate) group relations and to safeguard their superior status within it.

How, then, can changes in the established structure of dominant/subordinate relations come about? What can invalidated members of subordinate populations do to improve their group status and opportunities and to regain their sense of human dignity? In Chapters 5 and 6, I employ both established social movement theory (Clark, Grayson and Grayson, 1975) and new social movement theory (Melucci 1980, 1996) in order to provide a sociological framework for my analysis of the development and achievements of two current, human-rights-oriented social movements: the women's and gay/lesbian rights and liberation movements.

Strategies for change

Group-level discontent

There are a number of effective strategies in the quest for human rights, liberation and empowerment which may be adopted by subordinate populations. However, before these can be effectively employed, members of subordinate groups must become organized into *pressure groups* designed to take collective action towards status improvement and towards the reclaiming of their right to human dignity (Kallen, 1995, ch. 8).

As long as members of subordinate groups remain "beaten into submission" by the self-fulfilling prophecy of invalidation, they may be very discontented, but they are not likely to act on this discontent. Having given up hope of status improvement, they are not motivated to do anything about it. Before group-level discontent can lead to demands for change, something must trigger a heightened group-level consciousness of oppression, abuse and degradation, to a point at which more and more members of the subordinate population reach an extreme of discontent which is experienced as intolerable. What typically provides the trigger to heightened discontent is a sudden or a radical change in social conditions which raises the hopes and expectations of members of subordinate groups for status improvement (Clark, Grayson and Grayson, 1975).

One of the major modern developments affecting inter-group relations on a global scale is the tremendous advance in the fields of transportation and communication. Whether through travel or telecommunication, members of subordinate groups are today constantly exposed to a tempting choice of new values, ideas and standards, many of which challenge established ways and entrenched authorities. Exposure to new ideas and values, and comparisons with other subordinate groups who have improved their status, raises expectations. As a result, increasing numbers of members of subordinate populations become critical of the existing system of unequal, dominant/subordinate relations and they begin to openly voice their discontent with their collectively disadvantaged, subordinate status within the established hierarchy.

A crucial aspect of modern communication for the triggering of group-level discontent is the provision of successful *role models* for subordinate populations throughout the world to follow. The achievement of independence and nationhood by formerly colonized peoples throughout Africa, following the Second World War, had a marked influence on the global rise of black nationalism. Black Power movements, in turn, influenced human rights-oriented protest movements among other subordinate populations: women, gays and lesbians, senior citizens and persons with disabilities, to name only a few.

Organization for protest

While rising expectations can raise group-level discontent to virtually intolerable levels, before this discontent can be mobilized subordinate groups must become *organized for protest* (Kallen, 1989, ch. 6; 1995, ch. 8). Frequently, protest organizations among subordinate populations find their roots in self-help groups. Initially, in order to help each other cope with their shared experience of invalidation and with their disadvantaged life conditions, members of subordinate groups may organize themselves into self-help groups designed to offer members mutual support and solace in order to make life under unsatisfactory life conditions more bearable. These groups are not, however, designed to change or to better the life conditions of subordinate populations.

According to Ponse (1978: 92) self-help groups in the lesbian world can be important in neutralizing and overcoming the stigmatizing effects of the negative judgment of the heterosexual world. Ponse distinguishes between two types of support groups among subordinate populations: *secretive* groups and *activist* groups.

In the lesbian community, Ponse contends, secretive (closeted) groups provide an opportunity for lesbians to socialize with each other in an atmosphere where closeted gay women can relax and possibly develop relationships with other gay women. While secretive groups often do not directly address lesbian identity as an issue, they must make sure members identify themselves as lesbian in order to ensure and protect the secret status of the group. Secretive groups often emphasize the need for gays to accommodate to their subordinate status, not to seek to change the status of the group. These groups stress the need for gays to harmonize with the "straight" world, and they emphasize the similarities between the two worlds.

In contrast, Ponse points out, activist groups, committed to gay liberation and/or feminism, reject the subordinate status of lesbians by challenging heterosexism. Changing the lesbian identity to a positive identity is the primary issue. Activist groups help women coming to terms with their lesbianism by starting with the assumption that being a lesbian is a natural alternative lifestyle. Activist groups therefore make a concerted attempt to instill feelings of lesbian pride. They use openly proud lesbians as role models (Ponse, 1978: 91). While activist groups encourage their members to come out and to label themselves proudly as lesbians, they will protect the identity of their members wishing to remain secret (Ponse, 1978: 91).

In general, while self-help groups among subordinate populations can serve to provide an initial base for the development of new, positive group identities, before collective protest can be organized effectively, substantial numbers of members of subordinate populations must be willing to overcome their deeply rooted fear of discriminatory retaliation at the hands of dominant authorities. They must attain sufficient self- and group pride and confidence to come out of the closet, to escape the trap of their subordinate status, in order to take concerted action against their more powerful oppressors.

Creating positive group identities

The key to mobilization for protest

In order to create positive collective identity, in the initial phase of protest organization leaders must focus on consciousness-raising efforts designed to convince members to reject dominant-imposed, invalidating labels and to replace them with new, *positive self-definitions*. This change in self-identity – from nigger to black, from faggot and dyke to gay and lesbian, from cripple to physically challenged – symbolizes a shift from negative to positive group identities, a shift which is essential in order to mobilize the discontent of subordinate groups around human rights and empowerment goals.

The next step in protest organization is for leaders to mobilize and to direct group discontent toward clearly defined *collective goals*. This is not an easy task, for despite their shared invalidated identities, members of subordinate populations may be very different in many other ways. They may vary in terms of their other group statuses; they may differ in terms of their political, economic, religious and lifestyle priorities. These intra-group differences are very likely to influence the opinions of individual members on issues of concern to the subordinate group as a whole. Leaders attempting to organize protest groups must therefore be able to develop commonly agreed-upon, community-wide strategies and goals which can override these potentially divisive differences among members.

For example, within the general population of same-sex-oriented persons, gender provides a major line of cleavage, dividing lesbians from gay men on many critical issues of common concern. Among same-sex-oriented persons, as among other subordinate groups, there are multiple dividing lines based on intra-group differences in age, lifestyle (in or out of the closet), religious persuasion, socio-economic status, race and so on. Among the general population of persons with disabilities, in addi-tion to lines of division based on gender, race, age and the like, a major line of cleavage divides persons with different disabilities – mobility-impaired, hearing-impaired, sight-impaired, mentally-impaired and so forth, each of which has distinctive special needs, which give rise to quite different demands for reasonable accommodation. These lines of division among members of subordinate populations pose formidable hurdles which leaders must overcome in formulating generally agreed-upon community-wide strategies and goals for human liberation and empowerment.

Human rights and liberation movements

Human rights movements represent a particular form and direction of collective protest (Kallen 1995, ch. 8). This type of social movement is most likely to emerge when the discontent of subordinate populations focuses on the inconsistency between declared societal ideals endorsing human rights principles and the non-implementation of these ideals in public institutions and in public practice.

When governments begin to replace discriminatory social policies and laws with anti-discriminatory, human rights-oriented instruments, the expectations of invalidated, subordinate populations escalate. However, what almost inevitably happens is an expression of *cultural lag*: legal and policy changes are not immediately followed up by parallel changes in public attitudes and practices. The expectations of subordinate populations for actual equality of societal opportunities and for recognition of their right to human dignity may then come to outstrip the real increase in achievements. When this happens, collective discontent rises markedly. Members of subordinate populations may then begin to voice their demands for redress against long-term, past discrimination and also to make demands for immediate measures to enable them to achieve the promise of full equality of opportunity and results.

The emergence and proliferation of human rights and liberation movements in North America since the 1970s provides ample evidence for this position. Collective protest by organized pressure groups representing a variety of subordinate populations – aboriginal peoples, non-white populations (e.g. blacks), subordinate ethno-linguistic groups (e.g. French-speaking Canadians and Spanish-speaking Americans), women, gays and lesbians, senior citizens and persons with disabilities, among others – initially demanded changes in public policies affecting their particular concerns. In North America, during the 1970s – the "human rights decade" in which anti-discrimination legislation was introduced at various governmental levels – protest increasingly came to incorporate demands for legal changes, such as the inclusion of particular human attributes (e.g. race, ethnicity, sex, sexual orientation, age and disability) among the enumerated prohibited grounds of non-discriminatory laws (human rights codes). In Canada, since the inclusion, in 1982, of a new Charter of Rights and Freedoms in the Canadian Constitution – the highest law of the land – collective protest has focused increasingly on constitutional changes, designed to guarantee equal or equivalent protection for the fundamental rights and freedoms of all populations, in every part of the country. However, actual achievements have lagged behind the soaring expectations of members of subordinate populations. Throughout North America, while legal protections for the human rights of *some* populations in *some* sectors of society (federal, state/provincial, municipal and so forth) have been secured, equal/equivalent protection for the fundamental rights and freedoms of *all* populations in *all* sectors throughout the country remains a "dream deferred". Accordingly, voiced discontent continues, in the form of continued lobbying for change, and in the form of legal claims for redress against past violations of human rights, put forward by organized protest groups representing the various unmet concerns of particular subordinate populations in particular regions of the country.

New social movements

What is a "new social movement"?

In 1980, Melucci introduced the concept of a "new social movement" into the sociological literature. This concept was applied to increasingly emerging forms of collective action on a global scale giving precedence to culture, meaning and identity which Melucci associated with feminism, ecological radicalism, ethnic separatism and other variants of "identity politics" (identity- and solidarity-seeking movements). Melucci's approach emphasizes the importance of the psychology of collective emotional experiences in the active construction of collective identity, and highlights the significance of global communication and information, especially the internet, in this process.

Melucci's thesis

A brief exposition of some of the central points of Melucci's thesis reveals that his "new social movement" theory can contribute significantly to our understanding of the social movements highlighted in this book. Melucci (1980, 1996) proposes that changes in the structure of advanced, post-industrial societies have given rise to a singular category of social movements, which he calls the "new social movements". In advanced societies, today, he argues, the dominant class has assumed control, and a capacity for intervention, in spheres of society well beyond that of the production structure. Their reach now extends into the areas of consumption, information, services and interpersonal relations. The control and manipulation of the centres of technocratic domination are increasingly penetrating everyday life, encroaching on the individual's possibility of controlling his or her time, space and relationships.

This expansion of the societal arenas of dominant control, Melucci says, has changed the form of expropriation of social resources. The movement for reappropriation of society's resources is therefore carrying its fight into new territory. Increasingly, what is deemed to be at stake in conflict between the agencies of social manipulation and the forces pressing for reappropriation is the personal and social identity of individuals. Defense of the identity, continuity and predictability of personal existence is beginning to constitute the substance of the new conflicts. In the new social movements, individuals are collectively claiming the right to realize their own identity and to control their personal creativity, their affective life and their biological and interpersonal existence.

Melucci points out several characteristics shared by the various new social movements which would appear to confirm his hypothesis, which sees in the appropriation of identity the key to understanding them. First, these movements reject the traditional separation between public and private spheres. Those areas traditionally confined to the private sphere – sexual relations, interpersonal relations, biological identity – have become stakes in conflict situations and now are foci of collective action. At the same time, individual needs and demands have penetrated the sphere of the public and political. Birth and death, illness and ageing have all become foci of collective action.

A second characteristic found in some of the new movements is what Melucci calls the "superposition of deviance and social movements". In response to dominant control, opposition takes the form of marginality and deviance. Public intervention tends to reduce conflicts to the status of pathology, by subjecting non-conformists to preventative therapies or to "rehabilitation".

Another characteristic suggested by Melucci is that the new social movements are not primarily focused on empowerment. Essentially, they are not oriented toward the conquest of political power or of the state apparatus. Rather, these movements are oriented toward the control of a particular social space where they have autonomy or independence *vis-à-vis* the system.

Solidarity as an objective is another characteristic of the new social movements. The struggle centres around the particularistic issue of group identity, based on ascriptive criteria such as sex, age, race and territory. The movements, Melucci point out, also have instrumental objectives, and seek political advantages, but this dimension is secondary to the expressive nature of the relations sought in the search for solidarity, the primary thrust of the movements.

Finally, Melucci mentions the characteristic of direct participation, and the rejection of mediation in some new social movements. The emphasis on direct participation galvanizes the spontaneous, anti-authoritarian, anti-hierarchical nature of the protests in these movements. However, Melucci suggests, it is these particular features which contribute to the risks of discontinuity and fragmentation which constantly threaten these new movements.

Clearly, all of the characteristics elucidated in Melucci's thesis are not found in every new social movement: Melucci presents them basically as common themes.

In order to illustrate the main points of our analysis of human rights-oriented social movements generated by members of subordinate groups, I will now outline the development of the women's rights and liberation movement in North America and in a global context.

The women's rights and liberation movement in democratic society

As a social movement, the women's movement represents the organized attempt by women as a subordinate group, to bring about social changes – changes in law, policy, practice and attitudes toward women – devised to promote their equal status and treatment as women and as human beings in all spheres of societal life. As in the case of social movements in general, any comprehensive analysis of the women's movement must take into primary account the ever-present, multiple lines of fragmentation among women as a subordinate population.

This having been said, in order to illustrate the development of the women's movement, I will center my discussion on the major ideological lines of division which have developed in Western democratic societies, throughout the twentieth century. For purposes of this review, I will focus my attention on the women's movement in North America (Burt, 1988; Adamson, Briskin and McPhail, 1989; Berkeley, 1999; Rosen, 2000). As an important part of this review, I will examine some of the major social changes which have come about in response to North American women's organized lobbying efforts.

Maternal or social feminism

Life in early twentieth-century North America was dominated by the sexist, paternalistic (patriarchal) belief that the division between the "separate worlds" of men and women into public and private spheres, respectively, was a "natural" division. That is to say, differential and unequal gender roles were believed to be dictated by biologically determined differences in the intellectual and psychological characteristics of men and women. Men, it was assumed, were endowed with the superior qualities of reason, strength and self-determination; hence it was "natural" for the world of men to be the public, decision-making world of politics and bread winning. Women, it was assumed, were endowed with the complementary, but inferior qualities of sentiment, nurturance and morality; hence it was "natural" for the world of women, under the protective dominance of the male head of household, to be the private, dependent world of home and hearth: the sphere of child-rearing and home-making. Internalization by women of this sexist notion of separate worlds affected women's orientations to politics and policy-making. For example, most of the women active within the suffrage movement agreed that the spheres of men and women were separate, but held that they were also equal. They argued that women were morally superior to men, and that it was the responsibility of women to apply their private morality to the public world, by becoming involved in politics. Enfranchising women, that is giving them the opportunity to vote, they argued, would provide greater scope for public regulation of morality. In this context, women's issues continued to be defined as family-related or private issues, such as legalization of contraception. This orientation characterized the first wave of the women's movement called "maternal or social feminism", where women as reformist crusaders worked to ameliorate what they saw as the decadent effects of the industrial revolution: the evils of intemperance, prostitution, family breakdown and decline in spiritual values.

Women's rights
The "double-bind"

By the 1960s, many women in North America found themselves in a "double-bind" situation, where their private sphere obligations and self-images had remained virtually unchanged, while their public sphere activities had increased dramatically. Most importantly, women had retained responsibility for the household and family, while at the same time they were participating in the paid labor force. Moreover, in the labor force, as in law and in public policy, women continued to be faced with sex discrimination. They were excluded from many areas of employment, and even when they did penetrate male-dominated careers, they were unequally rewarded for their work: they were paid significantly less and were far less likely to achieve promotion than were their male counterparts.

Liberal feminism

This situation gave rise to the second wave of the women's movement, with the emergence of liberal feminism. Liberal feminism was fueled by women's protest against sex discrimination in public life, and liberal feminists argued that women should be treated in the same way as men, without regard to sex, in the public sphere. They demanded that women and men be accorded equality of opportunity and equality of rewards in public life. The liberal feminism movement was and is essentially a women's rights movement. Its proponents seek equal recognition and protection of the human rights of women and men, in the public sphere. They argue that women must be represented equally with men at all levels within existing, public institutions.

Women's liberation

Gender role change

From the 1960s, feminist proponents of the women's liberation movement criticized liberal feminists for not going far enough in their demands for social change. While liberal feminists insist that women be represented equally with men throughout the ranks of public, decision-making structures, their apparent assumption has been that public institutions themselves need no modification. Proponents of the women's liberation movement criticize liberal feminists for their alleged failure to address the patriarchal and capitalist underpinnings behind existing public institutions. Further, and most importantly, women's liberationists criticize liberal feminists for their disregard of the necessity for *role change in the private sphere*. They argue that the liberal version of gender role equality created the stereotype of the divided woman, dominated in the private sphere by paternalistic values which sustain her dependency while, at the same time, governed in public life by egalitarian (equality rights) values which promote her independence. Liberationists insist that in order for women to become fully liberated from paternalistic (patriarchal) constraints, changes facilitating women's equality and independence in both public and private spheres must be put in place. From the view of women's liberation, then, gender role equality, in public life, on men's terms, is not enough; the ultimate goal of women's liberation must be gender role change, for men and women, in both public and private life.

Marxist/socialist feminism

While socialist feminists and radical feminists share a common commitment to the long-term goals of the women's liberation movement, their emphasis on both perceived determinants of sex inequality and on strategies for change is quite different. Socialist feminists place their emphasis on eradicating capitalist structures, for they maintain that the capitalist economic system is the primary determinant of women's subordinate status. They argue that the capitalist economy categorically discriminates against women, just as it categorically discriminates against workers. Under capitalism, they argue, women's unpaid labor in the private sphere is considered worthless, because it has no monetary exchange value. Yet, they argue convincingly, the achievement of the goal of economic productivity endorsed by capitalism and patriarchy is predicated on the vital economic contribution made by women's private, unpaid labour. Socialist feminists argue, further, that entry into the paid work force is not automatically a liberating experience for women. Many women who enter paid employment simply find themselves doing double duty: they work for wages in the public sphere and continue to do unpaid labour in the private sphere. Socialist feminists argue that what is necessary in order to facilitate women's liberation is a radical restructuring of societal institutions that involves alternatives both to capitalist modes of production and to the patriarchal structure of public and private social institutions.

With many other feminists, socialist feminists see the paternalistic (patriarchal) nuclear family as the cornerstone of women's subordinate status because it plays so central a role in perpetuating women's dependent status. They argue that the private sphere must be radically restructured so as to include stable, cooperative and collective arrangements for child care and domestic tasks which would liberate women from the discriminatory constraints of the paternalistic, nuclear family.

Radical feminism

Radical feminists agree with much of the socialist feminist analysis of the structural sources of women's subordinate status, but they differ on a fundamental question of emphasis. While they agree that the disadvantaged political, social and economic position of women is an outcome of patriarchal capitalism, they argue that *sexism* is at the root of all other forms of discrimination. Indeed, the self-designation "radical" means "at the root". Radical feminism grew out of women's disillusionment with the politics of the New Left in the 1960s, when women, fighting for equality and human rights in the American civil rights movement and in the anti-Vietnam war movement found themselves treated as inferior persons and exploited as sex objects by their male counterparts within the organizations in which they were active. In response, they divorced themselves from male-dominated organizations and formed their own women's organizations dedicated to the eradication of sexism. Sexism, as manifested in sexist language, gender stereotyping, pornography, paternalistic family arrangements and wife and child abuse became the focus of radical feminist concern. Radical feminists rejected the liberal feminist view that men and women should be treated in the same way, i.e., they rejected the traditional, liberal assumption that equality rights are predicated on sameness. Instead, they reconfirmed the *biological uniqueness of women* and insisted that differences between men and women should be celebrated, and should not be used to rationalize discrimination against women.

From a human rights view, the radical feminist argument takes into account the principle of equivalence, which provides a basis for "special treatment" of women in some instances. The principle of equivalence applies in instances where certain human characteristics can be shown to limit opportunities for the bearer, unless specially compensated for. In such instances, special, compensatory mechanisms must be put in place in order to ensure the bearer full and truly equal access to opportunities. Standard treatment, in the sense of affording the bearer of limiting characteristics the same opportunities as others without limiting characteristics, would be discriminatory. Under Article 11(2) of the Convention on the Elimination of All Forms of Discrimination against Women (UN, 1981), the principle of equivalence is implemented in order to ensure that states take appropriate measures to prevent discrimination against women on the grounds of marriage or maternity, and to ensure their effective right to work. Article 11(2) prohibits dismissal on the grounds of marital status, pregnancy or maternity leave; it requires the provision of maternity leave with pay and without loss of former employment status or benefits; it encourages the provision of support services for working families such as child care facilities and it insists that special protection be afforded pregnant women in potentially harmful work environments.

The issues addressed under Article 11(2) of the Convention are of central concern to radical feminists, for they have declared that "the personal is political". They argue that many forms of discrimination against women relate not only to public but also to private gender roles. Radical feminists have drawn public attention to the fact that the bulk of human rights abuses of women and children operate within the private sphere of domestic and familial relations, a sphere protected from political scrutiny by the paternalistic ideology of sanctity and privacy of home and family life. Before radical feminists placed it on the public agenda, domestic violence was regarded as a private matter in which the law ought not to meddle. Not only have radical feminists been in the forefront of the battle for legal protection against violence toward women and children, but they have also been actively involved with provision of hostels and counseling services for female victims of public and family violence.

Sexuality and reproduction

Among the common themes and agendas which have come to unite socialist and radical feminists under the umbrella of women's liberation, a major issue of common concern is that of women's sexual and reproductive freedom. Feminists have been active and notably successful in claiming women's right to abortion on demand; in insisting upon reliable means of birth control; in challenging sexist/paternalistic control over child birth and child rearing and in affirming the right to sexual relationships – with a partner of the opposite sex or of the same sex – that deny and defy the sexist, paternalistic norm.

The women's movement and social change

To what extent has the rise of the women's movement influenced changes in law, social policy and social practice in North America?

Enfranchisement

The first wave of feminism, represented by the early twentieth-century suffrage movement, after decades of struggle, eventually managed to achieve its goal of the enfranchisement of women, in Canada, in 1918, and in the USA, in 1920.

Women's rights and liberation

The second wave of feminism (women's rights and liberation) focused on government's responsibility to take an active role in addressing discrimination against women. In the USA, in 1963, pressured by women's lobbying groups, President Kennedy convened a Commission on the

Status of Women, naming Eleanor Roosevelt as its chair. The report issued by that Commission in 1963 documented discrimination against women in virtually every area of American life. State and local governments quickly followed suit and established their own commissions for women, to research conditions and recommend changes that could be instituted. Following from this initiative, Title VII of the 1964 Civil Rights Act was passed, prohibiting employment discrimination on the basis of sex as well as race, religion and national origin. With its passage, the Equal Employment Opportunity Commission was established to investigate discrimination complaints.

The ERA

The next step was the re-introduction of the Equal Rights Amendment (ERA) for the United States Constitution, originally drafted by the National Woman's Party in 1923, in order to ensure that men and women would have equal rights throughout the USA; the ERA had languished in Congress for almost fifty years. Then, in 1972, the ERA was finally passed and sent to the states for ratification. The wording of the ERA was simple: "Equality of rights under the law shall not be denied or abridged by the United States or by any state on account of sex." This issue came to each state to decide individually, and its ratification required thirty-eight states.

The campaign for state ratification of the ERA provided the opportunity for millions of women across the nation to become actively involved in the women's rights movement in their own communities. But, despite polls consistently showing a large majority of the population supporting the ERA, it was considered by many politicians to be just too controversial. When the deadline for ratification came in 1982, the ERA was just three states short of the thirty-eight needed to write it into the US Constitution (Equal Rights Amendment. Encyclopedia entry, see website references).

Feminism in Canada
Equality rights provisions

In contrast to the USA, women in Canada have fought for and gained constitutional protection for equality with men. With the enactment of the Charter of Rights and Freedoms in 1982, constitutional protection for the equality of women and men is guaranteed under s. 28, as well as under the more general (non-discriminatory) equality rights provisions (ss. 15 (1) and (2) of the Charter. In 1985, affirmative action programs for women received constitutional sanction.

Women's rights and women's liberation

In Canada, the second wave of feminism, as represented by the women's rights (liberal feminist) and women's liberation (socialist and radical feminist) movements, had also managed, by 1966, to overcome their internal disparities sufficiently to enable members of the various organizations they represented to cooperate in the organization of a Committee for Equality for Women. This committee was given the mandate to obtain a federal government enquiry into the status of women in Canada. In response, the federal government established The Royal Commission on the Status of Women.

The Royal Commission reported in 1970. Much to the surprise (if not consternation) of the federal government, it grounded its recommendations in the four underlying principles which encompassed the double set of demands of the liberal and radical feminists of the second wave: (1) that women should be free to choose whether or not to take employment outside the home; (2) that the care of children was a responsibility to be shared by the mother, father and society; (3) that society had a permanent responsibility for "special treatment" of women because of pregnancy and childbirth; and (4) that society had an interim responsibility to provide "special treatment" for women in order to overcome the adverse impact of systemic discrimination against them (i.e. the provision of programs of affirmative action). By 1987, most of the Royal Commission's recommendations regarding legal inequalities had been implemented at the federal level. However, progress towards full equity for women still continues (*Status of Women Canada*, 1995).

Abortion

With regard to the controversial issue of abortion, the 1973 US decision in the landmark *Roe* v. *Wade* abortion case (*Roe* v. *Wade*, 1973) decreed that for the stage in pregnancy prior to approximately the end of the first trimester, the abortion decision and its effectuation must be left to the medical judgment of the pregnant woman's attending physician. This decision, the Judge pointed out, left the state free to place increasing restrictions on abortion as the period of pregnancy lengthened, so long as those restrictions were tailored to the recognized state interests. In Canada, by way of contrast, in January 1988, the Supreme Court struck down the federal/criminal abortion law as unconstitutional under the Charter of Rights and Freedoms, because it violated women's right to reproductive freedom (*R* v. *Morgentaler*, 1988). Since that time Canada has had no legislation prohibiting abortion, and women are free to choose whether or not to pursue this option in the case of an unwanted pregnancy (Duhaime, website, November 2, 2002).

The backlash

Pro-life women

Probably a majority of women today, whether or not they identify themselves as feminists, would support the human rights-oriented goal of
equality/equivalence of opportunity for women and men. Many
women, however, strongly object to and oppose other priorities and
goals of the second wave of feminism. In North America, and to varying
degrees, elsewhere, there are an increasing number of women's groups
whose members espouse alternate views and who feel that their particular group interests have not been addressed by the women's movement.
Anti-abortionist/right to life organizations such as REAL Women in
Canada and the National Right to Life and Feminists for Life groups in
the USA, which continue to accept the paternalistic (patriarchal) family
yet seek to obtain recognition for the distinctive abilities of women,
actively oppose the struggle for sexual and reproductive freedom of the
second wave of the women's movement.

Visible and immigrant women

Black feminists, speaking for women of color, have criticized the
women's movement for failing to address the situation of double jeop-
ardy facing non-white women, who are discriminated against on the
basis of both race and sex. Black feminists have been especially articulate in pointing out that mainstream, middle-class, white feminists
frequently display an insensitivity to the enormous power differential
between black and white women manifested in the lower income and
restricted options of black women (Stasiulus, 1990). Echoing these sentiments, immigrant women, together with women of color, have begun to
challenge the women's movement's strong middle-class and racist biases
(Agnew, 1996).

After the millennium

Women, feminism and social protest in a global context

By the 1990s, virtually all of the self-definitions of the protest movement
for women's rights and liberation – ranging from the early suffragettes,
through the various versions of feminism – had come under critical
question. The movement had become a reflective one, which involved a
rethinking of previous positions and approaches (Caine and Pringle,

1995: x). Most significantly, in contrast to earlier approaches, the 1990s
witnessed a new move toward inclusiveness, an attempt to expand the
framework of feminism to encompass difference and diversity among
women throughout the globe (Caine 1995). In direct contrast to earlier
assumptions of women's common identity as women, which gave rise to
goals of an united global sisterhood, it is precisely this homogenizing
idea of sisterhood which has come under attack from within feminism
itself (Ang, 1995). In the 1990s, it was widely acknowledged that significant differences between women, produced by the intersections of class,
race, ethnicity, religion, nationality and so forth, undermined the homo-
geneity and continuity of "women" as a social category. Accordingly,
"difference" became an obligatory tenet in feminist discourse in the
1990s and feminism's ability to "deal with difference" was increasingly
held to be a condition for its survival as a movement for social change.

The shift from unity to diversity

This shift in emphasis from unity to diversity raises the issue of precisely
the kinds of conflicts which can develop from the tension between individual rights and collective cultural rights. I addressed these in the
Introduction to this book, in both my discussion of the debate over the
universality of human rights in cross-cultural context, and in the case
study of women's rights in a multicultural society (Case Study 2.1).

How, then, do twenty-first-century feminists propose to "deal with
difference"? Ang (1995), among others, suggests that the way difference
should be dealt with is typically envisaged by the white/Western/
middle-class feminist establishment through such benevolent terms as
"recognition", "understanding" and "dialogue".

For Ang, and like-minded spokespersons for non-white/non-Western
women, to focus on resolving differences between women as the ultimate
aim of dealing with difference would mean the absorption/containment
of the "other" (non-white/non-Western women) in an inclusive, already
existing mainstream feminist community without challenging the legitimacy of the established structure of that community. Ang contends that
white/Western hegemony (whether male- or female-imposed) is the
systematic consequence of an historic, global development over the last
500 years – the expansion of European capitalist modernity throughout
the world, resulting in the subsumption of all "other" peoples to its
economic, political and ideological agenda. The white/"other" divide,
Ang insists, is an historically and systematically imposed structure which
cannot, yet, if ever, be superseded. From the perspective of "other"
women, the nature of global capitalist modernity is such that "other"

peoples are left with two options: either enter the game or be excluded. At the national level, either integrate/assimilate or remain an outsider; at the international level, either westernize or be ostracized from the world community. This ensures that the "other" in a white/Western-dominated world is always dependent on and defined in relation to dominant white/Western cultural norms. Seen this way, Ang argues that the politics of difference, while bitterly necessary in face of the increasing insistence of "other" voices, has not resulted in a new feminist consensus, and never will. There will always be a tension, she insists, between difference as benign diversity and difference as conflict, disruption and dissension.

Taking diference seriously

Taking difference seriously, Ang contends, necessitates the adoption of a policy of partiality, rather than a politics of inclusion (Ang, 1995). A politics of partiality, she says, accepts the principle that feminism can never be an encompassing political home driven by an ambition for universal representation of all women's interests. This is not only because different groups of women have different and sometimes conflicting interests but, more radically, because for many groups of "other" women, other interests, other identifications, are sometimes more important and politically pressing than, or even incompatible with, those related to their being women. In short, as Butler (1990: 4) points out: "the premature insistence on a stable subject of feminism, understood as a seamless category of women, inevitably generates multiple refusals to accept the category. It compels us [non-white/non-Western women] to say 'I'm a feminist, but . . . '" (quoted in Ang, 1995: 73).

Case Studies 5.1 to 5.3 will illustrate the significant diversities in feminist viewpoint among women in very different national and cultural contexts.

Case Study 5.1   The past is the present: thoughts from the new South Africa

"The Past is the Present", the theme of Maitse's paper, is based on her central argument that in today's newly liberated South Africa, men have a claim to the past, present and future, while women are confined to the mythic past of African culture that promotes, condones and glorifies gender inequality. She argues that South Africa's drive for national unity, "at all costs", with its emphasis on reconciliation and forgiveness has served to deny women who have borne the agony of both racial and gender oppression the opportunity to voice their experiences of sexual, physical and emotional violence by the police, comrades and both known and unknown men. While the themes of forgiveness and reconciliation are admirable ones, in practice, Maitse claims, these themes translate only into forgiving visible crimes carried out by the apartheid regime: they do not include the largely invisible crimes committed by men against women, acts such as beatings and rape by husbands and strangers, forced sterilization, forced insertion of birth control devices into women's wombs, as well as continuing harassment, molestation and humiliating sexist jokes.

Maitse argues further that identification with the goal of nationalism can be both progressive and reactionary, for it includes both the oppressor and the oppressed. Nationalism, she suggests, fails to acknowledge that within the nation there are two categories of people, men and women, whose relationship with each other is that of the dominator and the dominated. Hence, instead of offering women protection against male violence, nationalism serves to "keep women in their place".

In South Africa, Maitse continues, the emergence of nationalism paved the way for women's entry into the "nationalist political family". Women identified with men as the oppressed and exploited nation. However, this political family, like the domestic one, continued to be dominated by men. Nationalism, Maitse suggests, deploys new and old forms of men's control over women by merging traditional with new values in ways which exalt the primary role of woman as wife/mother/child bearer and rearer, traditional African cultural values which existed prior to colonization and apartheid.

In conclusion, Maitse contends that South Africa's projected national image as a liberated, democratic, non-racist and non-sexist society can never be realized simply by the cessation of the racially oppressive regime of apartheid. Non-sexism, she contends, requires a complete social change in gender relations. Such a change, in turn, requires not only a willingness by men to acknowledge the equal dignity and worth of women as human beings, but also a critical re-thinking of those cultural values which dehumanize women and a concomitant re-structuring of the male-dominated hierarchy in both the family and society, towards a new form rooted in gender equity.

Source: Maitse (1996).

Case Study 5.2   Freedom and democracy – Russian male style

In opening her arguments, Mamonoca reports that 50,000 very young women from Eastern Europe came to Germany in the 1990s, only to become prostitutes, 10,000 of them allegedly against their will. Some teenagers were sold to the West and several others were killed trying to escape. These human rights abuses, she suggests, were condoned by the Commonwealth of Independent States (CIS) media. One male commentator, disappointed with his experiences with the performances of contemporary prostitutes working in strip joints, reportedly argued that contemporary prostitution stemmed entirely from the greed of the young women selling themselves. He expressed no revulsion whatsoever for the men, the "pimps" who run and profit from these strip joints.

Unfortunately, Mamonoca points out, most Russian women have not had the opportunity to acquaint themselves with feminism. "Choking in *glasnost*", the CIS woman now rushes between trying to get lipstick and trying to get married, preferably to a foreigner and especially to an American. Businesses such as the Grooms by Mail Agency have capitalized on this apparent demand and are growing rapidly. Brochures spell out the desirability of Russian women, who allegedly have not been "ruined by feminism" and whose expectations of marriage and of life in general are much more reasonable than those of American women. Mamonoca suggests that the current outpouring of pornographic publications in Russia demonstrates how far the "maleocracy" has gone: young women learn to be sex objects for profit.

However, some of the few outspoken feminists in Russia are reportedly trying to reverse this trend. They echo the sentiments of Western feminists, who argue that a man who buys a woman is buying power, not sex and that it is a primitive, vulgar power of dominator over dominated. Others trying to reverse the trend have published research findings which reveal a direct correlation between pornography and rape. Although there is ample evidence that violence against women, including multiple rapes and forced prostitution, is on the rise, Soviet women are starved of information that could empower them with knowledge of their rights. Consequently, for example, very few women have resorted to the judicial process in the event of a rape.

Mamonoca contends that both Russia and America are "maleocentric" societies where the subordinate/dominated status of women is nearly analagous. When asked about the difference between Russian and American women, Mamonoca responds ironically that "in Russia women's consciousness lags behind the laws, and in America the laws lag behind women's consciousness". Unfortunately, as a direct result of Russian women's low level of consciousness, she suggests, as *perestroika* and *glasnost* have turned Russian society inside out, sexism has moved on to the more blatant forms of violations of women's rights documented earlier: mass rapes, forced prostitution and participation in violent pornography of ever-younger women, and all carried out with relative impunity by dominant male perpetrators.

Source: Mamonoca (1996).

Case Study 5.3   Common language – different cultures: true or false?

Powhiri

Powhiri begins her story by telling of her experience of growing up in a traditional Maori family and community where both men and women had "public voices". She deplores the fact that some Maori men today, influenced by the male-dominated ethos of *pakeha* (white/Western) society imposed through *pakeha* socialization over the last 170 years or so, now tend to relegate Maori women to a position of subjugation and servitude – a position which Western patriarchy has forced many of its women to endure. In Maori society, Powhiri points out, the roles of men and women are not the same, but they are complementary and equitable. Growing up in a farm community, Powhiri reports that she listened to the women in her family making major decisions about the purchase or sale of livestock or machinery and all other major decisions. Growing up with Maori values of equity between men and women, Powhiri reports that she learned to question the monocultural, male-dominated *pakeha* power structure and to challenge it on two fronts: as sexist and as racist.

As one of the very few Maori women who has been able to "indulge herself" in *pakeha* feminist groups such as the Women's Studies Association of New Zealand, Powhiri suggests that she finds herself in unenviable situations. As a Maori, she identifies with the real-life struggles of the Maori underclass in New Zealand which prevent most Maori (men and women) from affording such luxuries as going off to a conference for a weekend. Her strong Maori identity, she says, also poses a dilemma at conferences when she has to choose between seminars focusing on feminist issues and those for Maori women/women of colour/black/First Nations, focusing on racism, when both seminars are scheduled at the same time. On such occasions, she comments, I would opt for the most disadvantaged group: non-white/women.

In Powhiri's view, until all feminists deal with the issues of racism, not only within society as a whole, but within the feminist movement in particular, this will be a constant source of irritation and frustration for many non-white, non-Western feminists.

Sigrid

Sigrid begins her story by telling of her experience of growing up in an anti-Nazi family in Germany during the Second World War. She recounts that her father was in exile, as a traitor, for most of the war because of his refusal to join the Nazi party or to work with the Nazis in any way, which marked him as a traitor. The family was reunited in 1949, and Sigrid suggests that her development as "a bit of a rebel" was supported by her parents' convictions that she should think for herself and develop her own individuality. In high school, her constant speaking out against perceived injustices at school met with a very negative reception from teachers and precipitated her leaving school before graduation.

For the next few years, she worked and studied in Belgium, France and England attempting to gain the qualifications for entrance into university. She eventually secured a scholarship to study at a university in Arizona, where she was given the opportunity to spend some time on a Navajo reservation. That time, she says, opened her eyes to the struggles of peoples torn from their heritages by all-powerful, self-righteous, blatantly racist authorities – both the state government of Arizona and the federal government of the USA. This experience, Sigrid relates, enabled her to see more clearly than ever, the history that she had to live with as a German – the history of the Third Reich. This strengthened her growing conviction that, as a German, she would strive to ensure that the voices of marginalized peoples would never again be silenced.

Sigrid, as a white European and feminist, began to question the white/Western/middle-class bias of mainstream feminism. After attaining a university post in Germany, she began the Women's Studies courses and the new English literature courses which eventually led her to the literature of Aotearoa/New Zealand and, in particular, to Maori literature in English. It was

this burgeoning interest which led her to meet and to form a working relationship with Powhiri, then living for an extended period of time in Germany.
Sigrid claims that being open to their cultural differences has led to a temper-
ing of both women's traditional cultural approaches to life. Sigrid's German
concern with formal rules and structures has been tempered by Powhiri's
Maori flexibility and questioning of authoritative rules and structures. At the
same time, she says, Powhiri's more casual approach has been tempered by a
new determination to set goals fueled by a need to be successful in a foreign
land, and in order to help others achieve success at home in New Zealand.
Sigrid contends that while the two women have cultural differences and are
learning to adjust to and accept them, they also have common meeting
places, including, importantly, their common identity as radical feminists,
"women focused women". In closing, Sigrid argues that the task for such
women is to challenge the patriarchal structure of oppression which imprisons
women and stifles their development as whole, fulfilled persons. Not until the
patriarchy supports the full liberation of women as persons, she contends, can
radical feminists give up their struggle.

Source: Rika-Heke and Markmann (1996)

Observations on Case Studies 5.1–5.3: views from the "other" women

The underlying contrast between Sigrid and Powhiri's views and priorities expressed in Case Study 5.3 serves to highlight and to support the
position put forward by Ang, detailed earlier, that feminism can never be
an encompassing political home driven by an ambition for universal
representation of all women's interests. As Ang so astutely points out,
this is not only because different groups of women have different and
sometimes conflicting interests but, more radically, because for many
groups of "other" women, other interests, other identifications, are
sometimes more important and politically pressing than, or even incompatible with, those related to their being women. The white mainstream
women represented in Case Study 5.2 and 5.3 by Mamonoca (from
Russia) and Sigrid (from Germany) strongly support the notion of international sisterhood and the current feminist movement for the full liberation of "women focused women". On the other hand, the "other"
(non-white, non-Western) women, represented in Case Study 5.1 and
5.3 by Maitse (from South Africa) and Powhiri (from New Zealand),
women who have experienced the oppression of both racism and
sexism, have other national/ethnic interests and identifications which
are just as important to them as their status as women. It is these cases
which most sharply illuminate the conflicts experienced by these women

between individual and collective cultural/national rights. Because of Powhiri's strong commitment, as an activist, to both Maori rights and women's rights, she frequently finds herself in situations where she must choose between the two. Maitse's situation is quite different. She does not have the same choice. While, as a black South African, she identifies with new, post-apartheid South African nationalism, she finds that her equally strong identity as a woman is suppressed within this movement. Unlike Powhiri, she has no access to feminist activities through which to express her commitment to women's rights. For Maitse, her commitment to nationalism, as a black South African, is incompatible with her strong identification as a woman and her expressed commitment to women's rights.

Concluding commentary

In this chapter, I have focused on the women's rights and liberation movement in Western/democratic and global contexts. In democratic contexts, far more than in others, despite the formidable obstacles posed by external discrimination and internal fragmentation, women's movements have been able to achieve a common sense of purpose and to pursue important community-wide, agreed upon goals which are perceived to be of benefit to all women in the society. As human rights-oriented social movements, some important political goals (franchise, birth control) have been achieved, and some human rights protections for women (equality rights in public life) have been secured. However, in both democratic, multicultural contexts and in a global context, the women's movement has become increasingly sensitive to the limitations on solidarity within the movement posed by racial and cultural diversity. In particular, the conflict between individual and collective cultural rights is increasingly apparent in the movement's new commitment to "dealing with difference".

My analysis of the women's rights and liberation movement at the national and global levels lends strong support for Melucci's (1980,1996) thesis which sees in the appropriation of identity the key to understanding new social movements. First, these movements, as Melucci suggests, reject the traditional separation between public and private spheres. For feminists "the personal is political", and previously private issues involving gender – identities and interpersonal relations – have penetrated the sphere of the public and political.

Solidarity as an objective, Melucci suggests, is another characteristic of the new social movements. The struggle centers around the particularistic issue of group identity, based on ascriptive criteria such as sex, age and sexual orientation. The movements, Melucci point out, also have instrumental objectives, and seek political advantages, but this dimension is secondary to the expressive nature of the relations sought in the search for solidarity, the primary thrust of the movements. While Melucci's thesis holds, in general, there are internal lines of division within the women's movement on the degree of emphasis placed on instrumental (political and economic empowerment) versus expressive (identity and solidarity) objectives. These divisions are primarily expressed in differences between liberal and radical feminists: the instrumental emphasis is particularly strong within the separatist sector of the radical feminist branch of the woman's movement. These qualifications having been noted, I wish to reiterate the point made at the beginning of this section that, as a whole, my analysis of the women's human rights and liberation movement in both democratic and global contexts lends strong support for Melucci's (1980) thesis which sees in the appropriation of identity and the building and sustaining of group solidarity the key to understanding new social movements.

In Chapter 6, I will focus my analysis on the gay and lesbian rights and liberation movement in democratic and global contexts. In concluding, I will compare and contrast the women's and gay and lesbian movements as human rights-oriented new social movements.

Equality/Equity-Seeking Protest Movements 2: Gay and Lesbian Rights

In Chapter 5, I used both classic social movement theory and new social movement theory in my analysis of the women's rights and liberation movement. In this chapter, applying the same theoretical frameworks for analysis, my focus will be on the gay and lesbian rights and liberation movement, in both democratic and global contexts. In concluding this chapter, I will compare and contrast the women's and gay and lesbian movements as human rights-oriented new social movements.

The gay and lesbian rights and liberation movement

A legally sanctioned homophobic environment

In my earlier discussion of the promotion of heterosexist hatred and harm against members of the same-sex-oriented population, I pointed out that much of the current invalidation ideology used to justify discrimination against members of this subordinate target group was based on pseudo-religious "evidence", and in particular, on the arguments put forward by proponents of homophobic, fundamentalist, "radical-right wing" Christian organizations. Historically, throughout Euro–Christian countries, this same kind of pseudo-religious "evidence" was used to justify cruel acts of discrimination against gay men and lesbians and, under Nazi policies and laws in Hitler's Germany, even genocide (Adam, 1995; 53–9). With the separation of church and state in many countries, including North America, the pseudo-religious myths used to justify heterosexist acts of discrimination became enshrined in law, and in many countries "homosexual acts" were prohibited under criminal laws (Lauristen and Thorstad, 1974).

In this legally-sanctioned homophobic environment, the lives of most gay men and lesbians were tightly closeted. Fear of public degradation and cruel punishment kept most same-sex oriented-persons in the closet, and clearly impeded any form of collective protest. It wasn't until social conditions changed, leading to the decriminalization of "homosexual acts" in various societies and/or states within societies, that some same-sex-oriented persons began to come out of the closet and to raise demands for human rights-oriented change.

In order to illustrate the development of gay and lesbian protest, and the rise of gay and lesbian liberation movements in democratic contexts, I will focus my discussion on the chronicle of events in Australia and Canada (Kallen, 1996).

Australia

From closeted networks to activism

Woolcock and Altman (1999) point out that, unlike some European countries, there was no lesbian and gay movement in Australia in the interwar years, and only very guarded references exist in pre-1970s literature. These authors argue that it was the impact of social and cultural changes in Australia after the late 1960s which were particularly significant for understanding the emergence and the relative success of the lesbian and gay movement in Australia: the impact of second-wave feminism; the impact of large-scale and diverse immigration and the growing integration of Australia into a global world order strongly influenced by the USA, but increasingly seeking contact with the booming economies of east and southeast Asia. The first two factors led to an increase in mainstream support for cultural and sub-cultural diversity which made it easier for gays and lesbians to challenge heterosexist assumptions about the "unnaturalness" of homosexuality. The third factor led both to an increase in Asian immigration, strengthening cultural diversity and, at the same time, increasing the cultural impact of American gay and lesbian communities on their Australian counterparts.

Woolcock and Altman (1999) report that while closeted homosexual networks emerged in Sydney after the First World War, and began to flourish after the Second World War, these existed only as underground networks. It wasn't until the late 1960s and early 1970s that the first gay and lesbian political organizations were established. By the late 1970s, however, gay liberation groups would be found in all major cities. Lesbians were active in the early stages of both the women's and the gay movement, but they found themselves in a subordinate status in both. Dominated by heterosexual women in the women's movement and by men in the gay movement, they struggled to fight for their own concerns as gay women. The gay community, itself was divided in its interests not only along lines of gender, but also between the activist arm (emphasizing political and legal change) and the growing social and commercial networks (emphasizing the gay community and sub-culture). The task of the movement by the late 1970s was to reach all sectors of the diverse same-sex-oriented world, including the majority of women and men who rejected association with a "too political" movement. Further, a clash in interests between activist men and women arose as women sensed a growing masculinization of the movement which seemed more concerned with reaching the commercial world than in maintaining a cosexual alliance. Partly in response, lesbian separatists developed their own forms of political activism, free of male agendas. Woolcock and Altman (1999) contend that the advent of the Gay Mardis Gras (later the Gay and Lesbian Mardis Gras) in 1978 was a critical step in reconciling the community and the movement. By crystallizing the perceived achievements of law reform and community diversity, the Gay Mardis Gras enabled the community and movement sectors to identify with an effective common bond. Today, the annual event has become a mass celebration, drawing hundreds of thousands of spectators and, because of its commercial success in attracting tourists, it has gained considerable mainstream media and political support. In Woolcock and Altman's words (1999: 331) "It is arguably the largest gay/lesbian street party in the world."

The quest for political and legal recognition of gay and lesbian rights

In Australia, the recognition of same-sex-oriented persons as an invalidated, subordinate population requiring human rights protection, rather than a category of behaviourally perverted persons deserving punishment, is a very recent phenomenon (Matthews, 1988). This change occurred to some extent in the early 1970s, as gay and lesbian activists began lobbying for legal protection of sexual orientation under anti-discrimination laws. The first success came in South Australia in 1972. By the 1990s, there was some form of protection (variable from state to state) in the statutes of all Australian jurisdictions except Tasmania and Western Australia (Adam, 1995). However, the recognition of the human rights of same-sex-oriented persons in Australia did not occur without a long, hard struggle.

For example, when the New South Wales Anti-Discrimination Act was first introduced into Parliament in 1976, homosexuality was included among the recommended anti-discriminatory grounds (Matthews, 1988). However, this ground, together with the several other non-traditional grounds, were rejected by the opposition. At this time, so-called "homosexual" acts between men were still treated as serious criminal offenses in New South Wales, and in most other states throughout Australia, regardless of the age of the participants or the consensual nature of the acts. Police entrapment of men alleged to have engaged in homosexual acts in public toilets was a common practice (Matthews, 1988). In July 1982, the New South Wales Anti-Discrimination Board released their Report on Discrimination and Homosexuality (New South Wales Anti-Discrimination Board, June 1982). Highlighted in the report were discrimination in the law, in law enforcement agencies, in the courts, in employment, in education, in the media and in religion. The report also documented the many areas of discrimination against gay men and lesbians resulting from the lack of legal protection for same-sex partnerships. As recommended in the report, the prohibition against discrimination on the ground of homosexuality was added to the enumerated prohibited grounds of the New South Wales Anti-Discrimination Act in 1982. This amendment represented a monumental achievement, the end result of years of lobbying by gay and lesbian groups. At about the same time, a new method of categorizing and dealing with all sexual offenses was introduced by the New South Wales Crimes Act. The decriminalization of homosexual acts between consenting adults was one of the changes introduced (Matthews, 1988). By 1990, all Australian states except Tasmania had decriminalized homosexuality (Adam, 1995).

Decriminalization of homosexuality resulted in changes in public attitudes toward same-sex-oriented persons, from open hostility to some degree of toleration. As a result, the fears of same-sex-oriented persons that open disclosure of their sexual orientation would bring retribution in the form of job dismissal, or in other ways, diminished. However, before substantial numbers of lesbians and gay men had ventured out of the closet, the movement towards openness was dramatically set back by the advent of AIDS and the irrational stereotyping of gay men as the primary carriers of the disease. This event generated an abrupt reversal in public attitudes, most vehemently expressed in the homophobic views of various right-wing church authorities who reportedly exclaimed that AIDS was God's punishment for the sins committed by homosexuals (Wotherspoon, 1992).

Canada

The decade of lesbian and gay rights

As in Australia, in Canada until the 1970s, a major heterosexist barrier to the recognition of the human rights of same-sex-oriented persons was that imposed by legal discrimination. In Canada, various prohibitions within the Criminal Code made homosexual acts a criminal offensce. In 1969, amendments to the Criminal Code came into effect, legalizing sexual acts between two consenting adults (over the age of 21) in private. While the word "homosexual" did not appear in the amendment, same-sex-oriented persons and others soon began to deem the document the "homosexual bill", for it clearly opened the door out of the closet for Canada's adult same-sex-oriented population (Foster and Murray, 1972). After the Criminal Code was changed, gay and lesbian organizations sprang up across Canada and their membership grew rapidly (Foster and Murray, 1972).

The 1970s have been hailed as the decade of lesbian and gay rights in Canada. This decade witnessed the development of an increasing number of political action groups – gay and lesbian caucuses and lesbian and gay rights lobbying groups which sought to persuade politicians and governments to amend and/or to create legislation which would recognize and protect the fundamental human rights of gay and lesbian persons. As was the case in Australia, in Canada, the 1970s was a decade marked by extensive lobbying efforts by gay and lesbian organizations to have "sexual orientation" listed among the enumerated non-discriminatory grounds in human rights legislation throughout the country.

The backlash

In Canada, with the single exception of the Quebec Charter of Human Rights, this effort was unsuccessful. By the end of the 1970s, the backlash of the "moral majority" against the new visibility of open (or, out of the closet) lesbians and gay men had begun to take serious hold. Sparked by the highly propagandized anti-gay and lesbian campaigns of "Born-again Christian" Anita Bryant and others, attacks on same-sex-oriented persons in the known gay and lesbian venues became more frequent and police harassment in these areas was stepped up (Jackson and Persky, 1982). For example, in 1981, Metro Toronto police organized and carried out a series of raids on gay bathhouses and arrested almost 300 men, under antiquated and rarely-invoked "bawdy house" laws. In these now infamous "bawdy house raids", police used sledgehammers to break windows and doors, and, after private property was smashed, "found-

ins" were charged and exposed to public ridicule, and "keepers" were
dragged through the courts (Steele, 1994).

It was also at the height of the Anita Bryant campaign in North
America that Australian police stepped up attacks on gay venues and
events. In 1978, police attacked a Gay Mardis Gras rally in Sydney,
beating demonstrators and arresting some of the participants (Adam,
1995). In response, a Gay Solidarity Group was formed to defend the
Mardis Gras. After several months of protests against the Mardis Gras
arrests, including a march on the Darlinghurst police station during
which many protesters were arrested, the police finally dropped most of
the charges.

The 1980s

In Canada, as in Australia, discriminatory attacks upon gay and lesbian
venues and events served to generate community and movement solidarity, spawning new solidarity and protest groups determined to protect
their community, its venues and its events, and to fight for protection of
their human rights. The day after the "bawdy house" raids in Toronto
and again two weeks later, 3,000 protesters marched on No. 52 Division
police station (Adam, 1995). These protest actions, gave rise to a Right
to Privacy Committee that became the largest gay organization in the
city in the 1980s. The Right to Privacy Committee was formed to
protect gay venues and to protest against outside interference with the
gay and lesbian community's "social space" (Hannon, 1980).

As in Australia, the 1980s in Canada was marked by a notable
increase in public homophobia owing to the advent of the AIDS
epidemic, which exacted a catastrophic toll, mainly among gay men. In
Toronto, as in Sydney – the cities with the largest gay and lesbian
communities in each country – discriminatory attacks upon the
gay/lesbian community arising from sensational media coverage about
the spread of AIDS, and linking this disease with the gay male population, spawned a variety of educational and anti-discriminatory defense
mechanisms within the target community (*Toronto Star*, June 4, 1994). As
in Australia, gay and lesbian organizations in Canada have raised funds
for research into the sources of AIDS; they developed public educational
materials designed to refute the prejudicial assumption that AIDS was a
"gay disease", and they were in the forefront of the movement to combat
the fear of AIDS and to protect its victims (homosexual and heterosexual alike) from the dehumanizing effects of social ostracization and isolation (Woolcock and Altman, 1999).

As was the case in New South Wales, a major front upon which the battle for gay and lesbian rights was waged in Ontario was that for legal protection. In Ontario, after almost a decade of lobbying efforts, including several briefs to the provincial government meticulously documenting widespread institutional discrimination against lesbians and gay men in all areas of public life (Coalition for Gay Rights in Ontario, 1978, 1981 and 1986), lesbian and gay rights activists, strongly supported by other human/rights activist groups, finally succeeded in their battle to gain legal protection on the ground of sexual orientation. In 1986, the government amended the Ontario Human Rights Code to include "sexual orientation" among the enumerated non-discriminatory grounds. This new, legal protection for their human rights enabled many long-closeted lesbians and gay men to "come out" and to openly declare pride in their sexual orientation and in their community.

At the national level, during the constitutional debates of 1980–2, despite considerable support from civil libertarian and other mainstream sympathizers, gay and lesbian lobbying efforts failed to have "sexual orientation" included in the enumerated non-discriminatory grounds of the equality rights provision (s. 15) of the constitutional Charter of Rights and Freedoms. Nevertheless, the battle continued at the provincial and federal levels and, in the 1990s, gay and lesbian activist organizations across Canada finally achieved success in obtaining protection for sexual orientation under the provisions of the human rights codes of eight of Canada's ten provinces, one of two territories and at the federal level.

Gay and lesbian communities in Sydney and Toronto

At the level of the local community, the primary base for grass-roots organizing, the cities of Toronto and Sydney represent the centers of greatest concentration of the gay and lesbian population, currently estimated to have reached almost a half million in number in each city. Members of both Sydney's and Toronto's gay and lesbian communities have created a broad range of organizations and a community infrastructure which has enabled members to maintain distinctive, same-sex cultural lifestyles and to create a community power base from which to fight discrimination and to organize efforts to secure and improve protection for their human rights (Kallen, 1996). Within both the Sydney and the Toronto gay/lesbian communities, there has been an increase in coalition-building in recent years, which has enabled gay and lesbian activists to lobby as a united front on most human rights issues of common concern, despite serious lines of internal division based on gender, class and political ideology. At the level of the same-sex-oriented community, gay men and lesbians have been able to come together in a wide variety of organizational contexts, beyond political lobbying, to build a solid community infrastructure to support their distinctive sub-cultures and lifestyles (Adam, 1995; Kallen, 1996).

Sub-cultures versus ethnocultures

A critique of the internationally endorsed concept of collective rights

At this juncture in my analysis, I wish to digress briefly, in order to pose a pertinent question. Should institutionally complete (Breton, 1964) non-ethnic communities, such as the lesbian and gay communities in Sydney and Toronto be able to put forward collective rights claims in order to protect their distinctive sub-cultures? In my earlier discussion of collective cultural rights in the Introduction to this book, I pointed out that under the provisions of current international human rights instruments, only *bona fide* ethnocultures (and not sub-cultures) are entitled to put forward these kinds of claims.

Limitations of the internationally endorsed concept of collective rights

In the introduction to Kallen (1989: 16), I suggested that the internationally recognized provisions of the minority rights article (s. 27, ICCPR) could be interpreted, from a social scientific perspective, so as to provide a basis of justification, in principle, for the collective cultural claims of some subordinate non-ethnic communities. I argued that those non-ethnic communities which have developed legitimate, viable sub-cultures, with an institutional infrastructure facilitating their continuance over time, were entitled to the same legal protections as parallel, ethno-cultural communities.

Development/maintenance of an ethnoculture/subculture

Guided by the concept of institutional completeness introduced by Breton (1964), I posited three prerequisites for the development and maintenance of a distinctive, subordinate community ethnoculture or sub-culture (Kallen, 1989: 171):

(1) a living community of collectively identified members committed to preservation of cultural distinctiveness;

(2) the development and maintenance of a viable institutional

infrastructure for intra-ethnic communication and interaction and
for transgenerational cultural transmission;
(3) sufficient political and economic resources (voting power and
     buying power) to defend the subordinate community against exter-
     nal discrimination and to lobby effectively for collectively desired
     social changes.

In Kallen (1989, ch. 6), I attempted to validate this position, using the
case of the gay and lesbian community in Toronto as my example
(Kallen, 1989: 171–6). In my view, a broader re-conceptualization of
culture and collective cultural rights which could include viable sub-
cultural communities would move the international system of human
rights protection an important step forward.

Gay and lesbian rights: critical issues for the twenty-first century

Legalization of relationships

Of primary concern among the many equality issues (legal recognition
and protection for equality rights) which continue to be raised by organizations of gay men and lesbians, are family-related, marriage and
parenting issues. Legalization of gay and lesbian relationships (that is,
legal recognition of same-sex relationships) is seen as the key to the
acquiring of equal benefits for homosexual and heterosexual partnerships with regard to child custody, adoption, fostering, artificial (donor)
insemination, hospital visiting rights, estates and wills, pension benefits,
social security benefits and health benefits.

Some victories have been won in both Canada and Australia in
redressing these issues. As Adam (1995: 137) points out, Australia and
Canada have a "patchwork" of domestic partners' rights precedents set
by city officials, local courts and provincial/state governments. For
example, in Australia, Immigration Department regulations now permit
citizens to sponsor foreign same-sex partners under their family reunifi-
cation policies. In Canada, a landmark ruling by the Supreme Court of
Canada on May 21, 1999 recognized same-sex spousal support. At issue
were provisions in the Family Law Reform Act regarding support
payments after the break-up of couples. The long-awaited decision by
the country's top court ruled that Ontario's definition of "spouse" –
which applies only to heterosexual couples – violates the equality guar-

antees in the Charter of Rights by discriminating against gays and lesbians (*Toronto Star*, May 21, 1999). The decision exerted pressure on federal and provincial governments to rewrite hundreds of laws across Canada that discriminate against same-sex couples. Shortly thereafter, Ontario, British Columbia and Quebec changed their laws to comply with the Supreme Court ruling, with British Columbia allowing gay couples to adopt. Nova Scotia and Alberta soon followed (*Globe and Mail*, July 9, 2001). Saskatchewan also announced that it is amending 24 acts to give unmarried, opposite-and same-sex couples the same legal rights as married couples (*Toronto Star*, June 5, 2001). On June 1, 2001, Bill 75, endorsing registration of same-sex partnerships, passed under new registered domestic partnership legislation in the Province of Nova Scotia (*Toronto Star*, June 5, 2001). Nova Scotia was the first province in Canada to legalize registration of same-sex partnerships.

However, the battle for legal recognition of same-sex marriages suffered a setback when the federal Government of Canada decided to appeal the (July 12, 2002) decision of three Ontario Superior Court judges who ruled that restricting marriage to two people of the opposite sex violates gays' and lesbians' Charter right to equality (*Globe and Mail*, Thursday, August 1, 2002). Certainly, powerful interests oppose recognition of same-sex marriages, including influential leaders of religious bodies such as the president of the Canadian Conference of Catholic Bishops, and, on behalf of Muslims, the director of the Centre of Islamic Education in North America. But very recently, the political tide has turned in favor of gay and lesbian rights.

On June 17, 2003, Prime Minister Jean Chrétien announced that same-sex marriages will be recognized as legal in Canada through a new federal government law that will re-write the traditional definition of marriage (*Toronto Star*, June 18, 2003; *Globe and Mail*, June 19, 2003). The Prime Minister pointed out that the draft bill will protect religious freedom and the rights of churches and religious organizations to sanctify marriage as they define it. The government will refer the draft bill, to be produced within weeks, directly to the Supreme Court of Canada for a legal opinion. The high court will be asked to rule on the constitutional validity of legislation that legally recognizes the union of same-sex couples, after which the bill will be put to the House of Commons for approval in a free vote.

Nine provinces say they are willing to accept the marriage of same-sex couples once the federal government changes the country's longstanding, traditional definition of marriage. Ontario is the only province currently registering same-sex marriages. The recent gay civil rights breakthrough in Ontario is causing a sensation across the continent. Toronto is suddenly the gay marriage capital of North America (*Toronto Star*, June 14, 2003). Since the Ontario Court of Appeal ruled that same-sex couples can marry legally, they reportedly have been "applying in droves", not only from Canada but also from the United States and elsewhere. Toronto city hall issued 89 licences to same-sex couples in the first week: 49 to male and 40 to female couples.

In Australia, with bi-partisan support for reform, the state parliament in Victoria voted in June 2001 to amended a raft of laws to give same-sex couples equal rights in areas such as insurance, state taxes, hospital visitation and workplace conditions (365gay.com website, June 14, 2001).Victoria now joins three other states – New South Wales, the Australian Capital Territory and Queensland – in rectifying many of the disadvantages experienced by same-sex couples.

The Australian government in June 2001 dropped legislation to restrict single and lesbian women's access to Invitro Fertilization treatment (365gay.com website, June 14, 2001). The bill as it stood would have been voted down by the opposition Labour party and the minor parties in the Senate and so the government shelved it. The bill to amend the Sex Discrimination Act to allow states to restrict women's access to IVF, introduced in 2002, divided the party on the issue of a conscience vote.

This latter episode raises a very important point with regard to the fragile status of hard-wrought legal protections for human rights, not only for gays and lesbians but for members of all subordinate protest movements. Changes in the political structure, especially changes in party affiliation of majority governments in power, can radically alter the political climate on prevailing social issues (Kriesi *et al*, 1995). While the lesbian and gay struggle for equality and justice continues, unabated, the specter of set backs – in the form of negative amendments to antidiscrimination legislation or repeal of antidiscrimination statutes – as has occurred in the United States (Epstein, 1999: 46–7) looms large.

To what extent does our analysis of the national, gay/lesbian human rights and liberation movements in the democratic contexts of Canada and Australia, apply internationally? In the next section of this chapter, I shall undertake a comparative examination of gay and lesbian movements worldwide. My analysis will highlight the similarities and differences in these new social movements, in both Western and non-Western, democratic and non-democratic societies.

World-wide gay and lesbian movements

A comparative analysis of gay and lesbian (G & L) movements in a wide variety of national contexts throughout the globe (Adam, Duyvendak and Krouwel, 1999b), reveals both the striking cross-national similarities and the fundamental differences in the development of G & L movements. In order to explain both the similarities and differences uncovered, a trajectory of factors, distilled from the national studies, is posited. A basic prerequisite for the development of G & L movements is the ability to secure a "social space" where gay and lesbian identities can be developed (Melucci, 1980, 1996), and the ability to construct a rudimentary organization beyond private circles of friends. Once these prerequisites are met, gays and lesbians can start to make political demands. Within each national, political context, movement leaders can seize opportunities only if and when they are available: thus, variations can occur with changes in the political climate, both within and between national contexts. Movement organization also tends to be very much influenced by developments elsewhere in the world. Through a process of "transnational diffusion", gay and lesbian movements influence and learn from each other. International organizations such as the International Gay and Lesbian Association (IGLA) actively diffuse ideas and models, stimulating national movements to learn from each other in terms of goals, action repertoires and strategies. Additionally, representatives of both national and international G & L organizations have crossed borders and exchanged visions for movement development.

Similarities

Similarities in issue emphasis are found globally in G & L movements. Virtually everywhere, movements pursue a double strategy of fighting discrimination in law, public policy and practice, and establishing their own "public spaces" – either to hide from the homophobic outside world, or to meet in a free cultural place. Significant cross-national similarities can also be found in the pattern of actions and events of national movements. Mass demonstrations, consciousness-raising groups, sit-ins and lobbying efforts are typical. In many countries, the movement "came out" as a result of a triggering event, notably, in the USA, the Stonewall riots of June 1969. Commonly a highly homophobic event triggers a storm of protest as a perceived "enemy" or "opponent" serves to galvanize and mobilize movement organizations. In most countries, a gender conflict between lesbians and gays tends to split the movement.

Differences

Despite striking cross-national similarities, there are impressive national differences in the way lesbians and gays experience their identities in political terms. In countries of British heritage with well-developed same-sex cultural communities, there tends to be a continuum between personal identity and community politics, whereas the northern European countries tend to be characterized by a split between a somewhat apolitical culture and a formalized movement. Non-politicized identities and non-political social interaction dominate in the eastern European context as well as in other parts of the world outside the western hemisphere.

County paradigms and national imprints

Almost everywhere, studies show how national characteristics mould movements in both their aims and strategies: in Canada, the separatist struggle in Quebec; in France, the republican idea of universalism; in Japan, the hegemonic traditional and conformist culture and so forth. In each country, the G & L movement also has to "fit" into the emancipation model used by other groups in the society and recognized by authorities as valid and justified. In some countries, G & L movements must present themselves as cultural minorities; in others, as part of a broad movement for human rights and equality.

Prerequisites and facilitating conditions in the societal context

There are enormous differences among countries in the meanings of sexuality and in the possibility of same-sex-oriented identity. A common recognition of a shared sexual and affectional orientation is a precondition for a G & L movement to develop. Partly related to the issue of sexual identity are the various meanings of the sex/gender systems in different countries. Generally speaking, movements tend to be weaker in countries such as Brazil and Franco-era Spain, where same-sex preference is constructed through the lens of gender. Patriarchal logic may reserve public and political agency for men, depriving all women and those men considered to be effeminate of civic participation. This serves to create an identity split between *Activos* (masculine gay men) and *Passivos* (effeminate gay men) which inhibits movement solidarity.

Another major source of influence is the relative density of civil society. In most of the advanced capitalist countries, civil society relies on a social fabric of trust and cooperation among social organizations which creates opportunities for social organization, coalition-building and protest. In contrast, in totalitarian systems, such as the east European societies, widespread public distrust hinders the emergence of collective action. Also important is the way in which a society deals with subordinate groups in general. In countries like Japan, where a homogeneous religious and political culture is dominant, group-level differences are not well tolerated and subordinate groups have considerable difficulty in gaining a place for themselves on the public agenda. Alternatively, in immigrant countries or traditionally heterogeneous societies, such as the USA, Canada, Australia and the Netherlands, there is some level of respect and tolerance for political demands from subordinate groups and cultures.

The relationship between organized religion and the state is of major significance to the rise of a G & L movement. Institutionalized religion plays a major role in policing public culture in many societies, and this hampers the liberation of lesbians and gays. In the southern, eastern and central regions of Europe and parts of Latin-America, where politics and society remain heavily influenced by Roman Catholic or Orthodox churches, the level of acceptance of same-sex orientation tends to be very low. In Italy, Spain, Portugal and Poland, the Catholic church contributes to this intolerance, but the Orthodox church in Russia and Roumania is even more homophobic. In countries such as Canada and the Netherlands, where organized religion plays a lesser role, gay and lesbian emancipation has progressed much further.

Other, related factors which highlight the differences between repressive states, inhibiting G & L emancipation, and more tolerant states, facilitating the movement, include the extent of freedom from the conformist constraints of tradition (greater freedom generally associated with urbanization and industrialization), the role of the press and the nature of public attitudes.

Role of the judiciary

Virtually everywhere, the "political space" of the G & L movement directly depends on the judicial status of same-sex orientation. Legal repression serves to mobilize G & L movements and to direct the activities of G & L groups toward the eradication of discriminatory legislation that imposes criminal penalties on same-sex acts and which marginalizes lesbians and gay men. Where official, legal and social repression is severe and is backed by political violence (as is the case in eastern Europe) or random violence is backed by homophobic "opponents" (as is the case in Latin America and South Africa), it is almost impossible for a G & L movement to get off the ground. However, as soon as legal and violent repression declines and a social opening is created, allies can be found among "liberating" forces and G & L movements can develop. In cases of severe national repression, processes of international diffusion play a significant role: foreign examples of liberation (and, I might add, the enactment of legal protections for sexual orientation provide) a source of inspiration and imitation.

International case studies

The challenge posed by G & L groups and movements worldwide – whether engaged in institutional politics or pressing their demands from outside – is to contest difference and deny/defy the established structure of power. Today's G & L movement shares with other new social movements a democratic initiative of drawing subordinate/disadvantaged populations into civil society and politics and, at the same time, attempting to engage them in processes of political and social change which will serve to empower the disempowered in their thrust for institutional justice and equity in society (Adam, 1995). Where the current G & L movement differs from other new social movements is in its particular pledge to rehumanize the competitive and alienated relationships that separate "men from men and women from women". The G & L movement now exceeds the boundaries of an "identity" movement and of a "minority rights" movement: as a worldwide movement it is engaged in a broad struggle for human rights and social justice which it shares with other long-subordinated and disempowered groups (Adam, 1995).

In order to highlight the differences between repressive states inhibiting G & L emancipation, and more tolerant states facilitating the movement, two case studies, of Japan and Brazil, will be presented. Case Studies 6.1 and 6.2 should serve to illustrate the status of the G & L movement in repressive states, in contrast to the status of the G & L movement in more tolerant states, such as Australia and Canada, analyzed earlier.

Case Study 6.1   Japan finding its way?

It was not until the 1990s that embryonic gay and lesbian groups in Japan began to "come out" as a developing movement. Why this very late emergence of G & L politics in the Japanese national context? It has been suggested that the considerable upheaval in parliamentary politics in the early 1990s created a new environment which opened up possibilities for tolerance of difference traditionally unheard of in the culturally homogeneous and conformist national context. Historical construction of same-sex orientation in Japan suggests that it was cast as disruptive to the social order in a way parallel to that of heterosexual activity, outside of marriage, and prostitution, in particular. In this sexually conformist context, the only appropriate place for sex was in marriage, and for the express purpose of procreation. All other sexual activities fell under the term of *asobi* (play), which was tolerated only if it was engaged in discreetly did not interfere with the actors' primary duties toward the family, the community and the state. *Asobi* could be condoned only so long as it was limited to clearly identifiable individuals (e.g. effeminate men and masculine women) or to clearly defined (private) contexts, both of which had virtually no influence on the social order.

Children were socialized from a very early age into primary values of conformity, harmony, cooperation and obedience to adult authorities, in all social contexts. This left no room for the development of skills for discussion and creative thinking, for these were perceived to be potentially disruptive to the social order. To be openly gay or lesbian in such a social environment would contradict everything society held sacred.

While the structure of Japanese society denies gays and lesbians the possibility to openly live same-sex-oriented lifestyles, popular attitudes do not explicitly condemn same-sex orientation – rather, they ignore its very existence. Traditionally, there was no conception of a lifestyle other than heterosexual marriage, and this served to isolate gays and lesbians and to prevent the development of positive same-sex identities – a precondition for G & L movement organization.

Discrimination against lesbians and gays is most clearly visible in the areas of housing and work. Landlords will often reject two men living together beyond student age and employers, especially in high corporate occupations such as banking, do not tend to trust unmarried men to assume important positions, because they have not assumed the duties and responsibilities of family life and are therefore not deemed to be "stable". These situations are less problematic for lesbians, as such, because women are discriminated against in the labour market regardless of their marital status. The Equal Opportunity Law which took effect in 1986 prohibits discrimination against women in employment, yet its effect was to create a gendered, double career track in which women occupy the subservient stratum, confined largely to part-time, dead-end jobs.

The 1990s witnessed years of political upheaval, leaving Japanese party politics in disarray and opening the door to debates on social and moral matters in the media and in the public arena. Groups began questioning the norm of heterosexual marriage and alternative partnerships began to be proposed. Also, in the 1990s, a number of books depicting the personal experiences of lesbians and gays played a major role in the coming out process. The books did not spark the violent, homophobic reaction feared by the authors, and this led the way for many others, especially young gays and lesbians, to come out in the mass media or in their own environment. What seems to play a major role here are the time-honoured Japanese values of honesty and openness (expressing "true inner feelings"). While these values do not directly encourage people to be "different", they can help people explain coming out as gay or lesbian in a positive way: that one is being honest and open about oneself.

G & L movement

The central Japanese values of harmony, cooperation and consensus mitigate against movement development of any kind. The general attitude about making use of the law to further one's goals is that this strategy is inappropriate and unnecessary. Disputes are preferably, and mostly, resolved by reaching consensus between the parties before going to court. Japan has no laws directed towards same-sex-oriented persons or acts, in particular, probably because the privatization of sex in general means that most gays and lesbians remain closeted. Also, the condemnation of "difference" inhibits political activity. While gay and lesbian groups have existed since the 1950s, they did not "come out" until the 1990s, and to a large extent they have not become politicized. The extensive proliferation of gay and lesbian venues and magazines is one of the reasons often given to explain why it is difficult to interest people in gay/lesbian politics. While there have been three Gay and Lesbian Pride parades, attendance at these events appears to be dwindling. The internal disagreements about themes and activities in the events highlights an opposition between two streams of Japan's G & L activists. One stream leans toward American gay politics and stresses the "normality" of gays and lesbians and their right to equal treatment with heterosexuals. This stream tries to achieve goals by influencing politicians and changing laws. The other stream is less concerned with politics and law: it stresses the right of gay/lesbian people to be "different", and emphasizes freedom of expression.

While there is now considerable activity in gay and lesbian politics, this has led to very little in the way of change. Since allowing people to engage privately in alternate lifestyles costs the state no money, great political opposition is not likely to develop. This lack of opposition, however, opens the door for discussion and debate, with each other, and with the general public. Over the long term, such discussion and debate holds much promise for change in Japanese society towards greater diversity of values and lifestyles. However, such change is not likely to occur in the immediate future.

Source: Lansing (1999).

Case Study 6.2   "More love and more desire": the building of a Brazilian movement

During 1978, the imminent demise of more than a decade of repressive military rule in Brazil provided a strategic opening for movement organization and led to the formation of the country's first "homosexual" rights organization, Action Nucleus for Homosexual Rights, renamed Somos in 1979. Within a year, the first major controversy in the emerging G & L movement would split Somos, by then the country's largest gay rights group. Lines of conflict were drawn over the question of aligning with other protest movements or maintaining political and organizational autonomy. But, before long, an aggressive G & L movement would explode onto the Brazilian political scene. Fifteen years later, in June 1995, with the attendance of over 300 national delegates, representing G & L groups in sixty countries worldwide, at the 17th Annual Conference of the International Lesbian and Gay association (ILGA) in Rio de Janiero, the Brazilian movement had come of age.

Backdrop to the movement: the role of law

Late nineteenth- and twentieth-century laws, while making no explicit reference to sodomy, restricted homosexual behaviour by prohibiting sexual activities between adults in a public setting. With "catch-all" wording, the law enabled the police and judiciary to define and punish "improper" or "indecent" actions that did not conform to heterosexual norms. Another method of regulating public manifestations of homosexuality was to charge a person with vagrancy. These two legal provisions gave the police the power to incarcerate those persons who transgressed socially sanctioned heterosexual norms. Homosexual activities, then, while not explicitly defined as illegal, constituted behaviour that could easily be contained and controlled by Brazilian police and courts.

Gay and lesbian life prior to the 1970s

Brazil's traditional gendered construction of homosexuality was (and, to a great extent, remains) hierarchical and role-based. Men who engage in same-sex activities are defined in one of two ways: as *homem* (real man) or *bicha* (fairy). This binary opposition mirrors the dominant gender role categories of *homem* (man/sexually active partner) and *mulher* (woman/sexually passive partner). In same-sex activities, *bicha* is stigmatized, *homem* is not. Similarly, women who transgress traditional gender roles are marginalized. Masculine lesbians are stigmatized as *sapatao* (big shoe). Until the late 1950s, there were no exclusively gay or lesbian bars or other venues in Brazil. Public "homosociability" centered on parks, beaches, cinemas, rest rooms and the like. The only time, during the year, when gays and lesbians could openly (and playfully) express their desires in public was during *Carnaval* . . . the unique four-day festival when "everything is allowed".

In 1964, the Brazilian military overthrew the populist government and initiated twenty-one years of authoritarian rule. While a closeted gay and lesbian sub-culture existed in this period, the military repression prohibited the development of a G & L movement.

The G & L movement

By the mid-1970s, Brazil's military dictatorship was facing mounting opposition, which led to a process of gradual liberalization. It was within this political and social climate that the first G & L Rights organization was founded. By the 1980s, however, the fledgling G & L movement was in decline. Apparently, most gays and lesbians considered political organization to be unnecessary during the liberalization that accompanied the eventual return to democracy. However, the dramatic increase of HIV infection and AIDS in the 1980s sparked a wave of violence against gays and lesbians. Homophobic Brazilians, like their counterparts in other countries, quickly began to associate HIV and AIDs with same-sex activities, and misinformation together with rampant homophobia combined to cause a panic. From the mid-1980s to the mid-1990s, violence against gay men and lesbians, including over 1,000 reported murders, escalated.

During this time, a number of developments contributed to the resurgence of G & L activism. Many different social movements began raising the question of how to democratize participation in a non-military, civil society. Local groups focused on consciousness-raising and discussion. This helped to politicize gays and lesbians, who began to organize in order to fight for their citizenship rights by protesting against homophobia, violence and discrimination. At the same time, the (traditionally "silent") media began to discuss same-sex issues, and the activities of the international G & L movement – including G & L Pride marches, debates about gays in the US military and AIDs issues – were brought to public attention. While homophobia has certainly not disappeared in Brazil, the G & L movement has expanded in many important areas and has developed nationally coordinated campaigns around such issues as violence, same-sex domestic partnerships and national anti-discrimination legislation. A major factor contributing to the flourishing of the G & L movement in Brazil has been the international G & L movement, with key leaders traveling to the USA, Europe, and other countries in Latin America to participate in conferences and to attend Pride demonstrations. The ILGA Conference in Rio de Janeiro in 1995 brought many activists in contact with international delegates, fostering a rich interchange of ideas and strategies for the movement.

Source: Green (1999).

Melucci's thesis

My analysis of the women's and gay/lesbian human rights and liberation movements at both the national and international level lends strong
support to Melucci's (1980, 1996) thesis which sees in the appropriation
of identity the key to understanding these new social movements. First,
these movements, as Melucci suggests, reject the traditional separation
between public and private spheres. Those areas traditionally confined
to the private sphere – identities and interpersonal relations based on
sexual orientation and gender – have become stakes in conflict situations
and now are foci of collective action and have penetrated the sphere of
the public and political.

   A second characteristic found in some of the new social movements is
what Melucci calls the "superposition of deviance and social movements". In response to dominant control and manipulation of daily life
– on the rules of existence and ways of life – opposition takes the form
of marginality and deviance. In some instances, public intervention
tends to reduce conflicts to the status of pathology, by subjecting non-
conformists to preventative therapies or to "rehabilitation". While this
characteristic has plagued the history of same-sex-oriented identities
and relations globally today, as our international-level case studies of
Japan and Brazil demonstrate, the stigmatization of gay/lesbian identities it is particularly evident in the case of gay/lesbian liberation movements in politically and/or religiously repressive non-democratic

societies. Our case studies reveal that an important difference between repressive states, inhibiting both women's and gay/lesbian emancipation, and more tolerant states, facilitating these new social movements, is the extent of freedom from the conformist constraints of tradition. Where the social context is characterized by the persistence of traditional patriarchal constraints, for example, both women's and gay/lesbian liberation struggles are impeded.

Another characteristic suggested by Melucci is that the new social movements are not primarily focused on empowerment. Essentially, they are not oriented toward the conquest of political power or of the state apparatus. Rather, these movements are oriented towards an objective of *solidarity*. The struggle centers around the particularistic issue of group identity, based on ascriptive criteria such as sex and sexual orientation. The movements, Melucci point out, also have instrumental objectives and seek political advantages, but this dimension is secondary to the expressive nature of the relations sought in the search for solidarity, the primary thrust of the movements. While Melucci's thesis holds, in general, for the women's and gay/lesbian movements, at both the national and international levels, there are internal lines of division among members within both movements on the degree of emphasis placed on instrumental (political and economic empowerment) versus expressive (identity and solidarity) objectives. Most importantly, as our analysis at the international level demonstrates, repressive regimes in non-democratic societies can still effectively block opportunities for empowerment, thus limiting movement strategies to the furtherance of expressive goals.

In general, Melucci suggests, expressive goals are perceived as far less threatening to the established power structure than are instrumental goals. Insofar as the main thrust of the women's and gay/lesbian movements is on the expressive goals of solidarity and identity, they are not perceived as highly threatening to the established power structure. Kriesi *et al.* (1995) make an important distinction between *high-profile* and *low-profile* policy domains. These authors contend that the more resources are involved and the more power at stake (high policy domain), the more threatening a social movement may be for political authorities. In general, my analysis of women's and gay/lesbian human rights and liberation movements supports the thesis that the viability of instrumental goals of new social movements is highly contingent on the openness or closedness of the prevailing political opportunity structure.

Concluding commentary

In Chapters 5 and 6, my analysis of equality/equity-seeking human rights and liberation movements has focused on the women's and gay/lesbian rights and liberation movements – new social movements predicated on the grounds of gender and sexual orientation.

In Chapter 7, I will shift the focus of my analysis to aboriginal (also referred to as "indigenous", "native" and "First Nations") rights and liberation movements. In contrast to equality/equity-seeking human rights and liberation movements such as the gay and lesbian and women's movements, whose claims focus on obtaining redress for violations of fundamental individual rights, aboriginal rights and liberation movements are essentially *equivalence-seeking* movements, whose claims focus on obtaining redress for violations of collective cultural and national rights. These movements champion each aboriginal people's collective right to be culturally different – that is, to govern themselves as internal nations within Euro/Western societies in ways which differ from the norms of the dominant Euro/Western culture.

CHAPTER 7

The Roots of the Aboriginal Movement: Colonialism and Cultural Genocide

Introduction

In contrast to equality/equity-seeking human rights and liberation movements such as the gay and lesbian and women's movements, whose claims, as we have seen in Chapter 6, focus on obtaining redress for violations of fundamental individual rights, aboriginal (also referred to as "indigenous", "native" and "First Nations") rights and liberation movements are essentially equivalence-seeking movements, whose claims focus on obtaining redress for violations of collective cultural and national rights. These movements advocate the need for recognition and protection for the right of aboriginal ethnic groups to carry on their distinctive ethnocultural practices, to reside and to seek their livelihood on the lands within the territory of their ancestral ethnic "homeland" and their "inherent" collective right to self-government. They champion each aboriginal people's collective right to be *culturally different* – that is, to govern themselves in ways which differ from those of Euro/Western Governments and in accordance with cultural norms which differ from those of the dominant Euro/Western culture.

Precursors of aboriginal protest

Colonialism and cultural genocide

Aboriginal peoples throughout the globe have been victims of massive institutional human rights violations, initiated through colonial rule, in many cases, allegedly tantamount to genocide and/or cultural genocide.

Blauner (1972: 11) contends that, unlike other subordinate populations, colonized peoples are subject to three conditions. First, they become part of a new larger society through coercion. Colonized peoples are conquered, enslaved, or pressured into movement. Secondly, colonized peoples are subject to various forms of external control and manipulation that restrict their mobility and power. Thirdly, the cultural policy of the colonizer disrupts and ultimately destroys the aboriginal way of life (cultural genocide). The syndrome of *created dependency* which has derived from the destruction of aboriginal institutions and cultural practices, compounded by the denial of political, educational and economic opportunities in the new colonial-dominated society, has led to the more insidious, psychologically damaging aspects of *invalidated and subordinate status*. Internalization of the negative identity associated with invalidation has spawned widespread alienation, apathy and marginality among aboriginal communities. Over the long term, the impact of this alienation has resulted in domestic violence, alcoholism and drug abuse and high rates of suicide.

In the following analysis, we will present an overview of the history of human rights violations, including alleged genocide and cultural genocide, which has precipitated the rise of aboriginal protest movements in North America and in Australia.

The history of aboriginal genocide/cultural genocide

North America (*500 years of Indigenous Resistance*)

Aboriginal nations before colonial contact

Before the European colonization of the Americas, aboriginal nations inhabited every region of the continents and developed diverse cultural life ways, dependent on the diverse resources of the land area in which each aboriginal ethnic group resided (unnamed author, in *Oh-Toh-Kin*, 1992). Their numbers approached 70–100 million peoples prior to the European colonization. With a few exceptions, the hundreds of different aboriginal societies were classless and communitarian in form. Aboriginal cultures lacked written tradition: knowledge of the culture was passed on by word of mouth with children learning the distinctive skills and values of the community from their parents and other adults. While elders (senior members of the community) held a position of importance and honor for their knowledge, community decisions were most frequently made by consensus and discussions among the adult population as a whole.

Destructive impact of European colonization
Beginning with the arrival of Christopher Columbus upon the island of
Guanahani in the Caribbean region on October 12, 1492, wave upon
wave of colonizers, first Spanish, then Portuguese, Dutch, French and
British followed. All, like Columbus, were bent on fully exploiting the
lands and their peoples. Despite the relatively small number of
European colonizers present during the first 100 years of the colonization process, their effects were overwhelming. In this 100-year period,
the populations of the indigenous peoples declined from 70–100 million
to around 12 million. The demise of the aboriginal population was due
in part to the introduction by Europeans of diseases such as smallpox
and measles, for which aboriginal peoples had developed no immunity.
Once the effects of the epidemics were realized, however, deliberately
infected blankets and other textiles allegedly were supplied by colonizers
to indigenous peoples. However, wars, massacres, slavery, scorched-earth
policies and the subsequent destruction of subsistence agriculture and
food-stocks, all contributed to the accompanying starvation, malnutri-
tion and dismemberment of communally based indigenous cultures.
The continuing resistance of aboriginal nations to inhumane colonial
rule met with military force, and resulted in the destruction of aboriginal cultures and wholesale massacre of aboriginal peoples.

Expansion of colonization: competition for land
By the beginning of the seventeenth century, the Atlantic coast area of
North America was rapidly becoming colonized with British, French
and Dutch settlements. The growing European colonies quickly set
about acquiring land, and their expansionist policies led to fierce competition. This bitter struggle for domination of land and trade frequently
began and ended with attacks against aboriginal communities. It was at
this time that the concept of treaty-making between colonizers and
aboriginal nations, a measure designed to gain full possession of
resource-plentiful indigenous lands, began to take hold. The initial
English (and Dutch) settlers began the process of purchasing land,
supplemented as always with armed force against vulnerable indigenous
nations. It remains unclear as to what the aboriginal nations understood
• of the local purchasing process, but some points are clear: there was no
indigenous practice of private ownership of land, nor of selling land,
among or between the aboriginal nations' peoples prior to the arrival of
the colonialists; there were, however, agreements and pacts between
aboriginal nations with regard to access to hunting or fishing areas. This
observation would indicate that treaties were most likely understood by

aboriginal peoples as agreements between aboriginal and settler communities over *use* (rather than *sale*) of certain areas of land, as well as non-aggression pacts. However, the treaties were of little effect if they turned out to be less than honorable, and there allegedly was enough duplicity, fraud, and theft involved in the treaty-making that the treaties themselves could not be considered binding. As aboriginal peoples did not have a written tradition, fraudulent practices such as orally translating one version of a treaty and signing another on paper were frequent, as was taking European proposals in negotiations and claiming that these had been agreed upon by all – when, in fact, they were being negotiated. Violation of treaty agreements by settlers who encroached on indigenous land with impunity was also commonplace. Gradually, aboriginal nations along the Atlantic found themselves dispossessed of their lands, and victims of settler assault.

The late 1680s and the following 100-year period was to be a time of bitter struggle between European nations for domination in the Americas. The results were disastrous for indigenous nations. The fallout from those wars was the virtual extermination of some aboriginal peoples, a general militarization of the region with heavier armaments and combat veterans and the subsequent expansion of colonial settlements, pushing out many aboriginal nations and forcing them to relocate in unfamiliar and inhospitable territory.

With the defeat of France, the British had acquired vast regions of formerly French territory, on which lived many aboriginal nations. The British government seized the opportunity to consolidate its imperial position by issuing the Royal Proclamation of 1763, which was designed to conciliate "those disgruntled tribes" by recognizing their land rights, by securing to them control of unceded land and by entering into a nation-to-nation relationship with them. The Royal Proclamation of 1763 provided for a separate "Indian Territory" west of the Appalachians and the original Thirteen Colonies. Within this territory (now Canada) there was to be no purchasing of land other than by the Crown, in the presence of representatives of the aboriginal nations. As grand as these statements were, they were routinely violated by colonialists and rarely enforced. As the colonization process expanded westward, the real intent of the Royal Proclamation as a strategic document in the defense of British colonial interests in North America was starkly revealed.

"Manifest destiny" and the US Indian Wars

The eighteenth and nineteenth centuries marked a period of wars for independence that would force the European states out of the Americas.

Foremost among these wars was the independence struggle that led to the birth of the USA. While the USA was in the process of establishing itself as an imperialist world power, it was still struggling to consolidate itself as a continental base and meeting armed resistance by aboriginal nations. To counter aboriginal resistance, stringent legal measures were enacted aimed at relocating and isolating indigenous populations. Under the ideology of Manifest Destiny (the Divine right of white nations to rule the world), the USA was to launch a renewed period of war against those regions and aboriginal nations which remained unsubjugated.

The popular American history of this period, as graphically portrayed in "Cowboys and Indians" movies, inevitably depicted the aboriginal peoples as the "bad guys" and the settlers as the "good guys", and, of course, the cowboys always won the wars with the Indians (Brookeman, C., website, June 18, 2001). In reality, the "Indian Wars" of this period were by no means one-sided – the US forces suffered many defeats. But the US forces employed such effective measures as the deliberate spread of diseases; the use of informers and traitors; and the overwhelming strength of US forces in both weaponry and numbers of soldiers. These factors continued to erode the strength of once-powerful aboriginal nations.

The colonization of Canada
In contrast to the US campaign of alleged aboriginal genocide, the colonization process in Canada lacked the large-scale military conflicts that characterized the US "Indian Wars". Also, Canada did not fight a war for independence and remained firmly a part of the British Empire. Cultural genocide, however, was another matter. It formed an important ingredient of colonial aboriginal policy from the very beginning (Blauner, 1972; Kallen, 1995).

In British North America, after the US War for Independence, the military importance of the aboriginal nations was quickly eroded. With the influx of United Empire Loyalists from the new USA, the European population had grown substantially. The War of 1812 and US policies of relocating aboriginal communities also greatly diminished the power of the aboriginal nations by breaking up traditional confederacies. Most importantly, an official policy of "Christianization and civilization", at this time designed for forcible assimilation aboriginal peoples, was developed and enforced. By the 1850s, an instrument had been created to this end: The Gradual Civilization Act of 1857. Here, the "civilization of the tribes" referred to the destruction of aboriginal cultures (cultural genocide) (unnamed author, in *Oh-Toh-Kin*, 1992). At the same time, the

Crown was developing new methods of acquiring aboriginal lands. Beginning in 1850 and continuing into the twentieth century, a series of treaties were "negotiated" in which aboriginal nations ceded immense tracts of resource-plentiful land in return for (usually resource-poor) reserve land, hunting and fishing rights, limited "promises" of education and medical care and the payment of annuities.

As was the case in treaty-making south of the border, the colonizers knew what they wanted in proposing the treaties, but the aboriginal nations were unprepared for the duplicity and dishonour of the treaty-makers. The treaties were important aspects of the plan for the settler expansion of Canada westward and economic development based on resource extraction and agriculture. Expansion was seen not only as economically necessary but also politically urgent as the USA was expanding westward at the same time. The invasion of the prairie regions was not without settler/indigenous conflict. The most significant resistance in this period was that of the Metis peoples – descendants of primarily French and Scottish settlers and Cree Indians – in what would become Manitoba (Daniels, 1979a, 1979b). The Red River Rebellion (also known as the First Riel rebellion, after Louis Riel, a Metis leader) erupted following an influx of Euro-Canadian settlers and the purchase of the territory from the controlling Hudson's Bay Company by the Government of Canada. The rebellion was directed against the annexation of the territory of the Metis. Fifteen years later, in 1885, the Metis, along with hundreds of Cree warriors, were again engaged in widespread armed resistance against colonization. Their defeat marked the final chapter of armed aboriginal resistance in the nineteenth century. At this time, however, the use of military force in controlling aboriginal peoples was already being overtaken by the Indian Act of 1876. This Act, with subsequent additions and changes, remains the basis of legislation affording special, legal Indian status to a great many aboriginal persons in Canada today (Daniels, 1979a, 1979b).

Under the Indian Act, the federal government, through its Department of Indian Affairs, was given complete control over the economic, social and political affairs of Status Indian communities. More than just a legislative instrument to administer "Indian affairs", the Indian Act was and is an attack on the very foundations of the aboriginal nations. Besides restricting hunting and fishing and criminalizing independent economic livelihood, the Act also declared who was and who was not an Indian, removed *legal* Indian status from women who married men who did not have legal Indian status, under the Indian Act, and criminalized vital ritual aspects of aboriginal culture such as the potlatch, the sun-dance and pow-wow (Kallen, 1995). Everything that formed the political, social and economic bases of aboriginal societies was restricted; the culture was decimated because it stood as the final barrier of resistance to European colonization. In the area of political organization, a government agent was sent in to Indian reserves to supervise Indian affairs, usurping complete control over all matters from life to death. Indian leaders were summarily demoted to members of newly formed "municipal" councils with virtually no decision-making powers. In 1894, amendments to the Act authorized the forced reloca-tion of Indian children to residential boarding schools, which were seen as important agents of cultural genocide because they removed the chil-dren from the influence of the aboriginal community. Isolated children in the total control of Europeans were easier to break; aboriginal languages were forbidden and all customs, values, religious traditions and even clothing were to be replaced by European forms. Sexual and physical abuse were common characteristics of these schools, and their effects were devastatingly effective in seriously marginalizing generations of aboriginal peoples (*Residential Schools*, Contemporary Aboriginal Issues website, June 21, 2001).

Australia

Forced assimilation and cultural genocide
Like the impact of Euro/Western colonization on the indigenous peoples of the USA, the parallel impact on the aboriginal peoples of Australia has been postulated as genocide. The aborigines were the first human inhabitants of Australia. It is generally believed that they came from Asia around 60,000 years ago. The aborigines were nomadic hunter-gatherers. There were around 300,000 aborigines in about 250 tribal groups before the first European settlers arrived. Each group had its own territory, traditions, beliefs and language (*About: Aborigines. The First Australians*, website, August 8, 2001).

The aborigines lived in harmony with the natural world around them, but aboriginal peoples' communal co-existence with nature suffered a permanent alteration and near extinction with the advent of the Europeans beginning in the late 1700s. As more and more European settlers moved in and occupied the fertile lands, the aborigines were pushed further and further away from their traditional lands and into the harsh arid interior. (*About: Aborigines, ibid.*). Though the aborigines struggled to keep their land, their weapons were no match for British military technology and, as in North America, the Europeans brought many diseases that decimated the aboriginal population. In just over 100 years of European settlement, the number of aborigines in Australia plummeted 80 per cent to about 60,000. Battles with settlers and foreign diseases, such as smallpox and measles, were the main reasons for the decrease. The entire population of aborigines on Tasmania vanished completely (*About: Aborigines, ibid.*).

The Europeans also adopted a policy of forced assimilation/cultural genocide (Miller, 1998, see website references). They compelled aborigines to cover their bodies, providing clothes and blankets which the aboriginal peoples used unhygienically, resulting in their suffering from various new diseases. These factors contributed to a demoralization and to a high mortality rate within these groups which eventually caused them to die out. Another contributing factor to alleged aboriginal genocide was the forcible removal of children from aboriginal families and their adoption by Europeans. The 1997 Report of the Human Rights and Equal Opportunity Commission, *Bringing Them Home* (see website references), reveals that from 1910 until the 1970s, some 100,000 aboriginal children were "stolen" from their parents under the misguided belief that the aborigines were doomed and that saving the children was the only humane alternative. The reported experiences of stolen children expose shocking revelations of systemic denigration of aboriginal peoples and cultures, child abuse and neglect. On the basis of the incontrovertible evidence of extreme psycho-social damage to the children and their families from the experiences of forced removal, the Commission concluded that the actions of the authorities at that time amounted to genocide as defined by the United Nations.

For the majority of witnesses to the Commission, the effects were multiple and profoundly disabling, causing a cycle of damage from which it was difficult to escape unaided. Psychological and emotional damage rendered many stolen children less able to learn social skills and survival skills. The impairment of their ability to operate successfully in the world resulted in low educational achievement, unemployment and consequent poverty. These, in turn, caused their own emotional distress leading some to perpetrate violence, self-harm, substance abuse or anti-social behaviour.

After the Second World War
During the post-Second World War years, the policy of forced assimilation of aborigines was stepped up. (Assimilation Era, State Library of Queensland website, November 15, 2002). In 1951 "assimilation" was adopted as Commonwealth Government policy. To facilitate the process, all aboriginal people in the Northern Territory were declared "wards"

under the welfare ordinance of 1953, which gave the government legal rights over their movements, employment, residence, wages and even who they married. A network of government settlements was established to which any "wandering bush groups" were to be removed and where they were to be educated in the ways of mainstream society. By the late 1960s, however, the assimilation policy was increasingly being questioned, mainly because it failed to provide for the economic development of aboriginal people. The policy was based on an assumption that the aboriginal people would adopt the economic and cultural values of the Euro/White majority. To partake in development, aboriginal people were required radically to alter their distinct cultural practices, particularly their attachment to the land. As a result of forced assimilation, by the late 1870s most aborigines had joined white rural and urban communities. Yet, despite all government efforts to achieve cultural genocide, aboriginal cultures remained remarkably resilient.

Extermination/genocide and assimilation/ cultural genocide

Two methods, one goal

In Australia, though the aborigines struggled to keep their land, the fighting between aboriginal people and colonizers was highly unequal. Their weapons were no match for British military technology, and the Europeans brought many diseases that decimated the aboriginal population. In just over 100 years of white settlement, the number of aborigines in Australia, as we have seen, plummeted 80 percent to about 60,000.

In North America, colonization processes and policies also devastated aboriginal cultures and decimated aboriginal populations. In the early 1900s, the population of aboriginal peoples in North America had reached their lowest point. In the USA alone, this population had declined to some 250,000. Aboriginal peoples had been consigned to largely desolate land areas. The process of assimilation, endorsed through government agencies such as the Bureau of Indian Affairs, was implemented through residential schools, criminalization of aboriginal cultures and control of aboriginal political and economic systems. As in Australia, although to a lesser extent, forced removal of Indian children from their families and their adoption by Europeans also contributed to cultural genocide (Lyons, C., Eye website, January 31, 2000).

Aboriginal resistance and the germination of protest

In both North America and Australia, aboriginal resistance to forced assimilation continued in various forms. Traditional cultural practices and events were continued in secret and covert opposition to colonial control festered. Most importantly, by the 1970s, aboriginal peoples had begun to organize in order to express their discontent with their lowly status and disadvantaged life conditions, and to oppose government polices which kept them in a state of created dependency and favored the interests of Euro/white corporate powers now threatening serious encroachment and exploitation of aboriginal lands through major resource extraction projects.

The graphically documented history of continuing violations of aboriginal peoples' rights, already outlined in this chapter, provides the basis for aboriginal peoples' current collective rights claims expressed in their demands to regain political self-determination, economic viability and cultural sovereignty within their ancestral territories. The political, economic, cultural and legal issues involved in aboriginal cultural, land and self-government claims are highly complex, to say the least, and are very diverse, given the very different statuses and priorities of various communities of aboriginal peoples. What they all have in common, however, is a history of human rights abuses which, in many cases, is sufficient to substantiate claims for redress against genocide or cultural genocide. In order to simplify my discussion of these issues as much as possible for the uninitiated reader, I will begin by outlining the human rights principles which underscore the legal or quasi-legal bases of these claims.

Collective cultural rights

Cultural rights, aboriginal land rights and nationhood rights

Like members of other ethnocultural communities, aboriginal peoples can make claims for redress against past violations of their collective cultural rights – rights to language, religion and other features of their distinctive cultural heritage and life ways. The current cultural rights claims of aboriginal peoples rest on their well-documented history of cultural genocide at the hands of colonial authorities. (Kallen, 1995, Introduction).

Additionally, unlike those immigrant ethnic communities who can make no claim to territory (ethnic homeland or land of origin) within the country where they reside, aboriginal peoples whose collective rights to their ancestral territory have not been "officially" abrogated by some legal instrument wielded by government authorities can make *aboriginal rights* land claims. These land claims are collective claims based on *usufruct* – continuing use of aboriginal lands and their resources "from time immemorial", i.e. as far back as any living elders can remember.

Aboriginal *nationhood claims* rest on the established fact that, prior to colonization, aboriginal peoples were independent self-governing nations, occupying distinct territories – clearly recognized by other aboriginal nations. Each aboriginal nation developed and practised a distinctive culture which was passed down from one generation to another by word of mouth and by young people following the example set by elders of the community. From the aboriginal view, as currently put forward by aboriginal spokespersons, their right to sovereignty (collective right to self-determination) is an *inherent* right, which has never been and can never be surrendered. With colonization, they claim, their right to sovereignty was unjustly abrogated and their institutions of self-government systematically dismantled. As aboriginal nations, they are re-claiming their right to sovereignty: their right to create and adminis-ter their own forms of self-government, in accordance with their own, distinctive cultural values. From this aboriginal view, treaties made between aboriginal peoples and governments should be regarded as treaties between sovereign nations, in the sense of public international law. Aboriginal nationhood claims, which strongly emphasize the peoples' collective right to self-determination, are similar to the nation-hood claims of other subordinate national communities throughout the world, whose members can demonstrate a continuing link between their particular ethnic group, its distinctive culture and the ancestral territory it occupies or has a right to occupy. However, aboriginal claims are not precisely the same. What makes aboriginal nationhood claims unique is, first, the integral tie-in with their aboriginal land and its resources which is the very foundation of aboriginal ethnocultures and through which many aboriginal peoples continue to eke out a livelihood in culturally distinctive ways. The second way in which aboriginal nationhood claims are unique is that, as internally colonized nations, their aim is not to usurp control from existing governments, but to attain self-determina-tion as *internal nations* on aboriginal territories within existing post-colo-nial, Euro/Western dominated societies.

The International Human Rights Declarations

The collective claims currently advanced by aboriginal nations are based upon a forward-looking interpretation of a number of current interna-tional human rights declarations. Like other ethnocultural communities, the collective cultural rights of aboriginal groups are protected under the provisions for "minority rights" under Article 27 of the International Covenant on Civil and Political Rights (ICCPR). Legal interpretation of this article has recently shifted from a very narrow view, focusing on individual members of minorities, to a much broader position, focusing on minorities as *communities*. This broader position has gained considerable support since the adoption by the General Assembly of the United Nations, on December 18, 1992, of the Declaration on the Rights of Persons Belonging to National or Ethnic, Religious and Linguistic Minorities (UN, 1992). Of particular importance are Articles 4 to 7 of this Declaration, which outline the measures which ratifying states should take in order to protect the collective, cultural rights of their minorities.

Another key UN Declaration provides international protection for the collective right of self-determination of peoples. This declaration is protected under the provisions of Article 1 of both the International Covenant on Economic, Social and Cultural Rights (ICESCR) and the International Covenant on Civil and Political Rights (ICCPR). Until quite recently, legal definition of the term "peoples" was based on a very narrow concept of "people" which equated "people" with "nation" and which was interpreted even more narrowly, so as to support the right to self-determination of peoples only in cases of non-self-governing territories formerly under colonial rule by overseas states (i.e. externally colonized peoples). This restrictive interpretation afforded no support for the nationhood claims of peoples/nations living inside the territorial boundaries of recognized, sovereign states (i.e. internally colonized peoples).

Over the 1990s, however, largely in response to resolute lobbying by organizations and coalitions representing the world's internally colonized aboriginal (indigenous) peoples, there has been increasing support for a broader interpretation of Article 1 among international legal scholars. A draft proposal for an International Covenant on the Rights of Indigenous Peoples was adopted in Principle by the Third General Assembly of the World Council of Indigenous Peoples in May 1981. This draft proposal incorporated the right to self-determination of peoples (under Article 1) as a cardinal principle of the rights of aboriginal (indigenous) peoples. A preliminary document, the Draft Universal Declaration On Indigenous Rights, was introduced in August 1988. While this draft, and later drafts, leading to the present 1994 version of the Draft Declaration on the Rights of Indigenius Peoples (see Appendix B) recognize the collective cultural and aboriginal rights of indigenous peoples as well as their collective right to autonomy in matters relating to their own internal and local affairs, within states, the declarations fall short of an explicit recognition of the *inherent* right to self-government proclaimed by aboriginal nations.

Concluding commentary

In this chapter, as a prelude to our analysis of aboriginal human rights and nationhood movements, we have presented an overview of the history of human rights violations, including alleged genocide and cultural genocide, which has precipitated the rise of aboriginal protest movements in Australia, Canada and the USA. We have also examined the international human rights principles which underscore the legal or quasi-legal bases of aboriginal peoples' claims predicated on violations of their collective cultural and nationhood rights. In the next part of this analysis, to be presented in Chapter 8, we will focus on the current issues and claims put forward by spokespersons for aboriginal rights and nationhood movements in Australia and North America. We will then assess the outcomes and the prospects for the future of these equivalence-seeking, new social movements among aboriginal peoples.

Aboriginal Rights and New Nationhood Movements

Aboriginal protest movements as new social movements

From the perspective of "new social movement" theory, particularly as expounded by Melucci (1980, 1996) and Kriesi *et al.* (1995), as new social movements, current aboriginal rights and new nationhood movements manifest many of the characteristics of non-aboriginal, sub-cultural and ethnocultural movements within modern societies, yet they also differ in important respects. Like the other movements of this type – for example, the women's and the lesbian and gay movements – they place a strong emphasis on group solidarity and collective identity. Where they differ is in their territorial emphasis and their demands for political, economic and cultural sovereignty within the territories claimed as their ancestral homelands.

Kriesi *et al.* (1995) posit a hierarchy of political issues: they argue that the more material resources are involved, and the more power is at stake, the more threatening a social movement may be for political authorities. The non-aboriginal, sub-cultural and ethnocultural movements – such as the women's and lesbian and gay movements – Kriesi *et al.* suggest, can be categorized as "low-profile", posing no real threat to the high-priority policy domains of the dominant powers. In the case of the aboriginal movement, however, their overarching emphasis on control of land and land-based resources as an integral aspect of their aboriginal ethnocultures, and their determination to regain their status as independent and self-governing nations within their ancestral homeland territories, places them in a more "high-profile" category than the other movements. Thus, they are perceived as posing a palpable threat to the high-priority policy domains of the dominant powers. However, while aboriginal movements are in a real sense "nationalist" movements, as new social movements they depart radically from the traditional conception of post-colonial nationalist movements, such as those which have arisen among externally colonized peoples in Africa, India and other non-Western countries. These post-colonialist nationalist movements are highly instrumental and political in thrust: they aim to overthrow the colonial structure imposed upon them, to overtake the state apparatus and to usurp power for themselves (Connor, 1993). Unlike these post-colonial nationalist movements, the new nationhood movements generated by internally colonized aboriginal peoples are limited in their instrumental goals to attaining self-determination as internal nations on aboriginal territories within existing post-colonial, Euro/Western-dominated societies. Thus, while the new aboriginal movements are seen to pose a threat to dominant interests, they do not pose the threat of secession, nor do they pose the threat of usurpation of power from existing authorities, who will continue to rule the country as a whole, according to Euro/Western cultural standards of governance, law and justice.

Aboriginal rights and new nationhood movements

Australia

In the 1930s, a protest movement began which continues today (Horton, 1994; see website references). All of the restrictive legislation against aborigines, and the bodies formed to administer it, were state-based, and this tended to give aboriginal peoples within particular states a shared history, and a common target (Horton, 1994). Accordingly, despite their cultural differences, they began to develop a sense of regional (for example, Koori, Mufti, Nyungar) identity, and organizations began to develop which were also either regional or state-based.

The 1967 referendum for the first time gave the Commonwealth government power to legislate for aboriginal peoples. While this was largely a symbolic gesture, it did signal the beginning of action and organization at a national level. However, the continuing desire of the different aboriginal communities to maintain the essential uniqueness of their own ethnocultures has made it difficult for leaders of the aboriginal movement to organize, to unify and to form coalitions over and above the many lines of diversity among indigenous peoples of Australia. Accordingly, a nationwide aboriginal response to racist government policies resulting in aboriginal exclusion, subordination, disenfranchisement, impoverishment and cultural genocide, was slow to organize. However, it quickly gained momentum as aborigines and their supporters took two important steps to assert their rights (Miller, 1998; see website references).

Legal developments toward aboriginal rights

The first major assertion of indigenous rights began in 1971 as aboriginal groups filed lawsuits arguing that the taking of their land constituted a violation of their aboriginal or native title. Such legal challenges were uniformly refused by Australian courts under the doctrine of enlarged *terra nullius*, which stated that Australia was completely uninhabited when the British arrived in 1788. Historically, a racist interpretation of the doctrine of *terra nullius* by colonial governments and courts has considered as "unoccupied" territory in which live backward, primitive inhabitants, with the clear implication that the more advanced peoples are justified in dispossessing, if necessary, the less advanced. Accordingly, the courts deemed that the aborigines were indeed too backward to possess proprietary interests, and that the land was free for the taking (Miller, 1998).

When aborigines began asserting their rights in court, they traditionally emphasized the important point that aboriginal self-government has always existed. They claimed that indigenous self-government in Australia is the longest surviving egalitarian system of government possibly in the world. These claims were brought to light in *Coe* v. *Commonwealth of Australia* (1979) in which Paul Coe, an aborigine, filed suit against Australia and the UK on behalf of all Australian aborigines. In a sweeping complaint, he alleged that all historical claims to sovereignty by the British Empire and the Commonwealth of Australia were baseless and void. Not surprisingly, the Court dismissed the case. Nonetheless, it was *Coe* which foretold the filing of *Mabo* v. *Queensland* (1992), the watershed case which would change forever the outlook of Australian politics and aboriginal rights (Miller, 1998). However, as *Coe* and similar cases made their way through the Australian courts, the aboriginal rights movement continued its struggle outside of the judiciary as well.

Political developments toward aboriginal rights

The second major assertion of indigenous rights was quite activist in nature. In 1972, following the lead of the American Indian Movement and other indigenous movements around the world, aboriginal organizations, under the common rubric of the Aboriginal Embassy, pitched tents in protest on the front lawn of Parliament House in Canberra. The protesters had three primary demands: a greater voice in decisions for their future, an end to discrimination and recognition of their traditional claims on the land. The government agreed to discuss the first two demands but would not budge on the demand for recognition of land claims. The Aboriginal Embassy remained in place until 1975, when aboriginal and government leaders agreed to a compromise on land rights involving future legislation on the issue (Miller, 1998).

A significant shift toward the recognition of aboriginal rights came with the 1976 passage of the Aboriginal Land Rights Act, though the effectiveness of the law has proven limited over time. The Act shifted the aboriginal reserves of the federal Northern Territory to various legal entities established through the Land Rights Act in fee simple. These parcels of land are controlled and managed by localized groups of aborigines through the corresponding entities which own the land in trust, though the Commonwealth government maintains some measure of ultimate control (Miller, 1998).

Some of the extra-judicial events which have shaped the movement toward aboriginal rights have occurred outside the realm of Parliament and the state governments. In 1987, aborigines in parts of Queensland and New South Wales rioted against the state governments over abhorrent living conditions in their communities, including open pools of raw sewage, overcrowding, extreme unemployment and unabashed racism and segregation by local residents and schools. The riots and subsequent investigations turned the eyes of the world upon the plight of the aborigines but, once again, no real action followed. The government tabled the question of aboriginal rights.

However, on June 3, 1992, the relationship between the aborigines and the Australian government changed forever, thanks to the persistence of five Murray Islanders. In *Mabo* v. *Queensland*, the Australian High Court recognized the existence of aboriginal or native title and pronounced dead the doctrine of *terra nullius*. In the next breakthrough for the plaintiffs, the High Court found that the Murray Islanders did, indeed possess title to their ancestral lands. With this decision, the Australian judicial system officially recognized the land rights of the aborigines (Miller, 1998).

Reaction to the *Mabo* decision

Australians knew that the *Mabo* decision was a landmark, but it was unclear what the decision meant for Australia's future. Public reaction to the *Mabo* decision was marked by considerable confusion, doubt and resentment. In response, the Commonwealth government attempted to pass uniform national legislation which would clarify the concept of native title and effectively preclude any challenges from the states. The Native Title Act, passed on December 22, 1993, acted to clear the air in many ways. The legislation secured all existing freehold and most existing leasehold interests; it provided for a tribunal process to hear native title claims; and it provided funding for a number of programmes aimed at assisting or compensating those on both sides of native title controversies (Miller, 1998, see website references).

Aborigines celebrated the legislation as the most important first step in the process of reconciliation between black and white Australia. After the High Court upheld the validity of the Native Title Act, most Australians, white, aborigine, or otherwise accepted the new situation as permanent and as indicative of the future of their country. Unfortunately, there has been a noticeable backlash against the *Mabo* decision, the Native Title Act and aboriginal rights in general. There has been an upsurge of racist acts of violence and vandalism directed against aborigines, but even more disturbing than the individual acts of racism have been recent government moves to limit native title. In mid-1996, the federal government altered the Native Title Act to reduce aboriginal negotiating rights as a means to facilitate the exploration of a mine in Queensland, even as aborigines won recognition of native title on the Australian mainland for the first time.

Into the twenty-first century

In June 2000, three days of public events and official ceremonies were designated to mark the culmination of a nine-year process of reconciliation between the country's indigenous and non-indigenous populations (Tenenbaum, L., World Socialist Web Site (WSWS), June 17, 2001). As a major feature of the event, the Council for Aboriginal Reconciliation (CAR) handed over a document "Towards Reconciliation" to Liberal Prime Minister John Howard on the steps of the Sydney Opera House, before an audience of several thousand. The mandate of the CAR brief has been to tackle the country's racial divide.

On the day designated as National Sorry Day, thousands marched through major cities calling for an official government apology to Australia's aboriginal peoples for the genocidal policies carried out over the past 200 years against the aboriginal population. The march was led by members of the "stolen generation", the tens of thousands of aborigines forcibly separated from their families under the forced assimilation policy pursued by successive Australian governments until the 1960s, and the CAR. Howard was conspicuously absent from the march, and the apology was not forthcoming.

In a severe critique of the CAR agenda, documents and events celebrating them, WWSW highlights an apparent contradiction (Tenenbaum, L., *ibid.*). While tens of thousands were motivated to walk by deep concerns for social justice and equity, at the same time the events were supported to the hilt by the very politicians, business chiefs and media barons responsible for escalating social inequality.

The CAR's Documents of Reconciliation, Tenenbaum (*ibid.*) argues, emphasize economic empowerment of aborigines; however, not one reference is made to the need for decent-paying jobs, the most urgent demand of aboriginal workers in urban, regional and rural areas, where unemployment rates can reach as high as 100 percent. Instead, the CAR Documents' focus is on fostering select entrepreneurial partnerships with the business community.

With regard to aboriginal land rights, native title was promoted by the aboriginal leadership as a means of protecting important cultural and spiritual landmarks, in trust for future generations and for ensuring the right of impoverished aboriginal communities to live on traditional lands, without fear of eviction. But, in reality, Tenenbaum (*ibid.*) argues, native title renders alienable what was previously crown or common land, and endows it with a monetary value. Native title has become nothing more than a new private interest in land, that can be bought and sold on the capitalist market. It has become the vehicle through which long-term, capital intensive mining and tourism investments are able to be secured. Sacred sites already have been sold off by aboriginal land councils in exchange for ready cash. Not surprisingly, Tenenbaum (*ibid.*) points out, Corroborree 2000 and the Walk for Aboriginal Reconciliation were also sponsored by major corporate interests.

Further setbacks

In August 2000, an Australian court rejected a landmark claim for compensation launched in 1999 by two aborigines who claimed they were taken from their families as young children by the government. (BBC News, Friday, 11 August, 2000). The ruling constituted a major setback to hundreds of other claimants from the so-called "stolen generation", as well as to the aboriginal community, which is continuing to fight for the government to acknowledge past injustices. Prime Minister John Howard has refused to apologize on behalf of the government. The Australian government also dismissed a UN report on racial discrimination against aborigines (BBC News, *ibid.*).

In another milestone ruling in August 2002, the High Court in Canberra, Australia decided that aboriginal people did not have rights to oil or minerals found under tribal land now being used by mining companies (BBC News, Thursday, 8 August, 2002). The ruling was part of a decision on an eight-year-old land rights claim. The case covered nearly 8,000 square kilometers of land and water in northwestern Australia, which includes the Argyle diamond mine, the world's largest. The decision is seen as a landmark ruling on whether mining leases override native title rights, and it should determine the outcome of hundreds of outstanding native title claims (BBC News, *ibid.*).

Despite continuing setbacks, aboriginal concerns have become a valid, if not crucial, part of the political and social climate of Australia. The aboriginal rights movement has become transformed into a coalition of interests continuing the struggle to achieve goals of equity and justice for all aborigines.

North America

In the 1960s, in a global climate of national liberation movements in Africa, Australia, Asia and in the Americas, there was an upsurge in aboriginal people's resistance throughout North America (Kallen, 1995). As a result of government policies which continually prioritized Euro/white interests and neglected aboriginal concerns, aboriginal populations had become a marginalized underclass, and many reserve communities were characterized by unemployment, poverty, created dependency, cultural alienation, alcoholism and suicide. In addition, in this period, escalating resource extraction projects throughout the Americas were threatening to encroach on aboriginal lands, endangering the wildlife and threatening the livelihood and land-based ethnocultures of aboriginal nations. Vitally important for the cultural survival of aboriginal communities in the face of this threat were their struggles to protect their lands, the very roots of their aboriginal cultures, from outside exploitation by powerful corporate interests. Aboriginal protest was thus galvanized by escalating resource extraction projects. The reclaiming of traditional aboriginal nations' lands was a primary focus of this struggle in North America (Kallen, 1995).

Indigenous ("native") Americans and the US government

Conflicting government policies

The history of the interaction between American Indians and the American government has been shaped by a number of conflicting government policies (Brookeman, C., website, June 18, 2001). Early colonial policies of *separation* were designed to remove indigenous Americans from the lands that the expansionist white settlers coveted. At the same time, the government accorded recognition of the Indians' sovereign rights to their new territories. This policy was historically followed by one of *coercive assimilation* in which indigenous ways were to be replaced by dominant Euro/American cultural patterns. Coercive assimilation was reflected in the educational philosophy and techniques of the boarding schools for Indians established in the nineteenth century, where children from the same tribal community were separated and were forced to room with children from different tribal communities. This "mix and melt" technique was implemented together with instruction following a wholly Euro/American curriculum of study.

In the 1930s, in the liberal climate engendered by President Roosevelt's "New Deal" administration, the culturally oppressive policy of coercive assimilation of Indian peoples was replaced by a new policy of *tribal restoration* designed to protect and nourish "selected aspects" of Indian cultures. This policy was institutionalized in the Indian Reorganization Act of 1934, which was enacted to ensure the continued survival of the Indian tribal group, as both a reality and a legal entity.

Termination and tribal restoration
However, in the more conservative climate of the 1940s and 50s, the "special status" of Indian peoples came under critical question. This led to the adoption of a new federal policy of *termination* by which all the special arrangements made by the government for indigenous Americans in the field of education, welfare and so on were to be ended. In the 1950s, supporters of termination argued that the policy of tribal restoration had created a system of virtual dependency implemented by a top-heavy system of administrative bureaucracy. The idea that the Indian was a special case was now considered to be "un-American" in theory and practice. Termination was designed to ensure that they would become "Americanized", to their ultimate benefit.

By the 1960s and early 1970s, termination had lost support in government circles. Those who argued against termination suggested that it discouraged self-sufficiency among Indian groups. Another new policy, ushering in the *second phase of tribal restoration*, was put in place to ensure the continued viability of all Indian tribes and tribal governments. In accordance with this spirit the Congress passed the Indian Self-Determination Act of 1975, which reinforced the transfer of decision-making from the bureaucrats of the Bureau of Indian Affairs to the tribal councils.

　　　　　　　　　　SOCIAL INEQUALITY AND SOCIAL INJUSTICE

Divided reaction of indigenous peoples to government policies

Political activism and the rise of an indigenous American movement

A major issue confronting indigenous Americans in the immediate post-Second World War era was the continuing debate between the advocates of assimilation and those who favored some form of traditional tribal self-determination. For example; the American Indian Federation (AIF), representing highly assimilated Indians from Oklahoma, had opposed the Roosevelt administration's "New Deal" policies, and by 1944–5 was calling for termination. The AIF strategy was vigorously opposed by the National Congress of American Indians, a lobby group that had been organized in 1944 to represent indigenous Americans of all tribes. This organization demanded that the philosophy of tribal self-determination should be maintained.

Another important issue in this immediate postwar era was the long-running one of compensation. Many Indian groups had claims against the American government for lands and assets that had been unfairly seized. A coalition of interests including liberals and advocates of termination lobbied until Congress passed the Indian Claims Commission Act in 1946. But the plan soon ran into trouble. The three-person board could give money only for land; it could not take away lands that were now owned by the descendants of the original, often illegal white settlers.

Under the influence of the general rise of militancy associated with the Civil Rights Movements of the late 1950s and the 1960s, more direct action protest began to characterize the new generation of activist indigenous Americans who were often urban-based and college-educated. This new generation viewed the long and difficult process of seeking compensation through the courts as appeasement, "uncle Tomahawk" strategies that did not expose the abuses that many American Indians suffered through police harassment on the streets. It was these routine abuses of urban Indians which gave rise to the American Indian Movement, known as AIM, in 1968 (American Indian Movement (AIM) website, June 17, 2001).

Under the leadership of Chippewa Indian organizer Denis Brutus, AIM members began to patrol Minneapolis and St. Paul streets after dark in order to intervene on behalf of the many Indians who were being harassed by the police without justification. As a result of this activity, the number of weekend arrests dropped from a regular number of around 200 to just a handful. AIM also gained redress for Indians in cases involving blatant discrimination in the workplace, and in the area of federal funding for housing for urban Indians. AIM also conducted a seven-year campaign to establish a centre for Indian Culture in Minneapolis which would serve as a focus for the study and enhancement of indigenous American cultures, as a dynamic contribution to a pluralistic modern American society. AIM organized a whole range of direct-action sit-ins and occupations, from the taking over of Alcatraz Island in 1969 to the occupation of Wounded Knee in 1973. However, AIM did not speak for all indigenous Americans. More conservative Indians maintained their support for organizations like the Association on American Indian Affairs, the National Congress of American Indians and the Indian Rights Association. But AIM had shown that direct action could bring American Indians a greater share of the fruits of American capitalism and an enhanced sense of political power.

Finding a pan-Indian voice
Throughout the 1970s and 1980s, the American government struggled to legislate their way out of their ambiguous relationship and responsibilities with regard to indigenous Americans. It was the old conflict between termination and a colonial concept of federal supervision which carried with it a continuing responsibility to treat American Indians as wards, needing special protection of the Bureau of Indian Affairs (BIA). In 1978, the Carter Administration passed the Acknowledgement Project through Congress, a special program administered by the BIA to evaluate the claims of indigenous American groups unrecognized by the federal government as legitimate tribes. In 1981, the federal government formally recognized 283 tribes, entitling them to both federal and state grants. But nearly 175 indigenous American groups, especially those east of the Mississippi River, remained unrecognized.

One of the major problems for indigenous American leadership strategies is to devise ways to conduct negotiations with a collective pan-Indian voice, with representatives of Euro/American corporations or the federal government, while at the same time, preserving the autonomy of specific tribal peoples or nations. The rise of pan-Indian groups such as the National Congress of American Indians, the National Indian Youth Council, the National Tribal Chairmen's Association, the American Indian Movement and the Council of Energy Resource Tribes (CERT) represents both a common aspiration for national leadership and combined political pressure on an agreed agenda for all American Indians.

Energy resources
One issue that has sorely divided the dedicated nationalists and the supporters of the retention of decision-making by the individual tribal

or nation group has been that of the exploitation of the considerable energy resources that exist on Indian-owned land. In 1982, the CERT accepted the invitation of the BIA to draft, in cooperation with major oil and gas trade associations, a series of regulations governing tribal sever-ance taxes on mineral deposits. Many Indian groups feared that CERT would become an agent of multinational corporations, signing away rights that individual tribes should control.

The advent of Reaganism and Reagonomics in the 1980s brought particular pressures to bear on economic developments and philosophy within the American Indian community. While broadly endorsing the principles of tribal self-government that were signed into law in 1975 as the Indian Self-Determination and Education Assistance Act, President Ronald Reagan's American Indian policy statement also pointed out the negative consequences of "excessive regulation" under the 1975 policy which, he argued, had, by and large, inhibited the political and economic development of the tribes. He promised that his administra-tion would remove the obstacles to self-government and would promote the development of healthy reservation economies.

The main agent of this policy of promoting "healthy reservation economies" was James Watt, Secretary of the Interior, who argued that the appropriate strategy would be to open up more public and Indian land to commercial exploitation. In the 1980s, indigenous American leadership was put on the defensive by these policies which clearly gave support to the many economic pressure groups who held that the energy resources currently underneath the reservations were national assets. The underlying mood of indigenous American response to Reaganism, its policies and promises, was decidedly negative. Indigenous leaders emphasized the hardships caused to the American Indian community by the cuts in social programs initiated by President Reagan.

Indian (native) American policy in the 1990s

President Bush, in his 1991 Statement Reaffirming the "Government-to-Government Relationship Between the Federal Government and Indian Tribal Governments" (June 14, 1991, see website references), re-confirmed the earlier (1983) position of the Reagan–Bush administra-tion, and said that it would be the cornerstone of the Bush–Quayle administration's policy of fostering tribal self-government and self-determination. The President commented that the concepts of forced termination and excessive dependency on the federal government must now be relegated, once and for all, to the history books.

In similar vein, President Clinton, in his 1994 Presidential

Memorandum of April 29, 1994, "Government-to-Government Relations With Native American Tribal Governments", (see website references), emphasized that the United States government had a unique legal relationship with Native American tribal governments as set forth in the Constitution of the United States, treaties, statutes and court decisions. The President promised that he was strongly committed to building a more effective day-to-day working relationship reflecting respect for the rights of self-government due the sovereign tribal governments. The congenial rhetoric of government policy, in practice, however, continues to fall very short of the mark. The words of Birgil Kills Straight, of the Oglala Lakota Nation, spoken at the AIM 25th Anniversary Conference/International Peoples Summit on September 27, 1993, continue to apply as we enter the twenty-first century: "[The] Indian way is not tolerated in White America, because it is not acknowledged as a decent way to be . . . Sovereignty, Land and Culture cannot endure if a people is not left in peace" (American Indian Movement (AIM) website, June 17, 2001).

While the indigenous American movement continues in its struggle to improve the life conditions and to protect the rights of indigenous Americans, it appears that the heyday of activist protest is long gone. A statement from spokespersons for AIM suggests that while Native American activist groups continue to organize protests and demonstrations to protect the rights of all Native Americans, they fail to recapture the sympathetic audiences they once had during the peak of their cultural rebellion (AIM website, 17 June, 2001).

Canada
The colonial model

In Canada, until the 1960s, government policy towards aboriginal peoples had its roots and its continuing reality in the colonial model of government administration (Kallen, 1995, ch. 8). The racist rhetoric behind virtually all varieties of aboriginal policy, defining aboriginal peoples as culturally primitive and racially inferior, justified wholesale violations of their human rights. The long-term outcome was the political/economic/social subordination and marginalization of aboriginal peoples and destruction of their traditional ways – cultural genocide. The various Indian Acts (1896–1950) – paternalistic federal policies specifically designed for Indians legally defined as Status Indians – gave racist, colonial assumptions their clearest institutional expression. Further, the cultural and geographical fragmentation of Canadian aboriginal peoples that ensued from colonial "divide and rule" policies eased the way for the long-term continuance of colonial relations between administrative authorities and aboriginal peoples in Canada (Waubageshig 1970: 97; Frideres, 1993: Part 1). The end result has been the social construction of a culturally alienated, powerless, impoverished, degraded and dependent population living at the margins of Canadian society: in it, but not of it (Frideres, 1993).

The Status Indian reserve

The Indian Act has been the legal instrument responsible for the encapsulation, oppression, neglect and diminution of Status Indians within the total institution of the reserve (Kallen, 1995). Under this Act, the federal minister of Indian affairs, until recently, has had the ultimate authority over all decisions affecting the lives and destinies of Indians residing on reserves. The minister and his agents have dominated and controlled all of the bands' resources – land, housing, capital and income, livestock and equipment – and have wielded decision-making authority over medical services, employment, education, wills and virtually all aspects of Indian life. Even the decision of a Status Indian to give up legal Indian Status has had to be approved. While their special legal status gives reserve Indians some economic benefits, such as certain tax exemptions, it systemically violates their fundamental human rights by heavily restricting their freedom and by keeping them in a perpetual state of dependency. Under increasing pressure from Indian leaders, Indian affairs ministers have turned over more and more of the responsibility for the everyday administration of reserves to their elected band councils. Yet, ultimate decision-making authority remains in the hands of federal authorities. In response to increasingly vociferous demands for Indian self-government, the federal government has agreed to turn Indian reserves into self-governing units. But their model (based on delegated authority) still leaves ultimate control in the hands of the state, and it has been rejected by those Indian leaders who seek independent "First Nation" status and self-government on the basis of national group rights.

The long-term, unintended, yet disastrous consequence of paternalistic, colonial-style policies, laws and practices toward Indians – epitomized by the reserve – is the ugly reality of the self-fulfilling prophecy of white racism. From a human rights view, the Status Indian reserve in Canada can be seen as analogous to a total institution" (Goffman, 1961). Treated as irresponsible children, Indians living on reserves have suffered oppression: they have been denied their human right to make the critical decisions affecting their own lives. Assumed to be naturally racially inferior in intelligence to Euro/Canadians, they have been denied equal educational and economic opportunities and reserves have become riddled with neglect. Sub-standard housing, breeding disease and death; closed schools due to lack of teachers, heat, and/or running water are but a few examples of continuing, dehumanizing life conditions on many reserves. Status Indians' human right to dignity and respect as persons has been violated at every turn: it has been violated every time an adult Indian has had to ask permission to go about the ordinary business of life. It is not surprising, given these long-term paternalistic conditions, that many reserves have become centers of Indian cultural alienation, characterized by all of the symptoms of the self-fulfilling prophecy of colonialism – poverty, crime, alcohol and drug addiction, apathy and *anomie*.

Colonialism destroys incentive, stifles initiative and breeds dependency and despair. Over the years, the more the Canadian government pursued its paternalistic, colonial-style policies, the more the Indians' self-confidence and self-respect were undermined and the cost of paternalistic handouts increased. Nevertheless, as so many critics have cynically pointed out, the administration found it less expensive to keep them on welfare than to make the huge capital expenditure required to make Indian reserves self-sufficient, independent communities.

The 1969 White Paper

By the 1960s, the government of Canada appeared to be moving towards a more "liberal" approach with regard to aboriginal policy. Aboriginal peoples had been given the right to vote, the "pass laws" (governing the rights of Status Indians off their reserves) had been scrapped and potlatches were once again permitted. In fact, the Indian Act itself was being viewed by some as an impediment to the assimilation of aboriginal peoples. By 1969, the government went so far as to formally articulate its assimilationist goals in the aptly-named "White Paper" (Canada, Government of (1969) The White Paper. Statement of the Government of Canada on Policy). This document, purportedly intended to accord Status Indians and other aboriginal peoples full ethnic equality within Canadian society, proposed the abolition of the special constitutional and legislative status of aboriginal peoples; the repeal of the Indian Act; the phasing out of the reserve system; and the transfer of responsibility for services from the federal to provincial governments (Jackson, 1979).

Ponting and Gibbins (1980) argue that the White Paper clearly reflected the position of the Liberal government and Prime Minister of the time (P. M. Trudeau). His "liberal" ideology strongly endorsed the protection of individual rights but was antagonistic to the notion of collective rights. Thus, the White Paper emphasized the equality of aboriginal and non-aboriginal Canadians, as individuals, at the expense of the collective survival of aboriginal ethnic groups, as culturally distinctive peoples. With specific reference to Status Indians, the policy paper gave some recognition to treaty rights, but it interpreted the wording of treaties historically negotiated between Indian bands and the Crown as revealing only "limited and minimal promises" (Government of Canada, 1969: 11). Further, it virtually ignored the gigantic liabilities which Indians had accumulated as a long-term result of the self-fulfilling prophecy of racism. It did not attempt to compensate for the economic, political and social disadvantages which would continue to impede the integration of Indians as "ordinary citizens" within Canadian society.

What the Government did not count on was the fierce and virtually unanimous opposition of aboriginal peoples to the White Paper proposal. Aboriginal protest surfaced in a number of documents written by angry Indian leaders. In his path-breaking book, *The Unjust Society* (1969), Harold Cardinal charged that the program suggested by the White Paper represented "nothing better than cultural genocide". For the Indian to survive, Cardinal contended, he must become "a good little brown white man". In effect, the policy implied "The only good Indian is a non-Indian" (Cardinal, 1969: 1). Another document, *Citizens Plus* (1970), authored by the Indian chiefs of Alberta, strongly reinforced Cardinal's position by arguing that Indians should be recognized as "Citizens Plus", – i.e. citizens who possess additional rights as "charter" members of Canadian society – Canada's First Nations.

The White Paper proposals had their most immediate impact on Status Indians, for the recommendation to abolish the special legal status of Indians under the Indian Act threatened the special rights it provided, particularly with regard to the protection of their lands. Their over-riding concern – shared by Canada's other aboriginal peoples – is to protect their historical relationship with aboriginal lands, which they view as critical for the survival of their distinct cultures. But, very quickly, other aboriginal peoples were swept up in the aboriginal tide of protest, for the White Paper proposals also threatened any potential claims that might be based on aboriginal (land) rights. These aboriginal fears were intensified by a speech given by Prime Minister Trudeau, in which he said that his government would not recognize aboriginal rights. However, under mounting, concerted pressure from aboriginal organizations, and after many months of public debate, the government finally retracted the White Paper proposals in 1971.

Since then, the various associations within the aboriginal movement have, with one voice, demanded recognition of their special status as First Nations within Canada. Despite the considerable diversity among the kinds of claims put forward, representatives have argued that aboriginal communities have the fundamental right to political and cultural sovereignty, and that they have the right to retain ownership of sufficient aboriginal lands to ensure their independence and their economic and cultural survival.

As pointed out earlier, spokespersons for aboriginal organizations maintain that sovereignty is a gift of the Creator which has never been and can never be surrendered. Prior to the arrival of European agents, aboriginal peoples were independent, self-governing nations whose members lived and sought their livelihoods within clearly delineated territories. With colonization, they claim, their right to sovereignty was unjustly abrogated and their institutions of self-government systematically dismantled. But, as nations, they assert their sovereignty and their right to create and administer their own forms of self-government. From this aboriginal view, treaties made between aboriginal peoples and governments should be regarded as treaties between sovereign nations, in the sense of public international law.

The constitutionalization of political issues

The Aboriginal Nationhood movement

A benchmark in the aboriginal struggle for liberation from colonial oppression was reached in 1982, when the Charter of Rights and Freedoms was introduced into the Canadian Constitution. Aboriginal organizations had lobbied fiercely to get some form of constitutional recognition for aboriginal peoples and for aboriginal land and treaty rights in the amended Constitution. That they managed to achieve this, even in the form of wording which recognized the collective rights of aboriginal peoples *in principle only*, was due in large part to the strong support for their cause given by many non-aboriginal organizations representing other subordinate peoples in Canada. This constitutional recognition led to a marked change in strategy, whereby political negotiations with governments over outstanding land claims and claims to nationhood became constitutionalized, and gave rise to continuing court battles over aboriginal rights and title to land.

The Aboriginal Nationhood movement in Canada (as elsewhere) is highly fragmented not only by the traditional differences among the many, diverse aboriginal peoples and cultures, but also by the complicated tangle of legal status divisions imposed by colonial authorities. Despite the real obstacles to unity on aboriginal issues posed by these lines of fragmentation, the various associations within the Aboriginal Nationhood movement have, with one voice, demanded recognition of their special status as First Nations within Canada. This ideological thrust was clearly articulated in the initial proposals for settlement of land claims and for self-government put forward by representatives of the Dene Nation (1976) and the Inuit of Nunavut (1979). Both of these proposals underwent considerable alteration, over the years, during the attempt of the aboriginal nations to achieve negotiated settlements with the federal government. In both cases, original nationhood claims have been compromised in the process.

The Nunavut case

For purposes of illustration, I will focus on the Nunavut case, which in my view represents the strongest single case for nationhood, based on the demonstrably continuing links between the Inuit people, their distinctive aboriginal ethnoculture and their aboriginal territory/homeland which Inuit communities continue to occupy and use (Case Study 8.1).

Case Study 8.1   The Inuit of Nunavut: an aboriginal success story?

New Nationhood: the Nunavut proposals (1979–92)

In order for the Inuit to regain aboriginal nationhood status, the national Inuit organization, Inuit Tapirisat of Canada (ITC), deemed it essential that the Inuit people regain political, economic and cultural sovereignty within their aboriginal territory. Thus, it was necessary to validate their claim to national self-determination. What this involved at the outset, was to document their claim that their aboriginal right to their territory had never been surrendered by war or by treaty, and that the Inuit had continued to occupy and use their lands in their traditional ways, "from time immemorial". To fully document their nationhood claim, Inuit representatives had to provide evidence for the continuing integral links between the Inuit people, their aboriginal territory and their land-based, aboriginal ethno-culture. In other words, the Inuit nationhood claims rested on the premise that the collective cultural, aboriginal and national group rights of the Inuit people had never been abrogated in any "official" way.

The original ITC proposal was supported by extensive research studies documenting (among other things) actual Inuit land use and occupancy over the centuries. One study, directed by Dr Milton Freeman, an anthropologist at McMaster University, showed that, from prehistoric times, the Inuit have used and occupied virtually all of an estimated 750,000 square miles of land claimed as their aboriginal territory, as well as an estimated 800,000 square miles of northern ocean. This documentation was essential in order for the Inuit to validate their collective land claim, based on aboriginal rights.

With regard to Inuit nationhood claims, a number of proposals were circulated among the many dispersed Inuit communities before a widely agreed-upon position paper was drafted. The first agreed-upon proposal was put forward by the ITC in 1979, as a position paper entitled "Political Development in Nunavut". In this paper, the ITC outlined Inuit demands for a newly defined territory which would assume provincial status over a period of about fifteen years. The proposal made several important claims, among them the right to self-determination of the Inuit people, the right of the Inuit to conduct their affairs in their own language (Inuktitut), the right of the Inuit to their traditional lands, waters and resources therein, their right to preserve and use their traditional hunting, trapping and fishing resources, their right to define who is an Inuk (Inuk = singular of Inuit) and their right to economic compensation for past, present and future use by non-Inuit of Inuit lands, waters and resources.

From the beginning, the federal government rejected the conception of Nunavut as an "ethnic" province, to be administered by the Inuit in ways which differed from those of other provinces. Throughout the twenty years of negotiations, the federal government invariably divided the political and economic package proposed by the Inuit, and focused on providing economic compensation for non-Inuit use of Inuit lands and resources. The Inuit proposals, on the other hand, focused on the sharing of Inuit lands and resources with the federal government and the people of Canada, on the understanding that the Inuit would have a prominent voice on all matters within their territorial jurisdiction.

The first step toward Inuit self-government was the proposed creation of a new territory, Nunavut, on Inuit aboriginal lands in the Northwest Territories (NT). This proposal envisaged the division of the NT into two separate jurisdictions, with Nunavut comprising the Eastern Arctic jurisdiction, north of the treeline. The Inuit proposed an elected system of government for Nunavut, similar to that of the existing NT government. Since the vast majority of people within the jurisdiction would be Inuit, the Inuit would assume a substantial degree of control over their economic and cultural destinies.

In 1982, what seemed at the time to be a major breakthrough for the Inuit was the result of a NT plebiscite which approved division of the NT into two territories. The split received federal government approval in principle, subject to agreement on a boundary between the two new jurisdictions, and settlement of outstanding aboriginal land claims in the NT. However, the boundary dispute continued until October 1990, when Inuit and territorial government leaders finally reached agreement on how to divide the NT and create Canada's third territory – the territory of Nunavut.

At this point, the entire package still had to clear three outstanding hurdles: (1) a plebiscite on the proposed new borders by voters in the existing NT; (2)

ratification of the agreement by a majority of Inuit voters aged 16 and over, not just a majority of those who do vote; and (3) ratification of the details of the agreement by a vote in Parliament and the passage of legislation to create the territory of Nunavut.

On May 4, 1992, voters in the NT narrowly supported a controversial boundary to split the NT into two territories, Nunavut in the east and the Western Arctic (or Denendeh, as the Dene prefer) in the west. The plebiscite saw the eastern NT, where 80 percent of the population is Inuit, vote overwhelmingly in support of the boundary, while Western Arctic residents voted strongly against it. Only a low voter turnout in the west, where just 47 percent of voters cast ballots, permitted a victory for boundary supporters. Rejection of the boundary highlighted several long-term concerns of opponents: (1) complaints by the Dene in Saskatchewan, Manitoba and the NT that the boundary placed traditional lands used by Dene Indians under Inuit jurisdiction; (2) complaints by aboriginal (Indian) leaders such as Ovide Mercredit, national chief of the Assembly of First Nations, that the Inuit should have reserved their *inherent right to self-government* as part of the package, instead of setting a precedent of abandonment of self-government which could be harmful to other aboriginal nations seeking self-government as part of their land claim negotiations; and (3) fears of Western Arctic residents of the demise of a central government and the fragmentation of the territory into diverse, regional governments, together with the dire economic consequences of such an occurrence.

In November 1992, Inuit residents in the Eastern Arctic voted 69 percent in favor of the final Nunavut land claim package. The package gave the Inuit clear title to 350,000 square kilometers (140,000 square miles) of land, as well as $1.15 billion in compensation for land ceded, over a period of fourteen years. The Inuit also have the right to hunt, fish and trap in all of Nunavut, a region that is 2.2 million square kilometers (880,000 square miles) in extent. An accord signed prior to the vote between federal government and Inuit negotiators called for the legal establishment of Nunavut by 1999. In the summer of 1993, legislation was introduced to ratify the agreement and to establish the Nunavut territory.

Nunavut today

The territory known as Nunavut was established under the Statutes of Canada 1993, Bill C-132 – the Nunavut Act. It received royal assent on June 10, 1993. The Inuit had made the creation of the territory through this act a prerequisite to signing their land claim. The Nunavut Land Claims Agreement Act (NCLA) came into law at the same time as the Nunavut Act. The Nunavut Land Claims Agreement and the Nunavut Act – the Act that created the new territory and government – work together in several ways. First, the NLCA guarantees that Inuit participation in the civil service (85 percent, ultimately) will reflect the ethnic makeup of the territory. The ethnic breakdown of Nunavut's population (1996 Census of Canada) is: Inuit: 20,480: Non-aboriginal: 3,975. Also, under the NLCA, both Inuit and the territorial and federal governments have guaranteed representation on institutions of public government responsible for issues that are left to the federal government alone in Canada's territories – these include agencies such as the Nunavut Water Board and Nunavut Wildlife Management Board, which make decisions affecting Crown (federal) lands and offshore areas. It is hoped that provisions in the NLCA intended to kickstart Nunavut's wage economy will eventually make Nunavut less dependent on federal government transfers.

The government of Nunavut today – similar to the territorial administration in Yellowknife NT – is run on the dominant (Euro/Canadian) model, not on the model of traditional Inuit self-government. In other words, this model of government is not based on the right of the Inuit to self-determination as a distinctive people, culture and nation. It represents a compromise position. Nevertheless, given the fact that the Inuit make up some 85 percent of the population of the new territory of Nunavut, their voting power can now be used to ensure that the individual and collective, cultural rights of the Inuit people are recognized and protected. Inuit nationhood, however, remains a dream deferred.

Source: Kallen (2003, ch. 7).

Concluding commentary

The analysis of aboriginal movements in Australia and North America documented in this chapter provides strong support for the thesis posited by Kriesi *et al.* (1995), that, as new social movements, aboriginal movements are perceived as more threatening to dominant interests than are other sub-cultural and ethnocultural movements. Kriesi *et al.* argue that the more material resources are involved, and the more that power is at stake, the more threatening a social movement may be for political authorities. In the case of aboriginal movements, their territorial focus, heightened by their emphasis on political, economic and cultural self-determination as nations in self-designated territories within the state, places these movements within the "high-profile" category. They are perceived as posing a threat to the high-priority policy domains of the dominant powers. In general, this perceived threat to the overarching political, economic and territorial control wielded by the society's dominant powers has been and continues to be a major roadblock to the aboriginal quest for new nationhood in Australia, the USA and Canada. In all three countries, governments have afforded "lip-service" recognition to the concept of aboriginal peoples as "nations" and, to varying degrees, have accorded limited powers of aboriginal self-governance and control of resources at the community level, but always on the basis of delegated authority: the government retains ultimate control. Again, in all three cases, governments have favoured cash settlement of

outstanding land claims, thus retaining control over vast areas of traditional aboriginal lands and resources. The end result is that aboriginal
peoples still occupy the status of disadvantaged, internally colonized
populations in society, and the prevailing social conditions in most
aboriginal communities – high unemployment, poverty, cultural alienation, alcohol and drug addiction and so forth – continue to epitomize
their marginalized status in society.

The Nunavut case is unique in that the final settlement of their claim
left the Inuit with "shared" control over large areas of their ancestral
lands and resources, and paved the way for them to assume a dominant
role in the governance of the new territory. The Inuit have done what
many indigenous groups around the world can only envy. While many
peoples around the world have attained self-government in some form,
no other group can claim to dominate a separate political unit on an
equal footing with other governmental units. Yet, the legacy of colonialism – sub-standard living conditions, unemployment, marginalization –
continues to breed apathy, alienation and high rates of suicide, especially
among youth in Nunavut. Moreover, as pointed out earlier, the government of Nunavut is structured on the dominant Euro/Western model
entrenched across Canada. Thus, even in the case of Nunavut, the quest
for new nationhood based on aboriginal cultural premise remains a
"dream deferred".

The next, and concluding chapter of this book (Chapter 9), will focus
on an analysis of the strengths and weaknesses of the current international human rights system. As a prelude to this examination, I would
like to highlight some critical issues for readers to consider in assessing
the usefulness of the human rights paradigm as an interpretive framework for the social scientific analysis presented throughout this book.

- How has your understanding of international human rights principles contributed to your understanding of dominant/subordinate
  relations? How useful is an understanding of the human rights paradigm in attempting to resolve conflicts between individual and
  collective rights?
- Can an understanding of the international human rights paradigm
  benefit members of subordinate groups? What are the limitations of
  the international human rights system in ensuring legal protections
  for human rights of subordinate populations within states?

With these considerations in mind, we will turn our attention to the concluding chapter of this book.

CHAPTER 9

Conclusion: Strengths and Weaknesses of the Current Human Rights System

Introduction

In the Introduction to this book, I asserted that an important consideration in developing a human rights-oriented framework for the analysis of
group-level social inequality and social injustice within states was that it
provides members of subordinate populations with an internationally
recognized basis for making human rights claims to equitable treatment.
For subordinate populations, by definition, lacking the power to significantly change their disadvantaged status, the human rights approach
provides a positive avenue through which to seek redress for past human
rights violations and through which to seek new protections for their
fundamental human rights in law and public policy. In assessing both the
successes and the failures of particular subordinate groups in their struggle to achieve group-level equality/equivalence in society, my arguments
have indirectly revealed some of the strengths and the weaknesses of the
current, internationally endorsed human rights system.

My analysis of two equality/equity-seeking human rights and liberation movements, the gay/lesbian and the women's movements, has
shown that, in both cases, within the context of Western democratic
societies, despite formidable obstacles posed by external discrimination and internal fragmentation, members have been able to achieve
"unity above diversity" on some common issues, and to pursue
community-wide, agreed-upon goals which are perceived to be of
benefit to all members of the population. Again, in both cases, despite
many failures and setbacks, some equity goals have been achieved:
some discriminatory laws and policies have been struck down, and

some human rights protections for members have been secured in law and public policy.

With regard to equivalence-seeking aboriginal rights and nationhood movements, my analysis of these movements in Australia and in North America has shown that many of the points made above are again applicable. Despite serious lines of fragmentation and much disagreement over issues and priorities, aboriginal organizations have been able to gain recognition of aboriginal people's land rights, and many aboriginal communities have been able to achieve at least a limited (municipal/delegated) form of autonomy.

On the down side, much is left to be done. The bottom line is that the ultimate goal of group-level equality/equivalence is still a long way from realization. Many aboriginal peoples still live in highly disadvantaged life conditions characterized by joblessness, poverty, despair, alcoholism, drug use and high rates of suicide. Women are still plagued by sexism and working women still lag far behind men in political and economic status. Gay men and lesbians are still a highly invalidated population, harassed by homophobia and subject to hate crimes.

When we turn our attention to the situation of subordinate groups in non-Western, non-democratic societies, however, the gains achieved by their counterparts in the Western democratic context assume a far greater significance. It is in highlighting this international comparison that the importance of protections for fundamental human rights in law and their enforcement through public policy is demonstrated.

The relationship between national and international dimensions of human rights

In Chapter 1 of this book, I proposed that international human rights principles set down in the provisions of the various international human rights treaties and covenants are *prior to law*: essentially, they serve to challenge states to revise laws in ways which offer guaranteed protections for the rights of citizens, especially members of subordinate groups, against abuses of state power. I highlighted the observation that human rights principles are advocated by UN authoritative bodies as *moral guidelines*, the universal human rights standards, to which all systems of justice should conform.

Throughout this book, I have documented both the effectiveness and the limitations of the current human rights system. On the positive side, I have shown how subordinate groups within democratic states can use international human rights principles, endorsed by states, in order to lobby for legal protection of their human rights through the enactment and strengthening of the provisions of human rights legislation. On the negative side, I have shown how dominant authorities can block efforts by subordinate groups to gain legal protection for their human rights, despite the ratification by states of UN human rights instruments.

The latter observation highlights the fact that the power of international human rights instruments is limited to that of *moral persuasion*. States which ratify international human rights instruments are morally, but not legally, bound to enact and enforce laws which incorporate the human rights principles articulated in the provisions of these instruments. However, in the twenty-first-century world of international media attention to human rights abuses, moral persuasion can be a very powerful instrument of international embarrassment for states which openly profess support for international human rights, constraining them to make appropriate changes consistent with human rights principles. This point is most clearly demonstrated in cases where individual citizens, having exhausted available avenues of legal redress for alleged human rights violations before state courts, take their case beyond the state level, for consideration by international or multi-state courts.

Claims put forward to the UN Human Rights Committee under the Optional Protocol to the International Covenant on Civil and Political Rights

Nations that ratify the International Covenant on Civil and Political Rights (ICCPR) are expected to introduce laws that will reflect its provisions. The Optional Protocol to the ICCPR provides individual citizens with direct recourse to the United Nations. Persons who believe that their rights as specified in the Covenant have been violated can state their case before the UN Human Rights Committee. Such persons must first have exhausted all legal avenues within their own country. Cases brought forward under the Optional Protocol to the ICCPR show how the protection for human rights afforded under international human rights covenants can provide avenues of redress against human rights violations for citizens beyond the state legal system. Most importantly, these cases demonstrate how international pressure can be brought to bear on nations to amend or eliminate discriminatory laws which violate international human rights covenants.

To date, Canada is one of only a small number of the nations signing the Covenant which has ratified the Optional Protocol. A significant number of complaints have been filed by Canadian citizens against Canada, under the Protocol. Among the most significant of these, in terms of its eventual impact, was the very first case, that of *Lovelace* v. *Canada* (1980) (Case Study 9.1).

Case Study 9.1   The Sandra Lovelace case

The Sandra Lovelace case concerned an Indian woman from the Tobique Reserve in New Brunswick, Sandra Lovelace, who, upon marrying a non-Indian, had lost her Indian status as a result of s. 12(10)b) of the Indian Act, which declared that "the following persons are not entitled to be registered, namely . . . a woman who married a person who is not an Indian". Her case was accepted by the UN Human Rights Committee notwithstanding the fact that she had not exhausted all domestic remedies, i.e. by going to the Supreme Court of Canada. The Committee accepted the fact that in the 1973 *Lavell* case another Indian woman had already gone before the Supreme Court on a similar issue and had lost. Sandra Lovelace stated in 1977 that Canada had infringed a number of rights contained in the International Covenanton Civil and Political Rights, including the right to protection from discrimination as provided under Articles 2(1) and 26; equality of men and women under Article 3; protection of the family under Article 23(1); equality of rights and responsibilities in terms of marriage under Article 23(4); and, the right to enjoy her own culture under Article 27.

In its 1981 decision, the Human Rights Committee declared that Sandra Lovelace had lost her rights prior to the entering into force of the Covenant on Civil and Political Rights and that her right to enjoy her family was only indirectly at stake. However, the Committee concluded in her favour by ruling that the effects of her loss of rights continued after the Covenant had come into force and that the particular right being denied was the right to enjoy her culture in her community. Following the release of the statement of the Human Rights Committee, the Canadian government agreed to modify the Indian Act to bring it in to harmony with the Covenant. It took four years for Sandra Lovelace's case to be decided at the United Nations and another four years for the Indian Act to be amended. The Government of Canada first introduced legislation in June 1984 to amend the Indian Act in order to remove the discriminatory clause. The amendment was re-introduced in the new parliamentary session in 1985 and became law in June 1985, thereby putting an end to sexual discrimination in the Indian Act.

Source: Kallen, 2003.

The second case to be presented is that of a UK transsexual who, under UK law, was not recognized as a woman and was denied her right to marry (Case Study 9.2). She brought her case before the European Court of Human Rights, alleging that her fundamental human rights had been violated. The Court judged in her favor.

Case Study 9.2   UK transsexual wins right to marry

A British transsexual won her battle in the European Court of Human Rights to be recognized as a woman and to be allowed to marry (*BBC News*, 11 July, 2002): 65-year-old Christine Goodwin told the court that English law had denied her the right to a new sexual identity. However, the ruling does not immediately override UK law – it simply means it will have to be taken into account by judges in future. Ms Goodwin can now apply again to the British courts in the hope they will do so.

Judges' ruling
The judgment delivered in the Strasbourg court unanimously held that the UK's failure to recognize Ms Goodwin's new identity in law breached her rights to respect for privacy and her right to marry under the European Convention on Human Rights. The UK is one of four countries in the Council of Europe which does not recognize a sex change as legally valid. The others are Ireland, Andorra and Albania.

However, Ms Goodwin's solicitor, Robin Lewis, said that the decision would mean the British government would eventually be forced to change its laws. He pointed out that the judges had emphasized that the ruling was based on a continuing international trend in favor of the social and legal acceptance of transsexuals. The Court noted that there had been major social changes in the institution of marriage since the adoption of the European Convention as well as dramatic changes brought about by developments in medicine and science in the field of transsexuality. They said the fact that Ms Goodwin was still considered male by the authorities affected her life where sex was of legal relevance, such as in the area of pensions and retirement age. The court argued that the UK government's stance fell far short of the standards for human dignity in the twenty-first century.

A spokeswoman for the Lord Chancellor's Department said that the judgment would be taken seriously. She agreed with the sentiments expressed by Ms Goodwin's lawyer, that this judgment of the European Court eventually would require the government to change the law, and that any government practice which could lead to the history of a transsexual being identified would also have to be changed so as to respect the individual's right to privacy.

Source: BBC News.

While the foregoing cases demonstrate the influence which international human rights bodies can wield through moral persuasion to constrain ratifying states to change their laws and practices to conform to universally endorsed human rights principles, there remain formidable barriers to such change, particularly in non-Western countries where traditional religious values opposed to some Western/democratic concepts of human rights are legally entrenched. This impasse highlights the continuing tension between individual and collective rights in a global, cross-cultural context.

Universality of human rights in cross-cultural context

In Chapter 1 of this book, I explored the controversy surrounding the generally accepted concept of the universality of human rights in cross-cultural context. I noted that the most controversial aspect of this concept had to do with "private" rights. It is these provisions of the Universal Declaration of Human Rights that have not become universally accepted. The private sphere deals with issues such as religion, culture, the status of women, the right to marry, to divorce and to remarry, the protection of children, the question of choice as regards family planning and the like. These rights have traditionally been covered by religious law, and in some countries, they still are (Cerna, 1994). This tension between the universality of rights in the private sphere and the competing religious and/or traditional law means that some societies are unwilling to assume international human rights obligations in the private sphere.

To illustrate the kinds of conflicts which can develop from the tension between individual rights and collective cultural rights regarding private sphere issues, I will offer a stark example (Case Study 9.3).

Case Study 9.3   Sharia stoning sentence for Nigerian woman

LaShawn R. Jefferson, Executive Director of the Women's Rights Division of Human Rights Watch, has contended that the August 19, 2002 ruling by a Nigerian court of appeal to uphold the verdict of death by stoning of Amina Lawal for adultery is a cruel and inhuman application of Sharia (Islamic) law. The legal system, she alleges, is being used to punish adult women for consensual sex. While the death penalty is never an appropriate punishment for a crime, according to HRW, in this instance, the very nature of the crime is in doubt.

In March 2002, a Sharia court in the state of Katsina in northern Nigeria had sentenced 30-year-old Amina Lawal to death for having engaged in sex outside marriage. The government used her pregnancy as evidence of her having committed adultery. Ms Lawal, an unwed mother, now has an 8-month old child.

Over the past year, some northern Nigerian states have increasingly applied Sharia law to criminal cases, among them theft and adultery. Consequently, Nigerian Sharia courts have ordered amputations as punishment for theft and death penalty by stoning for adultery cases. To date, no stoning sentence has been carried out.

Jefferson urged the Nigerian government to commute the death sentence of Amina Lawal and drop the criminal charges against her.

In connection with an earlier, parallel case, involving alleged pre-marital sex, Human Rights Watch had urged the Court of Nigeria to reject the death penalty and the cruelty inherent in a punishment such as death by stoning (Human Rights Watch press release, March 26, 2002). In the earlier case, the court commuted the death sentence of Safiya Hussaini, who was sentenced to death by stoning by a Sharia (Islamic) court in October 2001. But the court decision was based on a technicality – that the alleged act of adultery had been committed before Sharia law was imposed in the region – and even as news of the decision was released, reports arose of another woman (Amina Lawal) in northern Nigeria being sentenced to death for adultery.

Human Rights Watch urged government authorities in Nigeria to ensure that other death sentences are also commuted and that courts refrain from sentencing people to cruel, inhuman and degrading punishments. Several other people have been sentenced to death since Sharia was extended to cover criminal cases in many parts of northern Nigeria. In September 2001, a man accused of sodomy for the rape of a 7-year-old boy was sentenced to death by stoning in Kebbi State. In January 2002, Nigeria saw the first execution under Sharia when a man accused of murder in Katsina was hanged. Sharia courts have also sentenced people to amputations and floggings.

Source: Human Rights Watch press release, New York, August 20, 2002.

Cerna (1994) commenting on the continuing tension between the universality of human rights in the private sphere and the competing religious and/or traditional law, as illustrated in the foregoing case study, concludes that achieving universal acceptance of international human rights norms is a *process*, and different norms occupy different places on the continuum. While the international community may censure countries for practices based on norms which violate human rights, they can not impose international human rights norms to replace traditional ones. It is important that the international supervisory bodies come to recognize that change and acceptance of these norms must come from within the countries themselves. It seems clear, in the twenty-first century, that international norms dealing with rights that affect the private sphere of life will take the longest time to achieve universal acceptance.

Coalition-building for recognition and implementation of the human rights of subordinate groups

In addition to legal human rights protection, it is important that social policy measures designed to ameliorate group level disadvantage among subordinate populations be expanded and implemented at all levels of government. Subordinate rights organizations and coalitions can play an important role here by lobbying for improved legal and policy measures directed toward equitable treatment.

Mullaly (2002: 194–5) argues that dominant members and organizations can help subordinate groups empower themselves and enhance their cultural identities by supporting alternative subordinate community services and organizations that are operated by and serve members of particular subordinate communities. These alternative services and organizations are usually established because their traditional, mainstream counterparts tend to be culturally specific – that is to say, they are set up by dominant members and operate in accordance with dominant norms, values and expectations. Alternative subordinate community services and organizations, Mullaly points out, are countersystems to mainstream agencies because they are founded on different cultural principles, values and ideals. They represent attempts by subordinate communities to gain control over their own destinies. Alternative services and organizations usually spring from the efforts of a particular subordinate community or movement such as women, gay men, lesbians, aboriginal people, persons with disabilities and so forth. Such alternatives include rape crisis centres, transition homes for battered women and children, urban aboriginal friendship centres and aboriginal community healing centres, gay and lesbian venues and the like. While alternative services and organizations generated by particular subordinate communities can provide a springboard for community action geared towards human rights-oriented goals, coalition-building among subordinate groups can greatly strengthen the empowerment base of the subordinate movement and can thus bolster the efforts of the movement to achieve common, human rights-oriented goals.

New social movements and coalition-building among subordinate groups

Mullaly (2002: 197) maintains that a major obstacle to coalition-building among members of new social movements is that these movements tend to have a single-stranded focus on the identity, community and culture of a particular subordinate group. Thus, a political challenge is posed in the formation of multiple identity groups and movements by the problem of forming alliances and building solidarity that transcends, rather than subjugates, their differences. The tendency of subordinate groups and movements to focus solely on their respective singular issues obscures their awareness of and identification with the potentially shared political interests of other subordinate populations.

Another obstacle to coalition-building is externally imposed. Mullaly cites Wineman (1984: 159), who contends that the biggest obstacle to coalition building among different subordinate groups is the 'divide and rule' strategy of dominant political and economic authorities, embedded in social policies that serve to create and sustain deep divisions among different subordinate groups. This dominant strategy engenders a competition among subordinate groups for resources and attention, a point well-documented in my discussion in Chapter 8 of the women's, gay and lesbian, and aboriginal movements.

Mullaly (2002: 198–200) suggests four strategies (originally developed by Wineman) designed to overcome internal and external obstacles to coalition-building among different subordinate groups. The first, and essential, element of coalition-building is the mutual identification of different subordinate populations as *groups* (albeit for different reasons) disadvantaged and subordinated by dominant agencies in the society. The second element is for members of different subordinate groups to recognize that they share a *common goal*: that of transforming the structure of society from one based on group inequality to one based on group equality. A third element, directly related to the second, is for members of different subordinate groups to understand that it is the same, mainstream *political and economic elites* who are responsible for the inferiorization and disadvantaged status common to all subordinate groups. A fourth element, critical for coalition-building, is the recognition that most subordinate group members experience subordinate status on *multiple grounds* (multiple minority [*sic*] status). This fact enables the development of caucuses of internal minorities (minorities within minority communities [*sic*]) that facilitate the development of links with other subordinate groups. For example, an aboriginal women's caucus within an anti-poverty group becomes a link between aboriginal nations, women's and anti-poverty organizations. These internal caucuses not only manifest overlapping subordinate statuses and identities, but also become the points of contact between various subordinate organizations, and can spearhead coalition-building through the development of common goals and joint actions. Coalition-building, in turn, can greatly strengthen the empowerment base of the subordinate movement and thus can bolster the efforts of the movement to achieve human rights-oriented goals.

Concluding commentary

In closing, I wish to highlight the critical factor in this process: as long as the unequal structure of dominant/subordinate relations persists, subordinate groups seeking empowerment and human rights protection will do so by making demands upon the existing powers-that-be. Dominant authorities can still wield their power in discriminatory ways. Should the current climate of endorsement for human rights change, anti-discriminatory laws could be repealed and replaced by discriminatory ones. Laws, after all, are not unalterable: they are made by human beings, and can be changed by human beings.

This cautionary note having been made, I want to close on a note of optimism. In the present era of support for human rights principles among the world's democratic nations, dominant human rights activists can do much to further the empowerment and renewed validation of subordinate populations. By openly supporting the efforts of organizations representing invalidated and disadvantaged subordinate groups, and by engaging in public education, community advocacy and lobbying activities, human rights activists can expose the cruel practice of justifying injustice, and can further the universal human rights goals of equity and justice for all.

Appendix A: Universal Declaration of Human Rights*

Whereas recognition of the inherent dignity and of the equal and inalienable rights of all members of the human family is the foundation of freedom, justice and peace in the world,

Whereas disregard and contempt for human rights have resulted in barbarous acts which have outraged the conscience of mankind, and the advent of a world in which human beings shall enjoy freedom of speech and belief and freedom from fear and want has been proclaimed as the highest aspiration of the common people,

Whereas it is essential, if man is not to be compelled to have recourse, as a last resort, to rebellion against tyranny and oppression, that human rights should be protected by the rule of law,

Whereas it is essential to promote the development of friendly relations between nations,

Whereas the peoples of the United Nations have in the Charter reaffirmed their faith in fundamental human rights in the dignity and worth of the human person and in the equal rights of men and women and have determined to promote social progress and better standards of life in larger freedom,

Whereas Member States have pledged themselves to achieve, in co-operation with the United Nations, the promotion of universal respect for and observance of human rights and fundamental freedoms,

Whereas a common understanding of these rights and freedoms is of the greatest importance for the full realization of this pledge,

Now therefore, the General Assembly proclaims

This Universal Declaration of Human Rights as a common standard of achievement for all peoples and all nations to the end that every individual and every organ of society, keeping this Declaration

---

* Adopted by United Nations General Assembly, December 10, 1948.

constantly in mind, shall strive by teaching and education to promote respect for these rights and freedoms and by progressive measures, national and international, to secure their universal and effective recognition and observance, both among the peoples of Member States themselves and among the peoples of territories under their jurisdiction.

Article 1

All human beings are born free and equal in dignity and rights. They are endowed with reason and conscience and should act towards one another in a spirit of brotherhood.

Article 2

Everyone is entitled to all the rights and freedoms set forth in this Declaration, without distinction of any kind, such as race, colour, sex, language, religion, political or other opinion, national or social origin, property, birth or other status.

Furthermore, no distinction shall be made on the basis of the political, jurisdictional or international status of the country or territory to which a person belongs, whether it be independent, trust, non-selfgoverning or under any other limitation of sovereignty.

Article 3

Everyone has the right to life, liberty and security of person.

Article 4

No one shall be held in slavery or servitude; slavery and the slave trade shall be prohibited in all their forms.

Article 5

No one shall be subjected to torture or to cruel, inhuman or degrading treatment or punishment.

Article 6

Everyone has the right to recognition everywhere as a person before the law.

Article 7

All are equal before the law and are entitled without any discrimination to equal protection of the law. All are entitled to equal protection against any discrimination in violation of this Declaration and against any incitement to such discrimination.

Article 8

Everyone has the right to an effective remedy by the competent national tribunals for acts violating the fundamental rights granted him by the constitution or by law.

Article 9
No one shall be subjected to arbitrary arrest, detention or exile.

Article 10
Everyone is entitled in full equality to a fair and public hearing by an independent and impartial tribunal, in the determination of his rights and obligations and of any criminal charge against him.

Article 11
(1) Everyone charged with a penal offence has the right to be presumed innocent until proved guilty according to law in a public trial at which he has had all the guarantees necessary for his defence.
(2) No one shall be held guilty of any penal offence on account of any act or omission which did not constitute a penal offence, under national or international law, at the time when it was committed. Nor shall a heavier penalty be imposed than the one that was applicable at the time the penal offence was committed.

Article 12
No one shall be subjected to arbitrary interference with his privacy, family, home or correspondence, nor to attacks upon his honour and reputation. Everyone has the right to the protection of the law against such interference or attacks.

Article 13
(1) Everyone has the right to freedom of movement and residence within the borders of each state.
(2) Everyone has the right to leave any country, including his own, and to return to his country.

Article 14
(1) Everyone has the right to seek and to enjoy in other countries asylum from persecution.
(2) This right may not be invoked in the case of prosecutions genuinely arising from non-political crimes or from acts contrary to the purposes and principles of the United Nations.

Article 15
(1) Everyone has the right to a nationality.
(2) No one shall be arbitrarily deprived of his nationality nor denied the right to change his nationality.

Article 16

(1) Men and women of full age, without any limitation due to race, nationality or religion, have the right to marry and to found a family. The are entitled to equal rights as to marriage, during marriage and at its dissolution.

(2) Marriage shall be entered into only with the free and full consent of the intending spouses.

(3) The family is the natural and fundamental group unit of society and is entitled to protection by society and the State.

Article 17

(1) Everyone has the right to own property alone as well as in association with others.

(2) No one shall be arbitrarily deprived of his property.

Article 18

Everyone has the right to freedom of thought, conscience and religion; this right includes freedom to change his religion or belief, and freedom, either alone or in community with others and in public or private, to manifest his religion or belief in teaching, practice, worship and observance.

Article 19

Everyone has the right to freedom of opinion and expression; this right includes freedom to hold opinions without interference and to seek, receive and impart information and ideas through any media and regardless of frontiers.

Article 20

(1) Everyone has the right to freedom of peaceful assembly and association.

(2) No one may be compelled to belong to an association.

Article 21

(1) Everyone has the right to take part in the government of his country, directly or through freely chosen representatives.

(2) Everyone has the right of equal access to public service in his country.

(3) The will of the people shall be the basis of the authority of government; this will shall be expressed in periodic and genuine elections which shall be by universal and equal suffrage and shall be held by secret vote or by equivalent free voting procedures.

Article 22

Everyone, as a member of society, has the right to social security and is entitled to realization, through national effort and international co-operation and in accordance with the organization and resources of each State, of the economic, social and cultural rights indispensable for his dignity and the free development of his personality.

Article 23

(1) Everyone has the right to work, to free choice of employment, to just and favorable conditions of work and to protection against unemployment.

(2) Everyone, without any discrimination, has the right to equal pay for equal work.

(3) Everyone who works has the right to just and favorable remuneration insuring for himself and his family an existence worthy of human dignity, and supplemented, if necessary, by other means of social protection.

(4) Everyone has the right to form and to join trade unions for the protection of his interests.

Article 24

Everyone has the right to rest and leisure, including reasonable limitation of working hours and periodic holidays with pay.

Article 25

(1) Everyone has the right to a standard of living adequate for the health and wellbeing of himself and of his family, including food, clothing, housing and medical care and necessary social services, and the right to security in the event of unemployment, sickness, disability, widowhood, old age or other lack of livelihood in circumstances beyond his control.

(2) Motherhood and childhood are entitled to special care and assistance. All children, whether born in or out of wedlock, shall enjoy the same social protection.

Article 26

(1) Everyone has the right to education. Education shall be free, at least in the elementary and fundamental stages. Elementary education shall be compulsory. Technical and professional education shall be made generally available and higher education shall be equally accessible to all on the basis of merit.

(2) Education shall be directed to the full development of the human personality and to the strengthening of respect for human rights and fundamental freedoms. It shall promote understanding, tolerance and friendship among all nations, racial or religious groups, and shall further the activities of the United Nations for the maintenance of peace.

(3) Parents have a prior right to choose the kind of education that shall be given to their children.

Article 27

(1) Everyone has the right freely to participate in the cultural life of the community, to enjoy the arts and to share in scientific advancement and its benefits.

(2) Everyone has the right to the protection of the moral and material interests resulting from any scientific, literary or artistic production of which he is the author.

Article 28

Everyone is entitled to a social and international order in which the rights and freedoms set forth in this Declaration can be fully realized.

Article 29

(1) Everyone has duties to the community in which alone the free and full development of his personality is possible.

(2) In the exercise of his rights and freedoms, everyone shall be subject only to such limitations as are determined by law solely for the purpose of securing due recognition and respect for the rights and freedoms of others and of meeting the just requirements of morality, public order and the general welfare in a democratic society.

(3) These rights and freedoms may in no case be exercised contrary to the purposes and principles of the United Nations.

Article 30

Nothing in this Declaration may be interpreted as implying for any State, group or person any right to engage in any activity or to perform any act aimed at the destruction of any of the rights and freedoms set forth herein.

Appendix B: Draft Declaration on the Rights of Indigenous Peoples*

AFFIRMING that indigenous peoples are equal in dignity and rights to all other peoples, while recognizing the right of all peoples to be different, to consider themselves different, and to be respected as such. AFFIRMING ALSO that all peoples contribute to the diversity and richness of civilizations and cultures, which constitute the common heritage of humankind.

AFFIRMING FURTHER that all doctrines, policies and practices based on or advocating superiority of peoples or individuals on the basis of national origin, racial, religious, ethnic or cultural differences are racist, scientifically false, legally invalid, morally condemnable and socially unjust.

REAFFIRMING also that indigenous peoples, in the exercise of their rights, should be free from discrimination of any kind.

CONCERNED that indigenous peoples have been deprived of their human rights and fundamental freedoms, resulting, *inter alia*, in their colonization and dispossession of their lands, territories and resources, thus preventing them from exercising, in particular, their right to development in accordance with their own needs and interests.

RECOGNIZING the urgent need to respect and promote the inherent rights and characteristics of indigenous peoples, especially their rights to their lands, territories and resources, which derive from their political, economic and social structures and from their cultures, spiritual traditions, histories and philosophies.

WELCOMING the fact that indigenous peoples are organizing themselves for political, economic, social and cultural enhancement and in order to bring an end to all forms of discrimination and oppression wherever they occur.

* E/CN.4/Sub.2/1994/2/Add.1 (1994)

CONVINCED that control by indigenous peoples over developments affecting them and their lands, territories and resources will enable them to maintain and strengthen their institutions, cultures and traditions, and to promote their development in accordance with their aspirations and needs.

RECOGNIZING also that respect for indigenous knowledge, cultures and traditional practices contributes to sustainable and equitable development and proper management of the environment.

EMPHASIZING the need for demilitarization of the lands and territories of indigenous peoples, which will contribute to peace, economic and social progress and development, understanding and friendly relations among nations and peoples of the world.

RECOGNIZING in particular the right of indigenous families and communities to retain shared responsibility for the upbringing, training, education and well-being of their children.

RECOGNIZING ALSO that indigenous peoples have the right freely to determine their relationship with States in a spirit of coexistence, mutual benefit and full respect.

CONSIDERING that treaties, agreements and other arrangements between States and indigenous peoples are properly matters of international concern and responsibility.

ACKNOWLEDGING that the Charter of the United Nations, the International Covenant on Economic, Social and Cultural Rights and the International Covenant on Civil and Political Rights affirm the fundamental importance of the right of self-determination of all peoples, by virtue of which they freely determine their political status and freely pursue their economic, social and cultural development.

BEARING IN MIND that nothing in this Declaration may be used to deny any peoples their right of self-determination.

ENCOURAGING States to comply with and effectively implement all international instruments, in particular those related to human rights, as they apply to indigenous peoples, in consultation and co-operation with the peoples concerned.

EMPHASIZING that the United Nations has an important and continuing role to play in promoting and protecting the rights of indigenous peoples.

BELIEVING that this Declaration is a further important step forward for the recognition, promotion and protection of the rights and freedoms of indigenous peoples and in the development of relevant activities of the United Nations system in this field.

Solemnly proclaims the following United Nations Declaration on the Rights of Indigenous Peoples.

PART I
ARTICLE 1
Indigenous peoples have the right to the full and effective enjoyment of all human rights and fundamental freedoms recognized in the Charter of the United Nations, the Universal Declaration of Human Rights and international human rights law.
ARTICLE 2
Indigenous individuals and peoples are free and equal to all other individuals and peoples in dignity and rights, and have the right to be free from any kind of adverse discrimination, in particular that based on their indigenous origin or identity.
ARTICLE 3
Indigenous peoples have the right of self-determination. By virtue of that right they freely determine their political status and freely pursue their economic, social and cultural development.
ARTICLE 4
Indigenous peoples have the right to maintain and strengthen their distinct political, economic, social and cultural characteristics, as well as their legal systems, while retaining their rights to participate fully, if they so choose, in the political, economic, social and cultural life of the State.
ARTICLE 5
Every indigenous individual has the right to a nationality.

PART II
ARTICLE 6
Indigenous peoples have the collective right to live in freedom, peace and security as distinct peoples and to full guarantees against genocide or any other act of violence, including the removal of indigenous children from their families and communities under any pretext.
In addition, they have the individual rights to life, physical and mental integrity, liberty and security of person.
ARTICLE 7
Indigenous peoples have the collective and individual right not to be subjected to ethnocide and cultural genocide, including prevention of and redress for:
  a. any action which has the aim or effect of depriving them of their integrity as distinct peoples, or of their cultural values or ethnic identities;
  b. any action which has the aim or effect of dispossessing them of their lands, territories or resources;
  c. any form of population transfer which has the aim or effect of violating or undermining any of their rights;

d. any form of assimilation or integration by other cultures or ways of life imposed on them by legislative, administrative or other measures;

e. any form of propaganda directed against them.

ARTICLE 8

Indigenous peoples have the collective and individual right to maintain and develop their distinct identities and characteristics, including the right to identify themselves as indigenous and to be recognized as such.

ARTICLE 9

Indigenous peoples and individuals have the right to belong to an indigenous community or nation, in accordance with the traditions and customs of the community or nation concerned. No disadvantage of any kind may arise from the exercise of such a right.

ARTICLE 10

Indigenous peoples shall not be forcibly removed from their lands or territories. No relocation shall take place without the free and informed consent of the indigenous peoples concerned and after agreement on just and fair compensation and, where possible, with the option of return.

ARTICLE 11

Indigenous peoples have the right to special protection and security in periods of armed conflict. States shall observe international standards, in particular the Fourth Geneva Convention of 1949, for the protection of civilian populations in circumstances of emergency and armed conflict, and shall not:

a. recruit indigenous individuals against their will into the armed forces and, in particular, for use against other indigenous peoples;

b. recruit indigenous children into the armed forces . . . ;

c. force indigenous individuals to abandon their lands, territories or means of subsistence, or relocate them in special centres for military purposes;

d. force indigenous individuals to work for military purposes under any discriminatory conditions.

PART III
ARTICLE 12

Indigenous peoples have the right to practice and revitalize their cultural traditions and customs. This includes the right to maintain, protect and develop the past, present and future manifestations of their cultures, such as archaeological and historical sites, artefacts, designs, ceremonies, technologies and visual and performing arts and literature, as well as the right to the restitution of cultural, intellectual, religious and spiritual property taken without their free and informed consent or in violation of their laws, traditions and customs.

ARTICLE 13

Indigenous peoples have the right to manifest, practice, develop and teach their spiritual and religious traditions, customs and ceremonies; the right to maintain, protect, and have access in privacy to their religious and cultural sites; the right to the use and control of ceremonial objects; and the right to the repatriation of human remains.

States shall take effective measures, in conjunction with the indigenous peoples concerned, to ensure that indigenous sacred places, including burial sites, be preserved, respected and protected.

ARTICLE 14

Indigenous peoples have the right to revitalize, use, develop and transmit to future generations their histories, languages, oral traditions, philosophies, writing systems and literatures, and to designate and retain their own names for communities, places and persons.

States shall take effective measures, whenever any right of indigenous peoples may be threatened, to ensure this right is protected and also to ensure that they can understand and be understood in political, legal and administrative proceedings, where necessary through the provision of interpretation or by other appropriate means.

PART IV

ARTICLE 15

Indigenous children have the right to all levels and forms of education of the State. All indigenous peoples also have this right and the right to establish and control their educational systems and institutions providing education in their own languages, in a manner appropriate to their cultural methods of teaching and learning.

Indigenous children living outside their communities have the right to be provided access to education in their own culture and language. States shall take effective measures to provide appropriate resources for these purposes.

ARTICLE 16

Indigenous peoples have the right to have the dignity and diversity of their cultures, traditions, histories and aspirations appropriately reflected in all forms of education and public information.

States shall take effective measures, in consultation with the indigenous peoples concerned, to eliminate prejudice and discrimination and to promote tolerance, understanding and good relations among indigenous peoples and all segments of society.

ARTICLE 17

Indigenous peoples have the right to establish their own media in their own language. They also have the right to equal access to all forms of non-indigenous media.

States shall take effective measures to ensure that State-owned media duly reflect indigenous cultural diversity.

ARTICLE 18

Indigenous peoples have the right to enjoy fully all rights established under international labour law and national labour legislation.

Indigenous individuals have the right not to be subjected to any discriminatory conditions of labour, employment or salary.

PART V

ARTICLE 19

Indigenous peoples have the right to participate fully, if they so choose, at all levels of decision-making in matters which may affect their rights, lives and destinies through representatives chosen by themselves in accordance with their own procedures, as well as to maintain and develop their own indigenous decision-making institutions.

ARTICLE 20

Indigenous peoples have the right to participate fully, if they so choose, through procedures determined by them, in devising legislative or administrative measures that may affect them.

States shall obtain the free and informed consent of the peoples concerned before adopting and implementing such measures.

ARTICLE 21

Indigenous peoples have the right to maintain and develop their political, economic and social systems, to be secure in the enjoyment of their own means of subsistence and development, and to engage freely in all their traditional and other economic activities. Indigenous peoples who have been deprived of their means of subsistence and development are entitled to just and fair compensation.

ARTICLE 22

Indigenous peoples have the right to special measures for the immediate, effective and continuing improvement of their economic and social conditions, including in the areas of employment, vocational training and retraining, housing, sanitation, health and social security. Particular attention shall be paid to the rights and special needs of indigenous elders, women, youth, children and disabled persons.

ARTICLE 23

Indigenous peoples have the right to determine and develop priorities and strategies for exercising their right to development. In particular, indigenous peoples have the right to determine and develop all health, housing and other economic and social programmes affecting them and, as far as possible, to administer such programmes through their own institutions.

ARTICLE 24

Indigenous peoples have the right to their traditional medicines and health practices, including the right to the protection of vital medicinal plants, animals and minerals.

They also have the right to access, without any discrimination, to all medical institutions, health services and medical care.

PART VI

ARTICLE 25

Indigenous peoples have the right to maintain and strengthen their distinctive spiritual and material relationship with the lands, territories, waters and coastal seas and other resources which they have traditionally owned or otherwise occupied or used, and to uphold their responsibilities to future generations in this regard.

ARTICLE 26

Indigenous peoples have the right to own, develop, control and use the lands and territories, including the total environment of the lands, air, waters, coastal seas, sea-ice, flora and fauna and other resources which they have traditionally owned or otherwise occupied or used. This includes the right to the full recognition of their laws, traditions, and customs, land-tenure systems and institutions for the development and management of resources, and the right to effective measures by States to prevent any interference with, alienation of or encroachment upon these rights.

ARTICLE 27

Indigenous peoples have the right to the restitution of the lands, territories and resources which they have traditionally owned or otherwise occupied or used, and which have been confiscated, occupied, used or damaged without their free and informed consent. Where this is not possible, they have the right to just and fair compensation. Unless otherwise freely agreed upon by the peoples concerned, compensation shall take the form of lands, territories and resources equal in quality, size and legal status.

ARTICLE 28

Indigenous peoples have the right to the conservation, restoration, and protection of the total environment and the productive capacity of their lands, territories and resources, as well as to assistance for this purpose from States and through international cooperation. Military activities shall not take place in the lands and territories of indigenous peoples, unless otherwise freely agreed upon by the peoples concerned.

States shall take effective measures to ensure that no storage or disposal of hazardous materials shall take place in the lands and territories of indigenous peoples.

States shall also take effective measures to ensure, as needed, that programmes for monitoring, maintaining and restoring the health of indigenous peoples, as developed and implemented by the peoples affected by such materials, are duly implemented.

ARTICLE 29

Indigenous peoples are entitled to the recognition of the full ownership, control and protection of their cultural and intellectual property.

They have the right to special measures to control, develop and protect their sciences, technologies and cultural manifestations, including human and other genetic resources, seeds, medicines, knowledge of the properties of fauna and flora, oral traditions, literatures, designs and visual and performing arts.

ARTICLE 30

Indigenous peoples have the right to determine and develop priorities and strategies for the development or use of their lands, territories and other resources, including the right to require that States obtain their free and informed consent prior to the approval of any project affecting their lands, territories and other resources, particularly in connection with the development, utilization or exploitation of mineral, water or other resources. Pursuant to agreement with the indigenous peoples concerned, just and fair compensation shall be provided for any such activities and measures taken to mitigate adverse environmental, economic, social, cultural or spiritual impact.

PART VII

ARTICLE 31

Indigenous peoples, as a specific form of exercising their right to self-determination, have the right to autonomy or self-government in matters relating to their internal and local affairs, including culture, religion, education, information, media, health, housing, employment, social welfare, economic activities, land and resources management, environment and entry by non-members, as well as ways and means for financing these autonomous functions.

ARTICLE 32

Indigenous peoples have the collective right to determine their own citizenship in accordance with their customs and traditions. Indigenous citizenship does not impair the right of indigenous individuals to obtain citizenship of the States in which they live.

Indigenous peoples have the right to determine the structures and to select the membership of their institutions in accordance with their own procedures.

ARTICLE 33

Indigenous peoples have the right to promote, develop and maintain their institutional structures and their distinctive juridical customs, traditions, procedures and practices, in accordance with internationally recognized human rights standards.

ARTICLE 34

Indigenous peoples have the collective right to determine the responsibilities of individuals to their communities.

ARTICLE 35

Indigenous peoples, in particular those divided by international borders, have the right to maintain and develop contacts, relations and cooperation, including activities for spiritual, cultural, political, economic and social purposes, with other peoples across borders.

States shall take effective measures to ensure the exercise and implementation of this right.

ARTICLE 36

Indigenous peoples have the right to the recognition, observance and enforcement of treaties, agreements and other constructive arrangements concluded with States or their successors, according to their original spirit and intent, and to have States honour and respect such treaties, agreements and other constructive arrangements. Conflicts and disputes which cannot otherwise be settled should be submitted to competent international bodies agreed to by all parties concerned.

PART VIII

ARTICLE 37

States shall take effective and appropriate measures, in consultation with the indigenous peoples concerned, to give full effect to the provisions of this Declaration. The rights recognized herein shall be adopted and included in national legislation in such a manner that indigenous peoples can avail themselves of such rights in practice.

ARTICLE 38

Indigenous peoples have the right to have access to adequate financial and technical assistance, from States and through international cooperation, to pursue freely their political, economic, social, cultural and spiritual development and for the enjoyment of the rights and freedoms recognized in this Declaration.

ARTICLE 39

Indigenous peoples have the right to have access to and prompt decision through mutually acceptable and fair procedures for the resolution of conflicts and disputes with States, as well as to effective remedies for all infringements of their individual and collective rights. Such a decision shall take into consideration the customs, traditions, rules and legal systems of the indigenous peoples concerned.

ARTICLE 40

The organs and specialized agencies of the United Nations system and other intergovernmental organizations shall contribute to the full realization of the provisions of this Declaration through the mobilization, inter alia, of financial cooperation and technical assistance. Ways and means of ensuring participation of indigenous peoples on issues affecting them shall be established.

ARTICLE 41

The United Nations shall take the necessary steps to ensure the implementation of this Declaration including the creation of a body at the highest level with special competence in this field and with the direct participation of indigenous peoples. All United Nations bodies shall promote respect for and full application of the provisions of this Declaration.

PART IX

ARTICLE 42

The rights recognized herein constitute the minimum standards for the survival, dignity and well-being of the indigenous peoples of the world.

ARTICLE 43

All the rights and freedoms recognized herein are equally guaranteed to male and female indigenous individuals.

ARTICLE 44

Nothing in this Declaration may be construed as diminishing or extinguishing existing or future rights indigenous peoples may have or acquire.

ARTICLE 45

Nothing in this Declaration may be interpreted as implying for any State, group or person any right to engage in any activity or to perform any act contrary to the Charter of the United Nations.

References

Books and articles

Abella, R. S. and Rothman, M. L. (eds) (1985) *Justice Beyond Orwell*, Canadian Institute For the Administration of Justice.

Adam, B. D. (1995) *The Rise of a Gay And Lesbian Movement*, rev. edn, New York, Twayne Publishers.

Adam, B. D., Duyvendak, J. W. and Krouwel, A. (1999a) "Gay and Lesbian Movements Beyond Borders? National Imprints of a Worldwide Movement", in Adam, Duyvendak, and Krouwel (eds): 344–71.

Adam, B. D., Duyvendak, J. W. and Krouwel, A. (eds) (1999b) *The Global Emergence of Gay and Lesbian Politics: National Imprints of a Worldwide Movement*, Philadelphia, Temple University Press.

Adamson, N., Briskin, L. and McPhail, M. (1989) *Feminist Organizing for Change: The Contemporary Women's Movement in Canada*, Toronto, Oxford University Press.

Agnew, V. (1996) *Resisting Discrimination: Women from Asia, Africa and the Caribbean and the Women's Movement in Canada*, Toronto, University of Toronto Press.

Aldrich, R. and Wotherspoon, G. (eds) (1992) *Gay Perspectives: Essays in Australian Gay Culture*, Sydney, University of Sydney.

American Sociological Association (1982) "Report of the ASA's Task Group on Homosexuality", in *The American Sociologist*, 17, August: 164–80.

Ang, I. (1995) "I'm a Feminist but . . . 'Other' women and postnational feminism", in Caine and Pringle (eds) (1995): 57–73.

Baker, M. (1981) *The New Racism: Conservatives and the Ideology of the Tribe*, London, Junction Books.

Banton, M. (1967) *Race Relations*, London, Tavistock.

Barth, E. A. T. and Noel, D. L. (1972) "Conceptual Frameworks for the Analysis of Race Relations: An Evaluation", in *Social Forces*, 50, March: 333–46.

Barth, F. (1969) *Ethnic Groups and Boundaries*, Boston, Little Brown.

Becker, H. S. (1963) *Outsiders: Studies in the Sociology of Deviance*, New York, Free Press.

Bell, D. (1975) "Ethnicity and Social Change", in Glazer and Moynihan (eds) (1975): 141–74.

Bell, D. and Klein, R. (eds) (1996) *Radically Speaking: Feminism Reclaimed*, North Melbourne, Spinifex Press.

Bendix, R. and Lipset, S. M. (eds) (1953) *Class, Status and Power: A Reader in Social Stratification*, Glencoe, IL, Free Press.

Bennett, J. W. (ed.) (1975) *The New Ethnicity: Perspectives from Ethnology*, New York, West.

Berkeley, K. C. (1999) *The Women's Liberation Movement in America*, Westport, CN, Greenwood Publishing.

Biddiss, M. D. (ed.) (1979) *Images of Race*, New York, Holmes & Meier.

Blauner, R. (1972) *Racial Oppression in America*, New York, Harper & Row.

Bolaria, B. S. and Li, P. S. (1985) *Racial Oppression in Canada*, Toronto, Garamond.

Borovoy, A. (1978) *The Fundamentals of Our Fundamental Freedoms*, Ottawa, Canadian Civil Liberties Educational Trust.

Breton, R. (1964) "Institutional Completeness of Ethnic Communities and the Personal Relations of Immigrants", in *The American Journal of Sociology*, 70(1), 193–205.

Breton, R., Isajiw, W. W., Kalbach, W. E. and Reitz, J. G. (1990) *Ethnic Identity and Equality: Varieties of Experience in a Canadian City*, Toronto, University of Toronto Press.

Burt, S. (1988) *Changing Patterns of Women in Canada*, Toronto, McClelland & Stewart.

Butler, J. (1990) *Gender Trouble: Feminism and the Subversion of Identity*, London and New York, Routledge.

Caine, B. (1995) "Women's Studies, Feminist Traditions and the Problem of History", in Caine and Pringle (eds) (1995), 1–14.

Caine, B. and Pringle, R. (eds) (1995) *Transitions: New Australian Feminisms*, New York, St. Martin's Press.

Cairns, A. and Williams, C. (eds) (1986) *The Politics of Gender, Ethnicity and Language in Canada*, Toronto, University of Toronto Press.

Campbell, M. (1973) *Halfbreed*, Toronto, McClelland & Stewart.

Canada (1966) *Report to the Minister of Justice of the Special Committee on Hate Propaganda in Canada*, Cohen, M. (Chair), Ottawa, Queen's Printer.

Canada, Government of (1969) (The White Paper), Statement of the Government of Canada on Policy, Ottawa, Queen's Printer.

Cardinal, H. (1969) *The Unjust Society*, Edmonton, Hurtig.

Cardinal, H. (1977) *The Rebirth of Canada's Indians*, Edmonton, Hurtig.

Cerna, C. M. (1994) "Universality of Human Rights and Cultural Diversity: Implementation of Human Rights in Different Socio-Cultural Contexts", *Human Rights Quarterly*, 16: 740–52.

Chamberlain, H. S. (1899) *Foundations of the Nineteenth Century* (no publisher available).

Citizens Plus (1970) *Response of the Indian Chiefs of Alberta to the White Paper* (1969), presented to Prime Minister Trudeau in June.

Clark, S. D., Grayson, J. P. and Grayson, L. M. (1975) *Prophecy and Protest: Social Movements in Twentieth-Century Canada*, Toronto, Gage.

Clinard, M. B. and Meier, R. F. (1979) *Sociology of Deviant Behaviour*, 5th edn., New York, Holt, Rinehart & Winston.

Coalition for Gay Rights in Ontario, Briefs to the Members of the Ontario Legislature, Ontario Human Rights Commission.
    (1978) Discrimination and the Gay Minority.
    (1981) The Ontario Human Rights Omission.
    (1986) Discrimination Against Lesbians and Gay Men.

Connor, W. (1978) "A Nation is a Nation, is a State, is an Ethnic Group, is a . . . ", in *Ethnic and Racial Studies*, I,(4).

Connor, W. (1993) *Ethnonationalism*, Princeton, Princeton University Press.

Conrad, P. and Schneider, J. (1980) *Deviance and Medicalization: From Badness to Sickness*, St. Louis, C. V. Mosby.

Cotler, I. (1985) "Hate Literature", in Abella and Rothman (eds) (1985).

Cox, G. (1990) *The Streetwatch Report: A Study into Violence Against Lesbians and Gay Men*, Sydney, Gay and Lesbian Rights Lobby, April.

Daniel A., Helminiak, J. S. and Spong, A. (2000) *What the Bible Really Says About Homosexuality*, Alamo Square Press.

Daniels, H. W. (1979a) *We Are the New Nation: The Metis and National Native Policy*, Ottawa, Native Council of Canada, March.

Daniels, H. W. (1979b) *The Forgotten People: Metis and Non-Status Indian Land Claims*, Ottawa, Native Council of Canada, April.

Das Gupta, T. (1986) *Learning From Our History*, Toronto, Cross Cultural Communication Centre.

Deutsch, A. W. (1974) *The Eichmann Trial in the Eyes of Israeli Youngsters*, Israel, Bar-Ilan University Press.

Dworkin, R. (1977) *Taking Rights Seriously*, London, Duckworth.

Eberts, M. (1979) "*The Rights of Women*", in Macdonald and Humphrey (eds) (1979): 225–48.

Elliott, J. L. and Fleras, A. (1992) *Unequal Relations: An Introduction to Race & Ethnic Relations in Canada*, Scarborough, Prentice-Hall Canada.

Epstein, S. (1999) "Gay and Lesbian Movements in the United States: Dilemmas of Identity, Diversity and Political Strategy", in Adam, Duyvendak and Krouwel (eds) (1999), 110–32.

Espiell, H. G. (1998) "Universality of Human Rights and Cultural Diversity", in *International Social Science Journal*, UNESCO, December, 525–41.

Fishman, J. (1979) *Language and Ethnicity in Minority Sociolinguistic Matters*, Clevendon, Multilingual Matters Ltd.

Fleming, T. and Visano, L. A. (eds) (1983) *Deviant Designations: Crime, Law and Deviance in Canada*, Toronto, Butterworths.

Foster, M. and Murray, K. (1972) *A Not So Gay World: Homosexuality in Canada*, Toronto, McClelland & Stewart.

Frideres, J. S. (1993) *Native Peoples in Canada: Contemporary Conflicts*, 3rd edn, Scarborough: Prentice-Hall Canada.

Gibbins, R. and Ponting, J. R. (1986) "An Assessment of the Probable Impact of Aboriginal Self-Government in Canada", in Cairns and Williams (eds) (1986): 171–239.

Gilroy, P. (1991) *"There Ain't No Black in the Union Jack": The Cultural Politics of Race and Nation*, Chicago, University of Chicago Press.

Glaser, K. and Possony, S. T. (1979) *Victims of Politics: The State of Human Rights*, New York, Columbia University Press, 33.

Glazer, N. and Moynihan, D. P. (1970) *Beyond the Melting Pot*, 2nd edn, Cambridge MA, MIT Press.

Glazer, N. and Moynihan, D. P. (eds) (1975) *Ethnicity: Theory and Experience*, Cambridge MA, Harvard University Press.

Goffman, E. (1961) *Asylums*, New York, Anchor Books.

Goffman, E. (1963) *Stigma: Notes on the Management of Spoiled Identity*, Englewood Cliffs, NJ, Spectrum Books.

Gordon, M. (1961) *Assimilation in America: Theory and Reality*, New York, Oxford University Press.

Green, J. N. (1999) "'More Love and More Desire': The Building of a Brazilian Movement", in Adam, Duyvendak, and Krouwel (eds) (1999b), 91–109.

Hannon, G. (1980) "Taking it to the Streets", in *Body Politic*, 71: 9.

Herek, G. M. and Capitanio, J. P. (1996) "Some of my best friends": Intergroup Contact, Concealable Stigma, and Heterosexuals' Attitudes toward Gay Men and Lesbians", in *Personality and Social Psychology Bulletin*, 22(4), 412–24.

Herek, G. M., Gillis, J. R., Cogan, J. C. and Glunt, E. K. (1997) "Hate Crime Victimization among Lesbian, Gay, and Bisexual Adults: Prevalence, Psychological Correlates, and Methodological Issues", in *Journal of Interpersonal Violence*, 12(2), 195–215.

Herman, S. N., Yockaman, P., and Yuchtman, E. (1965) "Reactions to the Eichmann Trial in Israel", *Scripta Hierosolgmitana*, 14, Jerusalem, Magnes Press: 98–119.

Hill, D. G. and Schiff, M. (1988) *Human Rights in Canada: A Focus on Racism*, 3rd edn, Ottawa, Human Rights Research and Education Centre, University of Ottawa and Canadian Labour Congress.

Isaacs, H. A. (1975) *Idols of the Tribe: Group Identity and Political Change*, New York, Harper & Row.

Isajiw, W. W. (1977a) "Olga in Wonderland: Ethnicity in a Technological Society", *Canadian Ethnic Studies*, 9(1): 77–85.

Isajiw, W. W. (ed.) (1977b) *Identities: Impact of Ethnicity on Canadian Society*, Toronto, Peter Martin Associates.

Isajiw, W. W. (1999) *Understanding Diversity: Ethnicity & Race in the Canadian Context*, Toronto, Thompson Educational Publishing.

Jackson, E. and Persky, S. (1982) *Flaunting It: A Decade of Gay Journalism from the Body Politic*, Toronto, Pink Triangle Press.

Jackson, M. (1979) "The Rights of the Native People", in Macdonald and Humphrey (eds) (1979), 267–88.

Kallen, E. (1972) "Eskimo Youth: The New Marginals", in *International Biological Program: Human Adaptability Project*, Annual Report, 4, Anthropological Series, 11, Toronto, University of Toronto.

Kallen, E. (1989) *Label Me Human: Stigmatized Minorities & Human Rights in Canada*, Toronto, University of Toronto Press.

Kallen, E. 1992) "Never Again!: Target Group Responses to the Debate Concerning Anti-Hate Propaganda Legislation", in *Windsor Yearbook of Access to Justice*, XI, 47–73.

Kallen, E. (1995) *Ethnicity & Human Rights Canada*, 2nd edn, Toronto, Oxford University Press.

Kallen, E. (1996) "Gay and Lesbian Rights Issues: A Comparative Analysis of Sydney, Australia and Toronto, Canada", *Human Rights Quarterly*, 18(1), February, 207–23.

Kallen, E. (1997) "Hate on the Net", *Electronic Journal of Sociology*, 2, December.

Kallen, E. (2003) *Ethnicity and Human Rights in Canada: A Human Rights Perspective on Ethnicity, Racism and Systemic Inequality*, 3rd edn, Toronto, Oxford University Press.

Kallen, E. and Lam, L. (1993) "Target for Hate: The Impact of the Zundel and Keegstra Trials on a Jewish Canadian Audience", in *Canadian Ethnic Studies*, 25(1): 9–23.

Kaufmann (1966) *Report to the Minister of Justice of the Special Committee on Hate Propaganda in Canada*, Appendix II.

Kinloch, G. C. (1979) *The Sociology of Minority Group Relations*, Englewood Cliffs, NJ, Prentice-Hall.

Kriesi, H., Koopmans, R., Dyvendak, J. W. and Guigni, M. G. (1995) *New Social Movements in Western Europe: A Comparative Analysis*, Minneapolis, University of Minnesota Press.

Kymlicka, W. (1999) "Liberal Complacencies" Response to Susan Okin's "Is Multiculturalism Bad for Women?", in Okin *et al.* (eds) (1999), 31–4.

Laqueur, W. and Baumel, J. T. (eds) (2001) *The Holocaust Encyclopedia*, New Haven, CT, Yale University Press.

Lauristen, J. and Thorstad, D. (1974) *The Early Homosexual Rights Movement* (1864–1935), New York, Times Change Press.

Lemert, E. M. (1967) "The Concept of Secondary Deviation", in *Human Deviance, Social Problems and Social Control*, Englewood Cliffs, NJ, Prentice-Hall.

Lenski, G. (1966) *Power and Privilege*, New York, McGraw-Hill.

Li, P. S. (ed.) (1990) *Race and Ethnic Relations in Canada*, Toronto, Oxford University Press.

Lieberson, S. (1961) "A Societal Theory of Race and Ethnic Relations", *American Sociological Review*, 26, December, 902–10.

Lipset, S. M. (1968) "Approaches to Social Stratification", in D. L. Sills (ed.) *The International Encyclopedia of the Social Sciences*, 15, 296–316.

Lipstadt, D. E. (1994) *Denying the Holocaust: The Growing Assault on Truth and Memory*, New York, Plume.

Lunsing, W. (1999) "Japan: Finding Its Way?", in Adam, Duyvendak, and Krouwel (eds) (1999), 293–325.

Macdonald, R. St J. and Humphrey, J. P. (eds) (1979) *The Practice of Freedom*, Toronto, Butterworths.

Maitse, T. (1996) "The Past is the Present: Thoughts from the New South Africa", in Bell and Klein (eds) (1996), 436–40.

Mamonoca, T. (1996) "Freedom and Democracy – Russian Male Style", in Bell and Klein (eds) (1996), 441–47.

Matthews, the Honorable Justice, J. (1988) "Protection of Minorities and Equal Opportunities", *UNSW Law Journal*, 11(2), 1–30.

McLemore, S. D., Romo, H. and Baker, S. G. (2000) *Racial and Ethnic Relations in America*, Boston, Allyn & Bacon.

Melucci, A. (1980) "The New Social Movements: A Theoretical Approach", *Social Science Information*, 19(2), 199–226.

Melucci, A. (1996) *Challenging Codes: Collective Action in the Information Age*, Cambridge, Cambridge University Press.

Merton, R. K. (1949) *Social Theory and Social Structure*, Glencoe, IL, Free Press.

Miles, R. (1989) *Racism*, London, Tavistock.

Montagu, A. (ed.) (1999), *Race and IQ*, London, Oxford University Press.

Mullaly, B. (2002) *Challenging Oppression: A Critical Social Work Approach*, Don Mills, ON, Oxford University Press.

Murumba, S. K. (1998) "Cross-Cultural Dimensions of Human Rights in the Twenty-First Century", in A. Anghie and G. Sturgess (eds) *Legal Visions of the 21st Century: Essays in Honour of Judge Christopher Weeramantry*, The Hague, London, Boston, Kluwer Law International: 201–40.

New South Wales Anti-Discrimination Board (1982) *Discrimination & Homosexuality: Report*, June, Sydney.

New South Wales Anti-Discrimination Board (1992) *Report of the Streetwatch Implementation Advisory Committee*, Sydney, February.

Noel, D. L. (1968) "A Theory of the Origin of Ethnic Stratification", *Social Problems*, 16, 157–72.

Nozick, R. (1974) *Anarchy, State and Utopia*, New York, Basic Books.

Okin, S. M. (1999) "Is Multiculturalism Bad for Women?", in Okin *et al.* (eds) (1999), 7–26.

Okin, S. M., Cohen, J., Howard, M. and Nussbaum, M. C. (eds) (1999) *Is Multiculturalism Bad for Women?*, Princeton, Princeton University Press.

Parekh, B. (1999) "A Varied Moral World" Response to Susan Okin's "Is Multiculturalism Bad for Women?", in Okin *et al.* (eds) (1999), 69–75.

Park, R. E. (1950) *Race and Culture*, Glencoe, IL, Free Press.

Parsons, T. (1953) "A Revised Analytical Approach to the Theory of Social Stratification", in Bendix and Lipset (eds) (1953).

Patterson, E. P. (1972) *The Canadian Indian: A History Since 1500*, Toronto, Collier-Macmillan.

Ponse, B. (1978) *Identities in the Lesbian World*, London, Greenwood Press.

Pontell, H. N. (ed.) (1998) *Social Deviance: Readings in Theory and Research*, 3rd edn. Englewood Cliffs, NJ, Prentice-Hall.

Ponting, J. R. and Gibbins, R. (1980) *Out of Irrelevance: A Socio-Political Introduction to Indian Affairs in Canada*, Toronto, Butterworths.

Porter, J. (1965) *The Vertical Mosaic*, Toronto, University of Toronto Press.

Prus, R. (1983) "Deviance as Community Activity: Putting 'Labeling Theory' in Perspective", in Fleming and Visano (eds) (1983).

Rawls, J. (1971) *A Theory of Justice*, Cambridge, MA, Harvard University Press.

Remafedi, G. (ed.) (1994) *Death by Denial: Studies of Suicide in Gay and Lesbian Teenagers*, Los Angelos, CA, Alyson Publications.

Rex, J. (1983) *Race Relations in Sociological Theory*, 2nd. edn, London, Routlege & Kegan Paul.

Rika-Heke, P. and Markmann, S. (1996) "Common Language – Different Cultures: True or False?", in Bell and Klein (eds) (1996), 505–15.

Rosen, R. (2000) *The World Split Open: How the Modern Women's Movement Changed America*, New York, Viking Press.

Rosenthal, P. (1990) "The Criminality of Racial Harassment", in M. Boivin, J. Manwaring and D. Prouix (eds) *Canadian Human Rights Yearbook (1989–90)*, Ottawa, Human Rights Research and Education Centre University of Ottawa, 113–66.

Russell, B. (1972) *A History of Western Civilization*, New York, Simon & Schuster: xv.

Sagarin, E. (ed.) (1971) *The Other Minorities: Nonethnic Collectivities Conceptualized as Minority Groups*, Toronto, Ginn & Co.

Saller, Richard P. (1995) *Patriarchy, Property & Death in the Roman Family*, Cambridge, Cambridge University Press.

Sandel, M. (1992) *Liberalism and the Limits of Justice*, London, Cambridge University Press.

Satzewich, V. (1998) "Race, Racism and Racialization: Contested Concepts", in V. Satzewich (ed.), *Racism and Social Inequality in Canada*: 25–45.

Schaefer, R. T. (1995) *Race and Ethnicity in the United States*, Reading, MA: Addison-Wesley.

Schneider, M. S. (1988) *Often Invisible*, Toronto, Central Toronto Youth Services.

Shermer, M., Grobman, A. and Hertzberg, R. (2000) *Denying History: Who Says the Holocaust Never Happened and Why Do They Say It?*, Berkeley, CA, University of California Press.

Schermerhorn, R. A. (1961) *Society and Power*, New York, Random House.

Shibutani, T. and Kwan, K. M. (1965) *Ethnic Stratification: A Comparative Approach*, New York, Macmillan.

Silman, J. (1987) *Enough is Enough: Aboriginal Women Speak Out*, Toronto, Women's Press.

Simpson, G. E. and Yinger, J. M. (1972) *Racial and Cultural Minorities: An Analysis of Prejudice and Discrimination*, 4th edn, New York, Harper & Row.

Stasiulus, D. K. (1990) "Theorizing Connections: Gender, Race, Ethnicity and Class", in Li (ed.) (1990), 269–305.

Status of Women Canada (1995) The Royal Commission on the Status of Women in Canada: An Overview 25 Years Later, Ottawa.

Status of Women Canada (2000) *Fact Sheet on Women and Violence*, developed for Beijing + 5, Special Session of United Nations General Assembly, Ottawa.

Steele, S. (1994) "Coming Out", *Macleans*, May 18, 40–1.

Stonequist, E. V. (1937) *The Marginal Man*, New York, Scribners.

Swann, B. Jr, Langlois, J. H. and Gilbert, L. A. (eds) (1999) *Sexism and Stereotypes in Modern Society: The Gender Science of Janet Taylor Spence*, Washington DC, American Psychological Association.

Sydney Gay and Lesbian Mardi Gras Program, (1992) "'Sex Crimes' A Turbulent History of Police/Gay Relations", a pamphlet available at the event.

Taylor, C. (1995) *Philosophical Arguments*, Cambridge, MA, Harvard University Press, ch. 10.

Thompson, N. (2001) *Anti-Discriminatory Practice*, 3rd. edn, Basingstoke, Palgrave.

Time Magazine (1995) "Search for a Gay Gene", 145(24).

Trice, H. M. and Roman, P. M. (1970) "Delabeling, Relabeling and Alcoholics Anonymous," *Social Problems*, 17(4), Spring, 539–46.

United Nations (1945) *Charter of the United Nations*, signed at San Francisco on 26 June, 1945; entry into force October 24, 1945, in accordance with Article 110, New York.

United Nations (1959) *Declaration of the Rights of the Child*. Proclaimed by the General Assembly of the United Nations on November 26. (Resolution 1386 XIV).

United Nations (1978, 1988) *International Bill of Human Rights*.

United Nations (1981) *International Convention on the Elimination of All Forms of Discrimination against Women*. Adopted and opened for signature, ratification and accession by General Assembly resolution 34/180 of December 18, 1979; entry into force September 3, 1981, in accordance with Article 27(1).

United Nations (1982) Economic and Social Council Document: E/CN.4/Sub.2/1982/2Add.1 (contains *San Jose Declaration, 1981*).

United Nations (1989) *Convention on the Rights of the Child*. Adopted and opened for signature, ratification and accession by General Assembly resolution 44/25 of November 20, 1989; entry into force September 2, 1990.

United Nations (1992) *Declaration on the Rights of Persons Belonging to National or Ethnic, Religious and Linguistic Minorities*, adopted by United Nations General Assembly on 18 December.

United Nations (1994) *Draft Declaration on the Rights of Indigenous Peoples*. E/CN.4/SUB.2/1994/2/Add. 1.

United Nations Economic Social and Cultural Organization (UNESCO) (1978) *Declaration on Race and Racial Prejudice*. Adopted by the General Conference (Twentieth Session), Paris, November.

Van den Berghe, P. L. (1967) *Race and Racism*, New York, Wiley.

Van den Berghe, P. L. (1978) "Race and Ethnicity: A Sociobiological Perspective", *Ethnic and Racial Studies*, 1(4).

Wagley, C. and Harris, M. (1958) *Minorities in the New World*, New York, Columbia University Press.

Waubageshig (1970) *The Only Good Indian*, Toronto, New Press.

Wilson, W. J. (1973) *Power, Racism and Privilege*, London, Collier-Macmillan.

Wineman, S. (1984) *The Politics of Human Services*, Montreal, Black Rose Books.

Winslow, R. W. (ed.) (1972) *The Emergence of Deviant Minorities*, New Brunswick, NJ, Transaction Books.

Woolcock, G. and Altman, D. (1999) "The Largest Street Party in the World: The Gay & Lesbian Movement in Australia", in Adam, Duyvendak, and Krouwel (eds) (1999b).

Wotherspoon, G. (1992) "History Lessons: Social Responses to AIDS and Other Epidemics in New South Wales", in Aldrich and Wotherspoon (eds) (1992).

Yetman, N. R. and Steele, C. H. (1975) *Majority and Minority*, 2nd edn, Boston, Allyn & Bacon.

Website references

Aboriginal Australia: History, Culture and Conflict, available from http://In.info-please.com/spot/aboriginal1.html. (accessed June 16, 2001).

About: Aborigines. The First Australians, website, available from http://www.ozramp.net.au/~senani/aborigin.htm. (accessed August 8, 2001).

Abuse of the Disabled, Disability Resources website, available from http://www.disabilityresources.org/ABUSE.html (accessed November 12, 2002).

Abuse of Persons with Disabilities is a World Wide Problem, Inman, K., December 1, 2000, SocietyGuardian.co.uk website, available at http://society.guardian.co.uk/disabilityrights/story/ (accessed on July, 23, 2002).

ADL Website, Poisoning the Web/aryan nations, available from tp://www.adl.org/poisoning_web/aryan_nations.html (accessed July 7, 2002).

American Indian Movement (AIM), available from http://www-ersonal.umich.edu/~jmarcus/aima/html (accessed June 17, 2001).

Assimilation Era, State Library of Queensland website, available from http://www.slq.qld.gov.au/ils/100years/assimilation.htm (accessed November 15, 2002).

Basic Facts: The New Territory, October 1999, available from www.nunavut.com (accessed May 15, 2001).

Brookeman, C., *The Native American People of the United States*, available from http://www.americansc.org.uk/brookeman.htm (accessed June 18, 2001).

Child Abuse & Mental Health, available from www.soc-um.org/ca_mh.html (accessed June 3, 2001).

Duhaime, L. (July 1987) *Abortion Law in Canada*, available from http://www.duhaime.org/family/ca-abor.htm (accessed November 2, 2002).

Elder Abuse, available from http://www.aifs.org.au/institute/pubs/fm1/fm37mj.html (accessed November 7, 2002).

Elder and Vulnerable Adult Abuse, available from http://www.intac.com/~nspo/elder.htm (accessed June 3, 2001).

Equal Rights Amendment, Encyclopedia entry, available from http://encarta.msn.com/encnet/refpages/refarticle.aspx?refid=761579474 (accessed December 1, 2002).

Fact Sheets: Wife Abuse/Violence Against Women, Health Canada website, available from http://www.hc-sc.gc.ca/hppb/familyviolence/html/pubs_catalogue/english/wife_abuse.htm (accessed November 7, 2002).

500 years of Indigenous Resistance, author unnamed, reprinted from *Oh-Toh-Kin*, vol. 1, no. 1, Winter/Spring 1992. Available from http://www.dickshovel.com/500.html

Horton, D. R. (1994) *Unity and Diversity: The History and Culture of Aboriginal Australia*, Year Book Australia, 1994, available from http://www.abs.gov.au/aausstats/ (accessed June 16, 2001).

Human Rights and Equal Opportunity Commission Report (1997). *Bringing Them Home*, available from http://www.austlii.edu.au/special/rsproject/ rsjlibrary/hreoc/stolen/ (accessed June 22, 2001).

Human Rights Watch, website, available from http://www.hrw.org/ (accessed *passim* 2001–2).

Human Rights Watch, Women's Rights. Domestic Violence, available from http://www.hrw.org/women/domesticviolence.html

Human Rights Watch, "UK: New Anti-Terror Law Rolls Back Rights", HRW press release, New York, December 14, 2001.

Human Rights Watch, "Sexual Abuse of Women in US State Prisons", HRW press release, December 1996.

Human Rights Watch, "Sexual Abuse and Exploitation of Children", HRW press release, New York, August 20, 2002.

Human Rights Watch, "Sharia Stoning Sentence for Nigerian Woman", HRW press release, New York, August 20, 2002.

Ku Klux Klan website, available from http://www.kukluxklan.org/ (accessed July 7, 2002).

Lyons, C. *Stolen Nation* (January 31, 2000), Eye website, available from http://www.eye.net/eye/issue/issue_01.31.00/news/nation.html (accessed June 22, 2001).

Maria Campbell (Metis), available from http://www.library.csi.cuny. edu/users/lavender/389/noframes/metis.html (accessed November 3, 2002).

McCarthy J, Keren, D. and Morris, J., "66 Questions and Answers about the Holocaust: Nizkor's Response to the Institute for Historical Review and Ernst Zundel", Nizkor web site, available from http://www.nizkor.org/ qar-complete.cgi (accessed May 31, 2001).

Miller, M. C., *An Australian Nunavut? (1998)*, available from http://www.law. emory.edu/EILR/volumes/spg98/miller.html (accessed June 16, 2001).

National Elder Abuse Incidence Study, (1996) Final Report, September 1998, prepared for the Administration on Aging, US Department of Health and Human Services by the National Center on Elder Abuse, available from http://www.aoa.dhhs.gov./abuse/report (accessed June 5, 2001).

National Socialist White People's Party (NSWPP), "NSWPP on Revisionism" and "The NSWPP in its Own Words", available from http://www.nizkor. org/hweb/orgs/american/national-socialist-white-peoples-party/ (accessed 31 May, 2001).

Nizkor website http://www.nizkor.org (accessed May 31, 2001).

President Bush Statement on Indian Policy (1991), available from http:// bushlibrary.tamu.edu./papers/1991/91061402.html (accessed June 18, 2001).

President Clinton Statement on Indian (Native American) Policy (1994) available from http://www.epa.gov./indian/polin.htm (accessed June 18, 2001).

Preventing Elder Abuse – Statistics, available from http://www.sa.agedrights. asn.au/prevent/statistics.html (accessed October 4, 2002).

Residential Schools, Contemporary Aboriginal Issues website, available from http://www.school.net.ca/aboriginal/issues/schools-e.hml (accessed June 21, 2001).

Status of Women Canada website, available from http://www.swc.gc.ca (accessed June 15, 2001).

Tenenbaum, L. "A quarter of a million march in support of Australia's Aborigines. But who are the beneficiaries of "reconciliation"? (June 1, 2000), World Socialist Web Site, available from http://www.wsws.org/ (accessed June 17, 2001).

365gay.com website, available from http://www.365gay.com (accessed June 14, 2001).

Toothman, L., The Big Eight, available from http://www.tolerantescholen. net/toothman.htm (accessed 25 November, 2002).

Westboro Baptist Church website, available from http://www.godhatesfags. com/home.html (accessed July 9, 2002).

Zundel website http://www.zundelsite.org (accessed May 31, 2001).

Index